c o u r s e b o o k

Innovations

a course in natural English

Hugh Dellar and Andrew Walkley

with Darryl Hocking

THOMSON
✳ TM
HEINLE

United Kingdom • United States • Australia • Canada • Mexico • Singapore • Spain

Innovations Intermediate Coursebook
Dellar/Walkley/Hocking

Publisher: *Christopher Wenger*
Series Editor: *Jimmie Hill*
Editorial Manager: *Howard Middle/HM ELT Services*
Director of Development, ESL/ELT: *Anita Raducanu*
Director of Marketing, ESL/ELT: *Amy Mabley*
Development Editor: *Paul MacIntyre*
Sr. Production Editor: *Sally Cogliano*
Sr. Print Buyer: *Mary Beth Hennebury*
International Marketing Manager: *Eric Bredenberg*
Associate Marketing Manager: *Laura Needham*

Compositor: *Process ELT (www.process-elt.com)*
Production Management: *Process ELT*
Illustrator: *Peter Standley*
Photography Manager: *Sheri Blaney*
Photo Researcher: *Process ELT*
Copyeditor: *Process ELT*
Cover/Text Designer: *Studio Image & Photographic Art (www.studio-image.com)*

Printer: *Seng Lee Press*

Cover Images: Kandinsky: © 2003 Artists Rights Society (ARS), New York/ADAGP, Paris; Da Vinci: © Bettmann/CORBIS; Guggenheim Museum: *Tim Hursley/SuperStock*

Printed in Singapore.
1 2 3 4 5 6 07 06 05 04 03

For more information, contact Thomson Learning, High Holborn House, 50/51 Bedford Row, London WC1R 4LR United Kingdom or Heinle, 25 Thomson Place, Boston, Massachusetts 02210 USA. You can visit our Web site at http://www.heinle.com

For permission to use material from this text or product, submit a request online at:
www.thomsonrights.com

ISBN: 0-7593-9841-0
(Coursebook)

Photo Credits

Page 9 (middle row right) © Heinle, (bottom row left) © Heinle, (bottom row middle) © Heinle, (bottom row right) © Dorothy Littell, page 11 (photo A) © BananaStock, page 13 (bottom right) © Heinle, page14 (first) © Heinle, (second) © Wendell Metzen/Index Stock Imagery, (third) © Heinle, (fifth left) © Digital Vision, page 16 © AP Photo/Seven Senne, page 19 (right top) © Heinle, (right bottom) © Heinle, page 20 (photo F) © Heinle, page 22 (bottom left) © Heinle, page 26 (top right) © Jim Esposito/Index Stock Imagery, (bottom right) © BananaStock, page 31 (top) © Heinle, (middle right) © AP Photo/Dave Thomson, (bottom) © Heinle, page 36 (middle row left) © Heinle, (middle row middle) Heinle, (bottom row left) © Heinle, (bottom row middle) © John Burke/Index Stock Imagery, page 37 (top left) © Heinle, (top right) © Heinle, page 39 © David Beightol/Index Stock Imagery, page 42 (photo A) © AP Photo/Austin Gorum-Fashion Wire Daily, (photo C) © Creatas, (photo D) © AP Photo/Jacques Brinon, (photo E) © Walter Bibikow/Index Stock Imagery, (photo F) © AP Photo/Bob Child, page 43 (top left) © Creatas, (middle left) © Ron Chapple, (top right) © Creatas, (bottom) © Philip Coblentz, page 44 (photo C) © Garry Adams/Index Stock Imagery, (photo D) © Creatas, (photo E) © Heinle, (photo F) © Image Source, (photo G) © Kent Dufault/Index Stock Imagery, page 45 © Image Source, page 47 (top left) © SW Production/Index Stock Imagery, (bottom left) © IT Stock Free, (right) © Bill Bachmann/Index Stock Imagery, page 48 © Heinle, page 49 (top left) © Mick Roessler/Index Stock Imagery, (bottom left) © Royalty-Free/Corbis, (right) © Thomas Sutto/Corbis, page 50 © Benelux Press/Index Stock Imagery, page 51 (top left) © BSIP Agency/Index Stock Imagery, (top right) © Image Source Limited/Index Stock Imagery, (bottom left) © Frank Pedrick/Index Stock Imagery, (bottom right) © Steve/Mary Skjold/Index Imagery, page 53 (left) © MaXx Images/Index Stock Imagery, (middle) © Stewart Cohen/Index Stock Imagery, page 54 (photo A) © Stephen Saks/Index Stock Imagery, (photo B) © Philippa Lewis; Edifice/Corbis, (photo C) © Philippa Lewis; Edifice/Corbis, (photo D) © Nathan Benn/Corbis, (photo F) © Macduff Everton/Corbis, (photo G) © WildCountry/Corbis, (photo H) © Rudi Von Briel/Index Stock Imagery, page 56 (left first) © Barry Winiker/Index Stock Imagery, (left second) © Francie Manning/Index Stock Imagery, (left third) © Digital Vision, (left fourth) © John Wang/RubberBall Productions, (right) © Steven Emery/Index Stock Imagery, page 59 (top right) © Mark Gibson/Index Stock Imagery, page 65 (top) © BananaStock, page 71 (right) © Image Source, page 75 (top left) © Heinle, page 75 (bottom left) © Image Source, (bottom right) © Heinle, page 76 (photo B) © AP Photo/Stephan Savoia, (photo C) © Mark Andersen/RubberBall Productions, (photo D) © Heinle, (photo E) © William Sallaz, (photo F) © Arni Katz/Index Stock Imagery, page 79 © Heinle, page 80 © Digital Vision, page 81 (top left) © Marc Romanelli, (top right) © Bill Bachmann/Index Stock Imagery, (bottom) © Everett Johnson/Index Stock Imagery, page 82 (photo A) © Digital Vision, (photo B) © BananaStock, (photo C) © Benjamin F. Fink Jr., (photo D) © IPS/Index Stock Imagery, (photo E) © Bill Whelan/Index Stock Imagery, (photo F) © Tom Vano/Index Stock Imagery, (photo G) © Jonelle Weaver, (photo H) © David Ball/Index Stock Imagery, (photo I) ©

Great American Stock/Index Stock Imagery, page 83 (top left) © Heinle, (top, right) © Ron Chapple, (bottom) © Stewart Cohen/Index Stock Imagery, page 85 © Benelux Press/Index Stock Imagery, page 86 © Corbis Images, page 92 (top row left) © Heinle, (top row middle) © AP Photo/Ron Edmonds, (top row right) © AP Photo/Peter Cosgrove, (bottom) © AP Photo/Itsuo Inouye, page 93 (top row left) © AP Photo/Amy Sancetta, (top row middle) AP Photo/Dan Loh, (top row right) © James Lafayette/Index Stock Imagery, (bottom row left) © Elizabeth DeLaney/Index Stock Imagery, (bottom row middle) © Image Source, (bottom row right) © James Lemass/Index Stock Imagery, page 94 (second) © Henryk T. Kaiser/Index Stock Imagery, (third) © Creatas, page 97 (top right) © AP Photo/Jacques Brinon, (middle) © AP Photo/Itsuo Inoue, (bottom) © Digital Vision, page 98 (top left) © AP Photo/Greg Baker, (top right) © Heinle, page 101 © BananaStock, page 104 (first top) © Katsumi Kasahara, (fourth) © IT Stock Free, page 105 © Pat Canova/Index Stock Imagery, page 107 © AP Photo/Beth A. Keiser, page 109 (top left) © Corbis Images, (top right) © AP Photo/Michael Caulfield, (bottom left) © AP Photo/Lisa Poole, (bottom right) © Tom Stillo/Index Stock Imagery, page 110 © AP Photo/Ade, page 111 © Dennis Lane/Index Stock Imagery, page 112 © Danny Daniels/Index Stock Imagery, page 115 © Philip Coblentz, page 122 (top left) © Royalty-Free/Corbis, (middle left) © ThinkStock LLC/Index Stock Imagery, (bottom left) © Franco Vogt/Corbis, (top right) © AbleStock/Index Stock Imagery, (middle right) © LWA-Dann Tardif/Corbis, (bottom right) © Craig J Brown/Index Stock Imagery, page 124 (top) © LWA-Dann Tardif/Corbis, (bottom) © LWA-Dann Tardif/Corbis, page 126 (photo A) © AP Photo/Diether Endlicher, (photo B) © AP Photo/Markus Schreiber, (photo C) © AP Photo/EFE Alberto Etevez, (photo D) © AP Photo/Andy Wong, (photo E) © AP Photo/Itsuo Inouye, (photo F) © AP Photo/John Russell, (photo H) © AP Photo/Max Nash, page 129 (top left) © AP Photo/David Langford, (top right) © Todd Powell/Index Stock Imagery, (middle) © AP Photo/Greg Baker, (bottom) © Bill Bachmann/Index Stock Imagery, page 131 © Bill Bachmann/Index Stock Imagery, page 131 (first) © AP Photo/Nick Ut, (second) © AP Photo/Damian Dovarganes, (third) © AP Photo/Jack Dempsey, (fourth) © AP Photo/Nick Ut, (fifth) © AP Photo/Max Nash, (sixth) © AP Photo/str, (seventh) © AP Photo/Roberto Pfeil, (eighth) © AP Photo/Alan Greth, (ninth) © AP Photo/Jonathan Evans, page 134 © Warner/Kobal Collection, page 136 © William Fritsch, page 138 (first) © Heinle, (second) © Ted Wilcox/Index Stock Imagery, (third left) © Pam Ostrow/Index Stock Imagery, (third right) © BananaStock, (fourth) © Diaphor Agency/Index Stock Imagery, page 139 © Image Source, page 140 (top) © AP Photo/Elaine Thompson, (bottom) Benelux Press/Index Stock Imagery, page 176 (first row left) © Thinkstock, (first row middle) © Image Source, (first row right) © Frazer Cunningham, (second row left) © Corbis Images, (second row middle) © elektraVision, (second row right) © Digital Vision, (third row left) © BananaStock, (third row middle) © Mark Cass, (third row right) © Steve Allen, (fourth row left) © Image Source, (fourth row middle) © Mark Cass, (fourth row right) © Image Source

All other photos are by Painet Inc.

To the student

How do you learn a language? There is no easy answer to this question. People learn languages in many different ways. The **Innovations** series starts from the basis of natural conversations people have every day, then teaches you the language you need to have similar conversations in English.

To make this process as interesting, motivating, and productive as possible, the **Innovations** series:

- contains numerous examples of the way grammar and vocabulary are naturally used. You can learn a lot of useful vocabulary from good grammar exercises, and good vocabulary activities will give you practice with the grammar of English.
- introduces you to many new features of spoken grammar and useful idiomatic language, followed by opportunities to practise them in meaningful contexts.
- includes reading texts that are intriguing and challenging, giving you plenty to talk – and think – about.
- features 'Learner advice' pages, which will help you study better.

We hope you find **Innovations** as fun and interesting to learn from as we did to write!

Acknowledgements

The authors and publishers would like to thank the following teachers for their valuable input on this material at various stages during production:

David Frank Barnes, The British Institute of Florence; Richard Booker, School of Professional and Continuing Education, University of Hong Kong; Michael Bowles, The British Council; John Cargill, The British Council; Alex Chevrolle, EF English First; José Olavo de Amorim, Colégio Bandeirantes; Audrey Don, Universidad Latina de America; John Eaglesham, British School of Milan; Frank Farmer, Universidad de Quintana Roo, Unidad Cozumel; Kirsten Holt, St Giles Eastbourne; Pamela Humphreys, The British Council; Maria Helena Primon Iema, Sociedade Brasileira de Cultura Inglesa São Paulo; Belgin Ogrek, Ozel Florya Koleji; Guy Perring, The British Council; Mark Rendell, EF English First; Mark Rossiter, American University of Dubai; Andre Joao Rypl, Cultura Inglesa Porto Alegre.

Andrew Walkley has taught mainly in Spain and Britain over the past twelve years. He currently divides his time between teaching general English, writing materials and maintaining a family life. He also does teacher training and regularly gives talks and workshops to teachers from all over the world. He would like to thank Macu, Rebeca and Santiago. Much love, and sorry for spending so much time in front of the computer!

Hugh Dellar has taught EFL, ESP and EAP in Indonesia and Britain, where he is now a teacher and teacher-trainer at the University of Westminster, London. He trains both native-speaker and non-native speaker teachers. He has also given papers and teacher development workshops all over the world. He would like to thank the following people: Lisa – for just being there; his mum and dad, Julian Savage, Maud Dunkeld, Andy Fairhurst, Nick Groom, Carole Patilla, Sally Dalzell, Nick Barrett, Darryl Hocking, Andrew Walkley, Rob Batstone, Ivor Timmis, Scott Thornbury, Chris Wenger, Howard Middle, Stuart Tipping, Michael Lewis and Jimmie Hill for their help, support, inspiration and enthusiasm over the years and Thierry Henry, Patrick Viera, Robert Pires, Curtis Mayfield, Pharoah Sanders, Iain Sinclair and Wong Kar-Wei for bringing beauty and joy to my rare moments of free time and for helping me get through!!

Darryl Hocking is a teacher and teacher-trainer in both ESOL and EAP, as well as a lecturer in art and design, at Auckland University of Technology, New Zealand. He specialises in developing academic literacies programmes in art and design and has also worked in this area at Goldsmiths, University of London. He would like to thank Rosemary, Lucia and Isaac.

Contents

1 Getting to know you

Using vocabulary

1 Fact-finding

Complete these questions 1–6 with the best missing word. Then match the questions to the answers a–f.

1. What .... you do?
2. .... are you from?
3. .... 's your birthday?
4. What do you do when you're .... working?
5. .... you like football?
6. .... you married?

a. Sweden.
b. April the fifth.
c. No, I hate it.
d. I work for IBM. I do web design.
e. No, not yet, but we're thinking about it.
f. Nothing much. Watch TV, go shopping, that kind of thing.

Now complete questions 7–12 and match them to the answers g–l.

7. .... old are you?
8. How long .... you staying here?
9. How .... have you been here?
10. How .... do you earn?
11. .... you got any brothers or sisters?
12. How long have you .... learning English?

g. Till next week. We're going back on Tuesday.
h. Twenty-five.
i. For six years on and off, but I'm still not very good.
j. It's nearly twenty years now.
k. Not enough!
l. Two brothers. One older, one younger.

Real English: Answering questions

When we answer questions like Where are you from? and How old are you? we don't usually reply with full sentences like I am from Brazil or I am sixteen years old. One word or short phrase is usually enough – Brazil or Sixteen. If we really do not want to answer a question, we can say: I'd rather not say, if you don't mind.

---

2 Speaking

Which of the twelve questions in Exercise 1 above would you ask ...

1. the first time you met someone?
2. once you knew them a bit better?
3. once you knew them really well?

Are there any questions which you would never ask? Why not?

3 More personal questions

If you want to ask a more personal question, you can add if you don't mind me asking. For example:

How old are you, if you don't mind me asking?

How much do you earn, if you don't mind me asking?

How long have you been learning English, if you don't mind me asking?

What happened to your hand, if you don't mind me asking?

🎧 **Listen to the questions above and practise saying them. Can you think of any other personal questions you could add the phrase if you don't mind me asking to?**

4 Speaking

In groups of three or four, use some of the twelve questions from Exercise 1 to find out the following.

1. Who is the oldest in your group?
2. Who is the youngest?
3. Who will be the next person to have a birthday?
4. Who has the most brothers and sisters?
5. Who has been studying English the longest?
6. Who has the best job?
7. Who does the most interesting things when they're not working?

Try to find the person in your class you have most in common with. Start by asking questions 1–12 from Exercise 1. Then make up your own questions to find out what you want.

5 | Listening

 **You are going to hear a conversation that took place during the coffee break in a language class. The conversation is between two English people, Jack and Lisa, studying Italian in England. Listen and find out which of the twelve questions in Exercise 1 they asked.**

With a partner, try to remember as much as you can about Jack and Lisa.

6 | Role play

Imagine you are one of the people in the pictures below. Think about how you would answer the twelve questions from Exercise 1. Now ask some other students. You might also find some other questions in the language strip at the beginning of the unit – or make up your own.

Reading

1 | Speaking

Everybody wants to know what the best way of learning a language is – and everybody has their own way of trying to study. Some ways, however, get much better results than others.

What are _your_ secrets for success? Write down five things you already do to improve your English. Use these sentence starters.

It's important to try to …
It's best to try to …
Don't worry too much about …
Make sure you …
It's better to try to … than it is to …

Compare your list with your partner's. Do you agree with each other's ideas? Why/why not?

Now read what a group of advanced foreign language learners and their teachers suggested when we asked them to do the same.

1. Did you come up with any similar ideas?
2. Are there any ideas you don't agree with? Why not?
3. Who do you think gives the most useful advice? Why?

The secret of success

Cissy (Taiwanese)
I think it's important to try to learn collocations – words which go together. It's much better than trying to learn single words. There are lots of words in English, like _get, give, go, make, do_, which mean different things in different contexts, so it's best to try to learn phrases like _get up, go shopping, make a mistake_.

Russell (Canadian)
Don't worry too much about your accent. So long as people understand you, it doesn't matter if you sound a bit Greek or Italian or Chinese or whatever. Everyone's got an accent – even the Americans, the Australians and the British! It shouldn't be a big issue. It's also more important to be able to pronounce whole phrases or words together than it is to be able to pronounce individual words on their own.

Sachiko (Japanese)
Make sure you revise what you study in class and try to remember what you've studied in the book you're using. It's more useful to make sure you really know what you've already done than to always try to learn more and more new words that you can't really use.

Miguel (Portuguese)
Of course grammar's important, but if you worry too much about it, you'll be too scared to say anything. It's important to be confident enough to try to say things without worrying too much about making mistakes.

Steve (English)
Don't worry about making a fool of yourself. When I first arrived in Peru to teach, I was visiting the headmistress of a local school and I wanted to try out my Spanish, so I told her in Spanish that she had a "buena escuela", which I thought meant "nice school". However, with my poor pronunciation, it turned out that I'd told her she had a "nice bum"! It was a bit embarrassing, but we both had a good laugh about it.

Gao (Chinese)
It's better to try to learn lots of words and phrases than it is to just worry about grammar all the time. You can do more with a big vocabulary than you can with good grammar!

Eduardo (Mexican)
Make sure you remember that being able to use a word involves more than just knowing its meaning. It's important to learn how and when you can use that word as well as what it means.

Eun-Sil (Korean)
Listen to as much English as you can, particularly things like soap operas, because they're full of useful, everyday English. Also, try to use your English as often as you can – in class, with your friends, on the Internet – so that you get better at using the language you already have.

2 | Common verb collocations

Cissy said it's important to try to learn collocations – words which go together. Which verbs in the box collocate with the groups of phrases below?

do	get	give	go	make

1. . . . . you a lift to the station
. . . . me a hand with my homework
. . . . you some advice

2. . . . . a mess
. . . . a lot of noise
. . . . a difference
. . . . sure

3. . . . . a lot of damage
. . . . very well in school
. . . . a bit of shopping
. . . . some research

4. . . . . better
. . . . angry
. . . . lost
. . . . home

5. . . . . skiing
. . . . grey
. . . . to church
. . . . for a walk

Which of the collocations above do these pictures illustrate?

3 | Classroom language

Match typical things your teacher will ask you to do 1–6 to the reasons for doing them a–f.

1. Underline the useful expressions
2. Compare your answers with a partner
3. Walk around the class and talk to as many people as possible
4. Practise saying these expressions aloud
5. Fill in the gaps
6. Cross out the odd one out

a. so that you can discuss any differences and learn from each other.

b. to share as many ideas as you can.

c. to make complete correct sentences.

d. so that you get an idea of what is not possible.

e. to highlight language to learn.

f. so that you learn stress and pronunciation at the same time as meaning.

4 | A quick quiz

How good are you at understanding classroom language? Do this quiz and find out!

1. Where is the main stress in these words?

collocation	embarrassed	mistake	surname

2. Listen to the words. How do you spell them?

3. How many syllables are there in these words?

chocolate	syllable	vegetable	vocabulary

4. How do you pronounce the words in question 3 above? Compare your pronunciation with what you hear.

5. What's the difference between the pairs of sentences?
   a. How long are you staying here?
      How long have you been here?

   b. I've been studying English for six years.
      I've been studying English for six years on and off.

   c. What do you do?
      What are you doing?

11

Using grammar

1 | Past simple and past continuous

When we tell stories about things that have happened to us, we often use the past simple and the past continuous. Can you find examples of each tense in the sentence below?

I was visiting my grandmother and I wanted to ask her about her childhood, but when I did, she told me the memories were too painful to talk about – even now.

When we tell stories about things that happened to us, we usually start by saying where we were and what we were doing at the time. We usually use the past continuous to do this. The kind of verbs we normally use are ones which can happen over an extended period of time – walk, visit, travel, live, stay, watch, and so on. For example:

Last week I was walking along the path beside the railway line and …

Last night I was jogging in the park when …

We use the past simple to give the details of the story. The kind of verbs we normally use to do this are ones which can happen quickly – hear, see, say, find, fall, feel, and so on. For example:

… I saw a dog attacking a boy.
… I suddenly got this terrible pain in my knee.

2 | Matching

Make sentences by matching the beginnings 1–4 to the endings a–d.

1. I was still packing
2. I was doing the washing-up
3. I was doing my homework
4. I was getting dinner ready

a. when my cat knocked coffee all over it and ruined it!
b. when I cut my hand on a knife.
c. when my taxi to the airport turned up!
d. when I knocked the noodles all over the floor.

Now make sentences by matching the beginnings 5–8 to the endings e–h.

5. While I was out looking for a birthday present for my girlfriend,
6. While I was driving to work the other day,
7. While I was cycling home the other day,
8. While I was cleaning up my flat the other day,

e. a car suddenly pulled out in front of me and knocked me off.
f. I found ten pounds down the back of my sofa.
g. I suddenly realised I'd actually already missed it!
h. I accidentally knocked a cyclist off his bike.

Now complete these grammar rules with simple or continuous.

9. We often use while + past . . . .
10. We often use adverbs like suddenly and accidentally with the past . . . .
11. We often interrupt a background action in the past . . . . by adding when + past . . . .

3 | Practice

Complete these stories by putting the verbs in brackets into the past simple or past continuous.

1. **Skiing**

   Last February I (a) . . . . (go) skiing in Spain – in the Pyrenees. I (b) . . . . (break) my leg on the first day of my holiday. I (c) . . . . (go) down a really steep slope when I suddenly (d) . . . . (realise) I was about to hit a tree in front of me. I (e) . . . . (try) to change direction, but I (f) . . . . (end up) crashing into another skier. I (g) . . . . (break) my leg – and his arm! So we both (h) . . . . (end up) in hospital.

2. **Going home on the bus**

   A few days ago, I (a) . . . . (go) home on the bus after school when suddenly this really crazy guy (b) . . . . (get) on and (c) . . . . (sit) down next to me. He (d) . . . . (start) talking to me, so I (e) . . . . (try) to read my book instead. Eventually, he (f) . . . . (get) bored and (g) . . . . (give up). About five minutes later, he (h) . . . . (change) seats and (i) . . . . (start) talking to someone else! I (j) . . . . (be) really relieved.

3. **A stupid thing to do**

   The most stupid thing I've ever done in a foreign language (a) . . . . (happen) while I (b) . . . . (live) in China a few years ago. One day, I was in a restaurant. I (c) . . . . (watch) English TV on cable and I (d) . . . . (enjoy) it a lot. I (e) . . . . (decide) I (f) . . . . (want) another beer, so I (g) . . . . (turn) round to one of the waiters and (h) . . . . (ask) him for one – but, stupidly, in English! He just (i) . . . . (stare) at me as if I was crazy until I finally (j) . . . . (realise). I (k) . . . . (feel) so stupid, I can tell you!

Did you notice that most of the verbs were in the past simple? This is because the past simple is a lot more common than the past continuous.

4 | Free practice

Now spend two minutes planning how to talk about one of these events. Remember to begin your story by saying where you were and what you were doing. Use the stories in Exercise 3 as models if you need help.

1. an accident you once had
2. something strange that once happened to you
3. a stupid mistake you once made
4. something really funny that once happened to you
5. something really frightening that once happened to you

> For more information on using the past simple and past continuous, see G1.

Go round the class and tell some other students your stories. Who told the best story?

Real English: I'm in the middle of ...

When we speak, we often use in the middle of.
I was in the middle of doing my homework when my computer crashed.

How many different ways can you complete this sentence?
Sorry I didn't answer the phone. I was in the middle of ...
Use the pictures below for ideas.

I don't do very much, really. • What do you do in your free time? • I suppose I'm a bit boring, really
I go to the gym twice a week. • I read a lot. • Well, actually, I collect stamps. • How long have you be
interested in jazz, then? • What've you been up to? • I've played ever since I was a kid. • My mum se
me to piano lessons. • I'm thinking of starting Chinese. • I work out every Friday. • I don't really have a
spare time at all. • I wish I went out more. • I'm a bit of a couch potato.
Are you watching the game tonight?

2 Free time

Using vocabulary

1 Evening activities

Look at these three patterns for talking about what you did last night:

a. I just stayed in and
- watched TV.
- read a book.
- wrote some letters.

b. I went out
- for dinner.
- for a drive.
- shopping.
- for a walk.

c. I went to
- the cinema.
- my brother's.
- the shopping mall.

Now use the three patterns above to complete these sentences.

1. .... for a walk round town.
2. .... tidied up my flat a bit.
3. .... for a run.
4. .... a friend's house for the evening.
5. .... did my homework.
6. .... clubbing.
7. .... the theatre and saw a great new play.
8. .... had an early night.
9. .... for a drink with some friends from work.
10. .... the Arsenal–Liverpool game.
11. .... took it easy.
12. .... the gym.
13. .... played PlayStation all night.
14. .... read a bit.
15. .... my yoga class.

Which of the activities above would you describe as doing 'nothing much'? Now with your partner, have short conversations using the sentences above. For example:

A: What did you do last night?
B: Nothing much. I just stayed in and tidied up my flat a bit and that's all, really. How about you?
A: Oh, I went out for dinner with some friends of mine.
B: Oh, that's nice.

2 | Free practice

Re-read the sentences 1–15 in Exercise 1. Tick the activities that you did yesterday. If you need to, add your own activities to the list.

Now find out what everybody did yesterday after class. What were the five most popular activities in your class? Which one was the least popular?

3 | Follow-up questions

Listen to six short dialogues. As you listen, complete these questions – one for each dialogue.

1. How . . . . do you do that, then?

2. How . . . . have you been doing that, then?

3. Where do you do . . . . , then?

4. Was it . . . . expensive?

5. Are you . . . . good?

6. Was it . . . . good?

Practise saying the questions 1–6 above. Then match the questions to the pairs of typical answers a–f.

a. • For quite a while now. Maybe four or five years.
   • Not very long. I've only just started.

b. • Yeah. It cost us about twelve pounds each.
   • No, not very. It only cost us a couple of pounds each.

c. • Not very, but I enjoy it anyway.
   • Yeah, not bad.

d. • Oh, it was all right – not brilliant.
   • Yeah, it was great.

e. • Quite a bit. About once or twice a week, I suppose.
   • Not that much. About once every couple of months, I suppose.

f. • At this place near my house.
   • At this place in the centre of town.

4 | Free practice

Make a list of six things you have done in the evening during the past month.

1. . . . .
2. . . . .
3. . . . .
4. . . . .
5. . . . .
6. . . . .

Ask some other people in your class what they did last night. If you had a very quiet night, use some of the ideas on page 14 or some of the ideas above and lie! Use whichever follow-up questions you think are appropriate. For example:

A: What did you do last night?
B: Oh, I went to the gym.
A: Oh, yeah? How long have you been doing that, then?
B: For quite a while now. It's really good.

Reading

1 An unusual hobby

Fritzi Korr is a female postman in the German town of Hildesheim. When she's not working, Fritzi spends most of her free time collecting china elephants and running a china elephant collectors' club.

Imagine you are going to interview her to find out a bit more about her unusual hobby. With a partner, write down five questions you would like to ask her.

1. ....
.................................?

2. ....
.................................?

3. ....
.................................?

4. ....
.................................?

5. ....
.................................?

Now read the interview and see if she answers your questions.

Interview with Fritzi

So, Fritzi, how did you get into collecting china elephants?

Well, it all goes back to when I was a kid. When I was about six or seven, one of my cousins gave me a small china elephant for my birthday, and I liked it so much I decided to start collecting them, so it all just started from there, really.

So, you've been collecting ever since?

Yeah, that's right. It's almost thirty years now. I know some people might think it's strange that I didn't grow out of it, but the more china elephants I bought, the more interested in them I got.

So, what is it that interests you about them?

I don't know, really. I like the fact that there are so many different kinds and I also like the fact that some of them are so beautiful. Also, I just really like elephants. They're amazing animals. There's something very special about them. In some cultures, they're sacred. Actually, I think I might have been an elephant in one of my past lives!

And how many have you got now?

I've got over five thousand. It's one of the biggest collections in the country, I think. I'm getting new ones all the time as well. I find them in second-hand shops, I buy them on the Internet and sometimes friends give me them as presents.

Where do you keep them all?

Well, I've got a special room in my house where I've got them all on display. I've got shelves and shelves of them! Actually, one day I'd like to open my own china elephant museum. I'm sure a lot of people would come and see it.

You also run a club, don't you? How did that start?

Well, back in the late 1980s, I just wanted to try to meet other collectors and find out more about the history of china elephants and about all the different kinds that exist around the world. I found out that there weren't really any books or catalogues on the subject, so I started my own club. It's just grown and grown and now there are about 125 members. We meet up from time to time and we swap elephants and things like that. It's great, and since we went online, collectors from all over the world have got in touch with us, which is great.

Do you have a favourite one?

I do, actually. It's one of the oldest one in my collection. It's from 1897, and it's a big black one with really sad eyes. It's so beautiful, it makes me want to cry – but in a good way.

Real English: run a club

If you run a club, you are in charge of it, you organise its events and you contact its members regularly. Look at these other things you can run:

He runs his own business.
My parents run a small family restaurant.
It's a charity. It's run by volunteers.

2 Speaking

How many of your questions did Fritzi answer? Change partners and tell your new partner what you can remember about her answers. If Fritzi ever does open a china elephant museum, would you like to go and visit it? Why/why not?

3 | Speaking

Fritzi's china elephant club now has over a hundred members. How many of these sentences can you complete about yourself?

1. I once joined a .... club.
2. I'm a member of the local .... club.
3. I go to a .... club every week.

If you cannot complete the sentences about yourself, can you complete them for a friend or a relative?

Here is a list of ten common clubs which you could find in many towns in Britain or the US. Which would you be interested in joining? Are there any you would never join? Why not? The following sentence frames may help you.

I'd quite like to join … . I think it'd be really interesting.
I wouldn't mind joining … . It might be fun.
I'd never join … . It's just not my kind of thing.

a golf club	a debating club
a tennis club	a conservative/ socialist/political club
a bridge club	
a chess club	a folk dancing club
a squash club	a local history club
a football supporters' club	

If you were going to start a club, what kind of club would it be? Why? Try to persuade other people in your class why they should join your club! Think of at least four reasons why they should.

4 | Vocabulary focus

Complete the paragraphs 1–6 below with the words and phrases in the boxes.

1.   album   fairs   get given   spare   swap

I've been collecting stamps ever since I was a kid. Sometimes I (a) .... them by friends and family, but I buy a lot at stamp (b) .... too. I've got stamps from all over the world and I keep them in a special (c) .... Sometimes, if I get (d) .... copies, I'll (e) .... them with other collectors.

2.   anything by   anything on   browsing   novels

I really love reading. I mainly read (a) ...., especially (b) .... John Grisham. Because I work in a bank, I also try to read (c) .... economics and that kind of thing. To be honest, I don't really do much else in my free time. Even when I go shopping, I always end up (d) .... round second-hand bookshops.

3.   fifty lengths   front crawl   pool   sauna

I don't have much free time, but I try to go swimming whenever I can. I usually go to the (a) .... near my house and I usually try to do (b) .... at least, swimming the (c) .... I've been trying to learn how to do the butterfly, but it's impossible. Afterwards, I like to go and have a (d) ....

4.   album   anything by   band   gigs   track

I'm really into music, especially (a) .... Funkadelic. I've got all their CDs, but my favourite (b) .... is 'Funky Dollar Bill', which is on their first (c) .... I go to lots of (d) .... as well. There's nothing better than hearing a good live (e) ....!

5.   fan   games   stadium   support

I'm a big baseball (a) .... and I (b) .... the New York Yankees. I don't go to many (c) .... because I don't live near their (d) ...., but I try to keep up with all the results and watch them on TV whenever I can.

6.   class   fit   gym   running machine   weights

Keeping (a) .... is really important to me, so I try to go to the (b) .... whenever I can. I usually do twenty minutes on the (c) .... and then do some (d) .... for a bit. I also joined a (e) .... recently, doing *tai chi*, which is nice and relaxing.

Are you similar to the people speaking in 1–6 above? Underline any sentences that are true for you. Rewrite some of the other sentences above so that they are true for you. Then tell a partner. For example:

I'm a big football fan and I support AC Milan.

Using grammar

1 Present perfect continuous and past simple

We can use both the past simple and the present perfect continuous to talk about a period of time. The past simple describes a period of time that is finished, while the present perfect continuous describes a period of time that continues up to and through the present. For example:

a. I played tennis for about five years. (but don't any longer)

b. I've been playing tennis now for about five years. (and still do)

Decide which question in these two short conversations is like a, and which is like b above.

1. A: How long have you been learning to play golf, then?
   B: For about three weeks now. I'm going for another lesson this afternoon.

2. A: How long did you do yoga for, then?
   B: Only three weeks. I didn't really enjoy it, so I stopped going to the class.

2 Practice

Practise saying these questions and then use one in each of the short dialogues below.

How long have you been doing that then?
How long did you do that for, then?

1. A: I'm doing this evening course to learn how to do web design properly.
   B: Oh really? . . . .
   A: Not very long. I only started it last week, actually. It's really good.

2. A: See you. I'm off to the gym.
   B: I didn't know you went to a gym.
   . . . .
   A: For quite a while now. Haven't you noticed I'm looking better?

3. A: When I lived in New Zealand, I used to work for a company that sold cooking equipment.
   B: Oh really? . . . .
   A: Oh, about three years, I suppose.

4. A: I used to do karate when I was younger.
   B: You! Karate! I don't believe it!
   . . . .
   A: For about eight years, actually. I managed to get my black belt.

5. A: I've got my first basketball game of the season on Saturday.
   B: Yeah, John mentioned you played.
   . . . .
   A: Oh, quite a while. This is my third season now.

6. A: I used to be quite a good marathon runner when I was younger.
   B: A marathon runner. Really? . . . .
   . . . .
   A: For years – until I had kids. I even ran in the New York marathon once.

3 Pronunciation: sounding interested

To show the person we are talking to that we are interested in what they are saying, we use quite high intonation. Listen and repeat the six responses and follow-up questions from Exercise 2. Make sure you try to sound interested!

1. Oh really? How long've you been doing that, then?

2. I didn't know you went to the gym. How long've you been doing that, then?

3. Oh really? How long did you do that for, then?

4. You! Karate! I don't believe it! How long did you do that for, then?

5. Yeah, John mentioned you played. How long've you been doing that, then?

6. A marathon runner. Really? How long did you do that for, then?

Now practise the short dialogues in Exercise 2 with a partner. Try to sound extremely interested!

4 Time expressions

There are two time expressions in each of these sentences. Cross out the wrong one. Then compare your answers with a partner and discuss how you made your decisions.

1. I've been playing tennis when I was at high school / since I was at high school.

2. I've been going to aerobics on and off for about two years / two years ago.

3. I've been trying to learn English for quite a while now / when I was in Canada.

4. I've been riding horses when I was a kid / ever since I can remember.

5. I've only been doing embroidery for a few months / last month.

6. I've been using e-mail since I got connected to the Net / before my computer died.

7. I've been doing it for ages now / ages ago.

8. I've been learning the violin for a few years now / two years ago.

Which two words commonly occur in time expressions that follow the present perfect continuous?

a. ....

b. ....

5 | Free practice

Make statements that are true for you using these sentence starters.

1. I've been learning English ....
2. I've been playing ....
3. I've been doing ....
4. I've been going (to) ....
5. I've been collecting ....
6. I used to do .... when I ....
7. I used to play .... quite a lot when I ....
8. I used to go .... quite a lot when I ....

With a partner, ask each other as many questions as possible about each activity.

6 | Talking about recent activities

We often use the present perfect continuous to explain why we haven't seen much of people recently. For example:

A: Hi, how are you? I haven't seen you for a while. What have you been up to?

B: Oh, I've been looking for a new place to live for the last few weeks. How about you? What've you been up to?

Now make answers using the words below.

1. I / work / a lot of overtime / recently
   ....
   ....

2. I / revise / my exams / the last few weeks
   ....
   ....

3. I / do / my flat up / the last month
   ....
   ....

4. I / sort out / my summer holiday / the last few days
   ....
   ....

5. I / look after / the kids / the last few months
   ....
   ....

6. I / try / find / new job / recently
   ....
   ....

Now have six short conversations with your partner using the ideas above.

Real English: I've been busy -ing
You can use the common structure I've been busy working/revising/ travelling in similar situations to the ones in the exercise.

For more information on using the present perfect continuous and past simple, see G2.

Where are you going this year? • Ever been camping? • It rained the whole time. • Never go on a cruise
– just take my word for it! • I'm too old to go backpacking. • Did you go up the Eiffel Tower? • I'd love
to see the Vatican. • It's time we had a break. • Did you fly? • We got a ferry across. • There's a lot to
see, isn't there? • The food's really cheap. • I hired a car. • Was it self-catering? • It was a total disaster.
We're off to Barcelona for a day or two. • Are you taking the kids? • You're
a little red on the shoulders.

3 Holidays

Using vocabulary

1 Speaking

Match the statements 1–8 to the pictures A–H below.

1. We went camping.
2. We went backpacking.
3. We had a fortnight in the sun.
4. We went on a skiing holiday.
5. We went walking in the mountains.
6. We had a week in Paris.
7. We rented a cottage.
8. We went on a cruise.

Have you ever been on any of these kinds of holiday? Where do you think the pictures are? Use these structures to make guesses:

It looks like it could be … , or somewhere like that.

I think it must be … because … .

2 Holiday activities

Which of these activities do you like doing when you go on holiday? Mark each one in this way:

✓ I really like it.   ✗ I don't really like it.

- lying on the beach all day, sunbathing
- going sightseeing
- walking in the hills or in the countryside
- going to markets and going shopping
- sitting around the pool with a drink
- meeting the locals
- reading and just having some time to myself
- sitting in the bar all day
- going surfing or windsurfing
- going clubbing every night
- driving around the country
- just taking it easy and relaxing

Compare your answers with a partner. Do you think you would enjoy going on holiday together? Now have conversations like this with a different partner.

A: I really like lying on the beach all day.
B: So do I. OR
   Oh, I'm afraid I don't.

A: I don't really like sightseeing.
B: Neither do I. OR
   Oh, don't you? Why not?

3 | Vocabulary practice

Complete the texts below with the words in the boxes. The first one is done for you.

1.

out	~~stayed~~	trips	went

We went on a family holiday to the south of France. It was me and my wife and all the kids. We (a) ..stayed.. in a little cottage and went out on shopping (b) .... to the market. We ate (c) .... quite a bit and one day we all (d) .... windsurfing.

2.

camping	campsite	tent	went

We went (a) .... in the south-west of England. It was great! We stayed at a small (b) .... and the weather was lovely for the whole two weeks. We (c) .... walking quite a lot – and for once the (d) .... didn't end up full of water!

3.

round	rucksack	took	went

We (a) .... backpacking (b) .... Thailand. We started off in Bangkok, (c) .... the train to Chiang Mai and then went down to Nan Phuket. It was really fun, but I got a bit tired of living out of a (d) .... all the time!

4.

cooking	cottage	fire	self-catering

We went on a (a) .... holiday in the Scottish Highlands. We rented a little (b) .... up in the mountains with a real open (c) .... In the evenings, after skiing, we all helped with the (d) .... It was really nice and cosy!

5.

flight	package	sitting	value

We went on a (a) .... holiday to St Lucia. It was really good (b) .... for money. We got the (c) ...., the hotel, and all the food for about seven hundred pounds each. I spent the whole week (d) .... round the pool, taking it easy.

6.

again	bored	cruise	scenery

We went on a (a) .... round Norway. The boat was lovely – swimming pool, gym, bar, four different restaurants. The (b) .... was incredible, but I got a bit (c) .... being stuck on board ship day after day. It was great, but I wouldn't do it (d) ....

Tell your partner about your last holiday. Spend two minutes preparing what you will say. Try to use some of the expressions from above.

Listening

1 | Speaking

In pairs, fill in this questionnaire about your partner.

1. **How often do you go on holiday?**
   a. once a year
   b. twice a year
   c. more than twice a year

2. **What kind of holidays do you most enjoy?**
   Type: . . . .

3. **What kind of holidays don't you like?**
   Type: . . . .

4. **What is the best place you have ever been on holiday? Why?**
   . . . .

5. **What is the worst place you have ever been on holiday? Why?**
   . . . .

Report what you have found out about your partner to the rest of the class.

With a partner, decide the best holiday for the four people in the pictures. Which of the four would *you* most like to go on holiday with? Why? This structure might help you:

He/she looks like the kind of person who'd enjoy ... .

2 | While you listen

You are now going to hear a conversation between two old friends, Rose and Steve. They are chatting about their plans for the summer. Cover the conversation below. As you listen, try to answer these questions.

1. Where are they going on holiday this year?
2. Have they been to these places before?

Now listen again and complete the gaps.

Summer holidays

Rose:	Are you going away this summer?
Steve:	Yes, we're going to Portugal.
Rose:	Oh, really? (1) . . . . ?
Steve:	We're not sure exactly. We're going camping, so we've just booked the flight. We're going to (2) . . . . when we get there. I suppose we'll probably go north of Lisbon – up the coast.
Rose:	That sounds great. It's (3) . . . . lovely there. Have you ever been there before?
Steve:	No, but my girlfriend's wanted to go for ages, so we thought we'd (4) . . . . What about you? Are you doing anything special?
Rose:	We haven't really decided yet. There's some really (5) . . . . to Ibiza at the moment. Or we might just go to Cornwall again.
Steve:	Oh, yes, Cornwall. It's really nice down there. We went a few years ago and had a great time.
Rose:	We rented (6) . . . . for a week last year. But you never know what the weather's going to be like, do you?
Steve:	No, I suppose not. But Ibiza? Really? Are you serious?
Rose:	Well, maybe. Why? Have you ever been there?
Steve:	No, but I've never really wanted to go, (7) . . . . It just sounds awful, from what I've heard. It's supposed to be full of British tourists getting sunburnt and drunk.
Rose:	Yes, I know, but at least we'd (8) . . . ., and it's not all like that. A friend of ours went last year and said there were lots of places where you can get away from all the clubbers.
Steve:	Oh, right.
Rose:	And there are (9) . . . . there for a hundred and fifty pounds for a week. And it's really cheap when you get there.
Steve:	Oh, well, it might be (10) . . . ., then.

3 Vocabulary

Complete these sentences with a word from the conversation on page 22.

1. Are you . . . . abroad this year?
2. We're not . . . . exactly when the train leaves.
3. We're . . . . camping in France.
4. I've just . . . . my flight to New York for Christmas.
5. We're going to . . . . a car when we get there.
6. St Lucia is . . . . to be a lovely place for a holiday.
7. We thought we'd . . . . Malta a try.
8. What do you think the weather's going to be . . . . ?
9. You can get a(n) . . . . holiday for two hundred pounds.
10. It might be . . . . a try.

Discuss these questions with a partner.

- Have you ever been to any of the places Rose and Steve mention?
- What did you think of them? Can you think of an adjective to describe each place?
- What problems do you think tourism can cause?

Real English: rent / hire

You can rent a car, a house, a flat, a villa, or a cottage. You can also hire a car, but you can't hire a house, a flat or any other kind of building.

4 Speaking

Have you ever rented/hired any of these things on holiday?

☐ a bike		☐ a moped
☐ a boat		☐ a motorbike
☐ a car		☐ a villa
☐ a cottage		☐ a windsurfer

5 Odd one out

Here are five groups of places to go on holiday. Which is the odd one out in each group? Why?

1. Texas   Mexico   California   New York   Florida
2. Rome   Paris   Tokyo   Shanghai   Buenos Aires
3. York   Bath   Cambridge   Edinburgh   Oxford
4. Victoria   Michigan   Garda   Nile   Geneva
5. The Alps   Kilimanjaro   The Andes
   The Pyrenees   The Himalayas

Mark where the strong stress comes in these place names.

The Himalayas	Geneva
The Pyrenees	Copenhagen
Michigan	Slovenia
Edinburgh	Buenos Aires
Victoria	Chile
Kilimanjaro	Brussels

Are there any place names which you are not sure how to pronounce? Have you ever been to any of the places mentioned above? When? What were they like?

6 Expressions with *place*

With a partner, discuss what kind of place you think is being discussed in these statements.

1. There's a nice little Italian place near my office which does great pasta.
2. I'm going round to Nick's place for dinner tonight.
3. It's a great place to go skiing.
4. Can you save my place? I'll be back in a moment.
5. If it's valuable, you'd better keep it in a safe place.
6. We're going to rent this little place in the countryside.
7. I couldn't find a place to park.
8. Are you still looking for a place to live?
9. He's always leaving his clothes lying around all over the place.
10. It's a great place for the kids to play in.

Tell your partner about somewhere you think is …

- a great place for a party.
- a great place for a picnic.
- a great place for a day-trip.
- a great place for old people.
- a great place to get married.
- a great place to eat.
- a great place to go shopping.
- a great place to live.
- a horrible place to live.
- a fairly boring place to visit.

Using grammar

1 | Present perfect: the best rule

Read these examples which use the present perfect.

I've just had some great news!

Have you ever been to Sri Lanka?

I've been to Australia twice now.

Read these explanations. All are true, but only one describes all three examples above. Which is it?

a. The present perfect is often used with just.

b. The present perfect looks back from the present.

c. The present perfect describes something in the recent past.

Now read this and see if you were right.

1. The present perfect has the auxiliary verb have/has in the present tense. This is followed by a past participle (e.g. been, done, lived, known).

2. It looks back on a period in the past and connects the past to the present.

3. Although the present perfect looks back on the past, it is not a past tense. The past simple is used to express past events without reference to the present. In the same way, we never use the present perfect with a finished past expression like yesterday, last week, twenty years ago. Here are some pairs of sentences which show the difference:

    I've known Jim for ten years. I met him ten years ago.

    We've lived here for ages. We moved here just after we got married.

    My father's been dead for ten years. He died when I was only fifteen.

Can you think of some more examples?

2 | Asking questions

Look at these questions and answers:

A: Have you ever been to Ibiza before?

B: No, but I've never really wanted to go.

A: Have you ever been camping?

B: Yes, and I'd never do it again! We got soaked!

Below are ten ways to answer the question: Have you ever been to (Egypt)? Complete each answer with Yes or No.

1. . . . . , but it's supposed to be brilliant.
2. . . . . , but I've always wanted to.
3. . . . . , but I'm not sure I'd go again.
4. . . . . , it's brilliant. You'll love it.
5. . . . . , I went once when I was a kid.
6. . . . . , but I'd love to.
7. . . . . , but it rained the whole time.
8. . . . . , but I've never really wanted to.
9. . . . . , and it was horrible!
10. . . . . , but a friend of mine has.

Listen and check your answers.

Ask your partner if they have ever been to these places. Try to use some of the answers 1–10 above.

- America
- Australia
- France
- Egypt
- Scotland
- Brazil
- Malta
- Thailand
- Hawaii
- Singapore
- Italy
- India

Try to find three countries you and your partner have both been to. Which did you enjoy most?

3 | Free practice

Look at this example:

A: Have you ever been on a cruise?

B: Yes, we went on one to Norway a few years ago. The scenery was fantastic and the food on the boat was superb!

Which tense was used in the answer? With a partner, have similar conversations about these holidays:

- a backpacking holiday
- a package holiday
- a camping holiday

4 | Position of adverbs

Rewrite these sentences. Put the words in brackets in the most natural place.

1. I've been to the south of Italy. (never)   . . . .
2. We've heard the news. (just)   . . . .
3. We've been good friends. (always)   . . . .
4. I've seen that film twice. (already)   . . . .
5. Have you seen their new baby? (yet)   . . . .
6. Has she been married? (ever)   . . . .

How many of the following are true about you?

☐ I've never been to Canada.

☐ I've never eaten squid.

☐ I've always liked the British.

☐ I've always wanted to go to India.

Make a list of the following things, then tell a partner about your list.

Places you've never been to, but would like to visit: . . . .
. . . .
Things you've never done, but would like to try: . . . .
. . . .
Things you've always liked: . . . .
. . . .
People you've always admired: . . . .
. . . .

Real English: really

Do you remember the sentence from the beginning of this unit?
I don't really like it. Really is a very common adverb in English.
Discuss in class the difference in meaning between:
I don't really like it.
I really don't like it.

Which is stronger? Why?

---

5 | Pronunciation: contrastive stress

🎧 **Listen to these short dialogues. Notice how have is stressed.**

A: Have you ever been to Singapore?

If the answer is no:
B: No, never, but I **have** been to Hong Kong.

If the answer is yes:
B: Yes, I **have**, actually.

With a partner, have similar conversations using these pairs of places or any others you can think of yourself:

Barcelona / Madrid	Naples / Venice	Munich / Berlin
Glasgow / Edinburgh	Tunisia / Morocco	Ankara / Istanbul

▶ For more information on how to use the present perfect simple, see G3.

4 Feelings

I'm really excited by all this. • Are you feeling all right? • You look a bit fed up. • I'm really sorry to he
that. • What a surprise! • I felt really sorry for him. • I've never felt so angry in all my life. • I really li
her. • He's not my cup of tea. • I was a bit irritated by what he said. • Are you sure you're all right?
What's the matter? • I'm feeling a bit depressed at the moment. • I'd rather not talk about it, if you dor
mind. • I love you. • Why are you always late? • Poor guy! • I'll get over it soo
• You're in a good mood this morning. • How's it been going lately?

Reading

1 | How's it going?

Sentences 1–4 are answers to the question 'How's it going?' Match the answers 1–4 to the follow-up comments a–d.

1. Actually, I'm feeling a bit ill.
2. I'm exhausted, to be honest.
3. To be honest, I'm a bit fed up.
4. I'm in a really good mood, actually.

a. I met this really nice guy/woman the other day.
b. I've had really bad food poisoning.
c. I got woken up at about two and couldn't get back to sleep.
d. It's this weather! I'm sick of it!

With a partner, see if you can think of two more follow-up comments for the answers 1–4. The pictures below might help you. Compare answers with another pair of students. Did you think of anything they didn't?

With a partner, use your ideas to have conversations like this:

A: Hi, how's it going?
B: I'm in a really good mood, actually.
A: Really? How come?
B: I met this really nice guy in a club last night.

Now read this text and see how the couple met. Do you think they will stay together? Why/why not?

The day that changed my life

When I saw Jim on the news, I didn't recognise him to begin with. He looked really thin and his hair was falling out. When I heard the reporter say his name, though, I looked a bit more closely and then I realised it was him. I just burst out crying. I was really surprised, because we were never really friends when we were at school together. He came from quite a poor family and his dad had been in prison. Maybe it was just because he was looking for attention, but I remember that he could be a bit loud sometimes in class and we were just very different, I suppose. But to see him there, looking so lost and alone, begging on the street! Well, it was just so upsetting. It broke my heart, it really did!

The next thing I knew, I was ringing the TV station which had run the report. I don't really know why – I just did it on impulse. Anyway, they gave me the address of a hostel for homeless people. I went down there the following day and it was really depressing. It was filthy and the whole place stank! Half the people there were either drunk or mad – or both! One of the workers showed me to where Jim was sleeping. What amazed me was that he recognised me at once and said, 'Oh, Andrea. It's you.' His voice sounded so sad, but, at the same time – and I can't explain this very well – it was like I could feel something pulling us together. I felt like it was destiny.

I'd like to say that things have been easy for us since then and that love has run its true course, but life doesn't work like that, does it? What happened to Jim when he became homeless was incredibly painful and he's had to fight to overcome his addictions. To begin with, my parents were very unhappy about our relationship. My father is a very successful businessman and I know he wanted me to marry someone with money. Still, they are slowly starting to accept my decision and now that they've met Jim a few times they can see that he is a good man.

We've had a lot of support from people who've seen our story in the papers, but we've also had a lot of negative comments too and we've both lost some friends. The media have also put a lot of pressure on us. I know Jim doesn't see it this way, but even now it still makes me angry the way the papers and the TV producers treat people. I just think back to that first story. Here was this completely broken man, living on the streets. They came along and did their story on him, and do you know what they gave him? Ten pounds and a cup of tea! That's it! And then they got back into their big cars and drove off, leaving him to go back to that awful hostel. They do these stories, but none of them really care about people. I can't forgive them for that.

Anyway, despite all that, we've managed to survive together. He's a wonderful person, and I love him with all my heart.

Now go back and underline any expressions which are new to you. Underline only whole expressions – not single words! Compare what you have underlined with what your partner has underlined.

2 | True or false?

Are these statements true or false? Why do you think so?

1. Jim was living on the streets when he first met Andrea. T / F
2. Andrea thought carefully before ringing the TV company. T / F
3. Jim still takes drugs. T / F
4. Andrea's parents wanted her to have an arranged marriage. T / F
5. Jim and Andrea agree that the media sometimes exploits people. T / F

3 | Speaking

Discuss these questions with a partner.

1. Is there much homelessness in your hometown? Why? How do you feel about it?
2. Do you ever give money to people who are begging?
3. Do you agree with Andrea that the media sometimes exploits people?
4. Why do you think some people made negative comments about Andrea and Jim's relationship?
5. Have you heard of any other love stories involving people from very different backgrounds?

4 | Expressions with *get*

Make sentences by matching the beginnings 1–8 to the endings a–h. All the sentences contain expressions with get. They are all connected with how Jim came to be homeless. Use your dictionary to help you if necessary.

1. They got married
2. She got killed
3. He got sacked
4. He got behind
5. He got addicted
6. She got pregnant
7. He got very depressed
8. He got evicted

a. to drugs.
b. with his work and couldn't catch up.
c. from his job.
d. in a car crash.
e. and was due to give birth in December.
f. in a registry office.
g. from his house because he couldn't pay the rent.
h. after his wife's death.

Real English: get / become

In spoken English get is much more common than become. In many expressions, such as get married, get angry, or get sick, get is almost exclusively used. We can use get with many adjectives. Become is used with nouns.
I became a teacher after I left university.
I gave up my job in the bank and decided to become a doctor.
She became a Muslim when she got married.

5 | Speaking

Discuss these questions with a partner.

1. Jim and his wife got married in a registry office. Where else do people typically get married?
2. What was the last wedding you went to? Where was it?
3. What would you say if someone told you they were pregnant? What questions might you ask?
4. Can you think of any other reasons why someone might get evicted?

6 | Free practice

With a partner, tell the story of how Jim became homeless. Use all of the expressions with get from Exercise 4 in any order you like, and add as much extra information as you can. You can start like this:

Things started going wrong for Jim a few years ago when he met a woman called Jan.

Compare your stories with another group.

Using vocabulary

1 Adjectives with two different forms

In the article, Andrea said: 'I was really surprised' and 'It was really depressing'. The pairs surprised/surprising and depressed/depressing are different in meaning. Some adjectives can end in either -ed or -ing. Do you know the rules for when we use each ending? Compare your thoughts with a partner and then read these rules.

a. There is only a small group of adjectives which end in either -ed or -ing, but many of them are very common.

b. We use the -ed form of the adjectives to describe people's feelings. People are surprised, bored, excited, etc.

c. We use the -ing form of the adjectives to describe things or situations. They are depressing, boring, exciting, etc. We often use the pattern I *find* + noun + *-ing* adjective. For example:
I found the party really boring.

Complete the pairs of sentences below with the pairs of adjectives in the box.

annoyed / annoying	frustrated / frustrating
bored / boring	surprised / surprising
confused / confusing	terrified / terrifying
depressed / depressing	worried / worrying

1a. Sorry, can you explain that again? I'm still a bit . . . . about it.

1b. I find English grammar really . . . ., especially the present perfect.

2a. He's got this really . . . . habit of tapping his foot all the time!

2b. I'm a bit . . . . that he didn't phone me! He promised me he would!

3a. I wish it would stop raining! This weather is really . . . .!

3b. His wife left him last year, and he's been really . . . . since then.

4a. That film was really . . . . I jumped out of my seat about five times!

4b. Sorry, but I can't look down. I'm absolutely . . . . of heights!

5a. Don't you think they should be here by now? Isn't it a bit . . . . that they haven't even phoned?

5b. I'm a bit . . . . about my exams next week.

6a. I was really . . . . when I arrived in Chicago. I thought it'd be much cleaner than it is!

6b. I thought the end of the film was really . . . . I mean, I wasn't expecting him to really be a woman.

7a. I get really . . . . when I can't say what I want to say. It drives me mad!

7b. I find talking to her very . . . . She never listens to anything I say!

8a. It was so . . . . that I fell asleep halfway through!

8b. I'm really . . . . with this! Can't we do something else?

Here are five other pairs of common adjectives with two different forms. Write one sentence for each to show the difference. Use your dictionary to help you if necessary. Compare your sentences with a partner's.

disappointed / disappointing	excited / exciting
scared / scary	stressed-out / stressful
upset / upsetting	

2 Speaking

Discuss these questions with a partner.

1. What kinds of things do you get worried about?
2. Have you got any annoying habits?
3. Is there anything that you're terrified of?
4. What things about English do you still find confusing?
5. What makes you depressed?

3 | Collocations

Match the adjectives 1–4 to the groups of nouns they collocate with a–d.

1. annoying
2. boring
3. disappointing
4. stressful

a. lesson / book / person / job / TV programme
b. day / job / week / situation
c. habit / person / noise
d. response / news / result / game

Now match the adjectives 5–8 to the groups of nouns they collocate with e–h.

5. confusing
6. scary
7. surprising
8. exciting

e. ending / answer / win / number of people
f. question / instructions / directions / plot
g. discovery / race / city / new development
h. monster / ghost story / ride

Which of the adjective + noun collocations above are new for you? With a partner, try to agree on a good example for each one. For example, an annoying noise could be the sound of water from a dripping tap or someone coughing a lot.

4 | Other kinds of feelings

We often turn down invitations because of how we are feeling. Make short dialogues by matching the questions 1–4 to the answers a–d.

1. Do you fancy going out for dinner later?
2. Do you fancy watching that film that's on later?
3. Do you fancy going jogging later?
4. Do you fancy going to that party later on?

a. No, I'm not really in the mood for a comedy.
b. No, I don't really feel like it. I'd rather just stay in and cook here.
c. No, I can't be bothered. It'll take ages to get there.
d. No, I'm too tired to do any exercise. I've been on my feet all day at work.

Listen and check your answers. Go back and underline the useful expressions in a–d above.

With a partner, practise the dialogues above.

> **Real English:** I can't be bothered
>
> I can't be bothered is a very common phrase which means you are either too lazy or too tired to do something.
> *I can't be bothered to cook tonight. Let's go out for dinner.*
> *Let's take the bus. I can't be bothered to walk there.*

5 | Free practice

With a partner, have conversations using these ideas.

1. A: fancy / get / something to eat?
   B: don't feel like / not hungry

2. A: fancy / go / theatre tonight?
   B: not / mood / a play / rather / go / the cinema

3. A: fancy / go swimming later?
   B: tired / work / all day

4. A: fancy / go / round to Kim's house later?
   B: bothered / not / mood

Using grammar

1 | Two uses of the present continuous

You are going to hear a conversation between two people who have just bumped into each other and have only met once or twice before. As you listen, try to work out:

1. where they are.
2. how they're feeling and why.

Look at the tapescript on page 149 and underline six examples of the present continuous. Decide if these examples fit use 1 or use 2 below.

Use 1: An unfinished action in the present

We often use the present continuous form of a verb to show that an action is not finished at the moment of speaking. For example:

A: What're you doing here? Are you going somewhere?

B: No, I'm just picking up a friend. He's coming down from Glasgow for the weekend. (The friend hasn't arrived yet.)

A: What are you doing at the moment? Are you still working for KFC?

B: Yeah, but I'm looking for something else now. (He hasn't found another job yet.)

A: Hello, it's Bill.

B: Hi. Listen, I'm sorry, I'm cooking dinner for some friends. Can I ring you back in about an hour? (The food is not ready yet.)

Use 2: An arrangement in the future

We also use the present continuous to refer to something we arranged before speaking, but which will happen in the future.

A: What are you doing later?

B: Oh, I'm meeting a friend of mine from school. He rang me last night, out of the blue. I haven't seen him for ages.

As you can see from the examples above, the present continuous is used to talk about both the present and the future.

2 | Practice

Decide if these sentences refer to:
a. an unfinished action in the present.
b. an arrangement in the future.

1. I'm meeting John later to discuss the plans for the party.
2. Listen, can you call me back in an hour or so? I'm cooking something just now.
3. I'm going to Australia in the summer.

4. I'm doing a lot of overtime at the moment. I'm trying to save as much money as I can.
5. I've got to get back home. I'm cooking dinner for everyone tonight.
6. Listen, I'm sorry, but I'm doing an extra shift at work tonight to cover for someone who's sick.
7. Let's wait a few minutes. It's pouring with rain outside.
8. I can't do it now. I'm writing this essay that's got to be in tomorrow.
9. I'm picking up my boyfriend from the airport at nine o'clock tomorrow morning.
10. Sorry, he's not in. He's doing some shopping in town, so he won't be back for a while.

Compare your answers with a partner. How did you make your decisions?

Use the following sentence starters to tell your partner a bit about what you're doing this week:

I'm meeting ...
I'm going ...

3 | Questions and answers

Make short dialogues by matching the questions 1–7 to the answers a–g.

1. What are you doing? Have you lost something?
2. What are you doing now? Are you still teaching?
3. What are you doing now? Are you going home?
4. What are you doing here? Are you looking for something special?
5. What are you doing here? Are you studying English?
6. What are you doing now? Are you very busy?
7. What are you doing here? Are you just having a drink?

a. No, I'm just window shopping, really. I haven't got much money at the moment.

b. No, I gave it up. I'm just temping in an office at the moment, until I decide what to do.

c. Yeah, I'm looking for my car keys. You haven't seen them anywhere, have you?

d. No, I'm just sorting out a few papers. I can leave it till later, if you want to talk now.

e. No, actually, I'm going to the cinema. I'm meeting a friend there. Do you fancy coming?

f. Yeah, I'm with some people from work. They're sitting over there.

g. No, I'm doing a computing course.

4 | Further practice

With a partner, have similar conversations to the ones in Exercise 3 on page 30, but change a bit of each answer. For example:

A: What are you doing? Have you lost something?
B: Yes, I'm looking for my glasses. You haven't seen them anywhere, have you?

A: No, sorry. Good luck! Hope you find them.

A: What are you doing now? Are you still teaching?
B: Yes, I am, but I'm working at a different school now.

5 | Free practice

With a partner, have the conversations you would have if you bumped into a friend in each of the places in the pictures below. For example:

A: Hi, Nick. What're you doing here? Are you going somewhere?
B: No, I'm just meeting a friend who's coming to visit.

6 | Speaking

Discuss these questions with a partner.

1. Have you ever bumped into someone you hadn't seen for a long time? When?
2. Do many people do temping work in your country? What kind?
3. Do you like window shopping? Why/why not?

7 | Negative responses

Here are eight negative responses, all using the present continuous. With a partner, decide what the question was. The first one is done for you.

1. A: *Dad, can I borrow the car tonight?*
   B: Actually, I'm using it later. Sorry.

2. A: ....?
   B: Not now. I'm watching TV. I'll do it later.

3. A: ....?
   B: I'd love to, but I'm meeting someone at six, I'm afraid.

4. A: ....?
   B: I'm terribly sorry, but we're having some problems with our computer.

5. A: ....?
   B: Sorry. I'm washing my hair tonight.

6. A: ....?
   B: I can't! I'm already seeing someone.

7. A: ....?
   B: No, I'm watching something.

8. A: ....?
   B: No, I'm listening to it.

Now ask other students your eight questions. They should respond using the negative answers above.

> For more information on how to use the present continuous, see G4.

Review: Units 1–4

1 Tenses

Complete these texts by putting the verbs in brackets into the correct tense. The time phrases will help you.

1. I (a) .... (do) an evening class on the history of film at the moment, and I
(b) .... (really / enjoy) it. It
(c) .... (start) six months ago, but I
(d) .... (miss) the first four classes, so I (e) .... (only / do) it for the last five months.

2. A: (a) .... (you / ever / be) to Syria?
   B: Yeah, I have, actually. I (b) .... (go) there about four or five years ago on holiday. It (c) .... (be) amazing. Actually, while I (d) .... (travel) around there, I (e) .... (meet) this man who's now one of my best friends. Why do you ask, anyway? (f) .... (you / think) of going?

3. A: What (a) .... (you / do) this weekend? Have you got any plans?
   B: Yeah, I have, actually. I (b) .... (meet) some old friends of mine tomorrow and we (c) .... (have) dinner together in the evening. I (d) .... (really / look forward to) it. I (e) .... (plan) to meet them for ages, but I just (f) .... (not have) the time.

2 Grammar review

Circle the correct words.

1. I was sleeping when / while suddenly my fire alarm went off.

2. I don't know about you, but I found the film a bit bored / boring.

3. A: Do you fancy going / to go out somewhere this afternoon?
   B: Yeah, that'd be nice. Did you have anywhere particular in mind?

4. I've been trying to get in touch with her since / for ages!

5. A: I've got my Danish class tomorrow.
   B: Oh, right. How long did you do / have you been doing that for, then?

6. A: Dad, can I borrow your car later on?
   B: No, sorry. I'm using / I'll use it tonight, I'm afraid.

7. The bomb attack happened while I was living / I have been living in London.

8. A: I used to play basketball professionally.
   B: Oh, really? How long did you do / have you been doing that for, then?

9. I'll meet / I'm meeting some friends of mine for a coffee later.

10. I've been doing aerobics since / for last spring.

Compare your answers with a partner and explain your choices.

3 Word order

Where in these sentences do the words in brackets go? Mark each spot with an arrow.

1. A: Have you been to Brazil? (ever)
   B: No, I've been anywhere in South America. (never)

2. A: Are you ready to go?
   B: No, I haven't finished writing this. (yet)

3. A: Do you know if Kate's in today?
   B: Yeah. I've seen her in the coffee bar. (just)

4. A: Do you fancy going to see Bad Times later?
   B: No, I've seen it, I'm afraid. (already)

5. I can't believe you've been abroad! (never)

6. A: How did you get into archery?
   B: I don't know. I've been into it, I suppose. (always)

4 Look back and check

Look back at Exercise 4 Vocabulary focus on page 17. Tick all the words and expressions you can remember. Ask your partner about anything you have forgotten.

Tell your partner as much as you can about how the rest of your family members spend their free time. Use as much of the language from this exercise as you can.

5 | Verb collocations

Match the verbs 1–10 to the groups of words and phrases they collocate with a–j.

1. give ▢
2. go on ▢
3. get ▢
4. work ▢
5. go out ▢
6. rent ▢
7. tidy up ▢
8. do ▢
9. go to ▢
10. go ▢

a. really depressed / married
b. for dinner / for a walk
c. my flat / my house
d. a lot of overtime / really long hours
e. grey / crazy
f. the cinema / church
g. a lot of damage / some research
h. a cruise / holiday
i. a cottage for a week / a bike for the day
j. it a miss / you some advice

You have one minute to memorise the collocations a–j. Now cover the exercise above. Your partner will read out the verbs 1–10. How many collocations can you remember?

With a partner, try to think of one more common collocation for each of the verbs 1–10.

6 | Adjectives

Complete the sentences below with the adjectives in the box.

annoying	pregnant
awful	scary
boring	stressful
great	strong
interesting	sunburnt

1. A: Have you heard? Reina's . . . .
   B: Really? Wow! When's it due?
2. My job's OK, but I wish I didn't have to go to so many long, ... meetings.
3. A: Where's he from?
   B: France. Can't you tell? He's got a really . . . . accent.
4. There's a nice restaurant in town we could hire. It'd be a(n) . . . . place for the Christmas party.

5. A: He's always promising to do things and then he never does!
   B: Oh, no. That must be really . . . .
   A: Yeah, it is. It drives me mad!
6. A: The train missed me by about twenty centimetres. I really thought I was going to die.
   B: Oh, no! That must've been really . . . .
7. One of the best things about my job is the fact that I get to meet lots of . . . . people.
8. A: I'm in charge of five hundred people where I work.
   B: Wow! That must be really . . . .
   A: Yeah, it is. That's why I'm going grey.
9. A: How was Crete?
   A: OK, but the weather was . . . . It rained almost non-stop.
10. A: You should've seen this guy! He was so badly . . . . he was almost purple.
    B: Really? People are so stupid! Why don't they just stay in the shade?

7 | Questions and answers

Match the questions 1–10 to the answers a–j.

1. How long have you been here? ▢
2. How long are you staying here? ▢
3. Was that film any good? ▢
4. Are you any good at volleyball? ▢
5. Hi. How's it going? ▢
6. What's the matter? ▢
7. How often do you do that, then? ▢
8. How did you get into that, then? ▢
9. Are you going away this summer? ▢
10. Have you ever been there before? ▢

a. Oh, it's nothing. I'm just a bit fed up with things at the moment.
b. About six more months, I think.
c. Yeah, we're going on a cruise round the Mediterranean.
d. Yeah, I'm not bad.
e. Fine, thanks. What about you?
f. About three months now.
g. I used to do it when I was at school, and I carried on after I left.
h. Oh, it was OK – not great.
i. No, never, but it's supposed to be lovely.
j. Quite a bit, actually. Maybe two or three times a week.

8 What can you remember?

With a partner, note down as much as you can remember about the texts you read in Units 1 and 4.

The secrets of success

The day that changed my life

Now compare what you remember with another pair of students. Who remembered more?

Which text did you enjoy more? Why?

9 Common expressions

Complete the sentences below with the words in the box.

exactly	fancy	given	makes	took
fan	give	grew	mood	wouldn't

1. I got . . . . it for my birthday.
2. It really . . . . me angry.
3. I'm in a really good . . . .
4. Do you . . . . going out somewhere later?
5. It was great, but I . . . . do it again.
6. I thought I'd . . . . it a try.
7. I just stayed in and . . . . it easy.
8. I used to, but I . . . . out of it.
9. Whereabouts is it . . . . ?
10. I'm a big . . . . of theirs.

Now discuss these questions with a partner.

11. Have you got given anything recently? What? Why?
12. What things make you really angry?
13. What kinds of things have you grown out of over the last few years?
14. What are you a big fan of?

10 Revision quiz

Discuss these questions in groups of three.

1. Can you think of three questions where you would use 'if you don't mind me asking'?
2. The answer is: 'No, I'm an only child'. What's the question?
3. What is collocation?
4. If you make a mess in your kitchen, do you need to tidy it up or wash it up?
5. Can you think of three ways to finish this sentence? I just stayed in last night and …
6. Can you think of three ways to complete this sentence? I went to … last night.
7. Can you think of three different kinds of club you could join?
8. What kinds of things do you do if you sort out your summer holiday?
9. If you go camping, where do you sleep?
10. Why are package holidays good value for money?
11. What's the difference between 'it's great' and 'it's supposed to be great'?
12. Where do you keep all your clothes and things if you go backpacking round the world?
13. Can you think of two reasons why you might be exhausted?
14. And two reasons why you might be a bit fed up?
15. Can you think of two famous soap operas?
16. Why might you get evicted?
17. What do you do when you give someone a lift?
18. Where would you do the front crawl?
19. Can you think of three things you could swap?
20. Why can learning a language be frustrating sometimes?

Learner advice: Recording and revising vocabulary

You probably already translate some of the new language you learn in class. However, you need to be careful how you use translation. Translating single words isn't a very good idea, because words have lots of different meanings depending on the other words you use them with. It's much better to translate whole expressions or collocations – words which go together.

Look at the page from a notebook below. On the left are twenty expressions from Units 1 to 4 of the *Innovations intermediate Workbook*. Translate them all into your language.

ENGLISH	MY LANGUAGE
I can take it or leave it.	
She's in her mid-thirties.	
It's just off the main road.	
That's a very difficult question to answer.	
Is it OK if I rub this off the board now?	
How long've you been doing that, then?	
I just stayed in and had an early night.	
not long after I graduated	
since I was a kid	
Is there anything good on?	
He's away on holiday at the moment.	
I don't really like going sightseeing very much.	
She's on a business trip.	
May the first is a public holiday.	
I wouldn't go there again even if you paid me!	
It's been ages. How've you been?	
Listen. I've got to go or I'll be late.	
I've got to get this essay finished by Monday.	
There's a lot of homelessness there.	
It was really scary!	

If possible, compare your translations with a partner who speaks the same language as you or with your teacher. You can test your memory by covering the left-hand side of the notebook up and just reading your translations.

Why don't you start keeping a notebook for translating lists of useful expressions?

What do you do? • How long have you been out of work? • I'm a traffic warden. • I'm thinking of leavi[ng] my job. • I've got a great boss. • What's the pay like? • I work on the assembly line. • That must b[e] interesting. • I'm in computers. • Is it part-time? • Have you ever been sacked? • We get four week[s] holiday a year. • I've just got a rise. • What's it like? • I work from 9 till 5 five days a week. • It's a full-tim[e] job. • I've gone freelance. • I work from home. • Congratulations on your promotio[n] • Desk jobs aren't for me. • Can I have your business card?

Using vocabulary

1 What do you do?

With a partner, discuss what you think the people in the pictures do for a living. Use these structures to make guesses:

He/she looks like a … or maybe a … .

I reckon she's/he's a … or perhaps a … .

🎧 **Listen and see if you were right. Note down any differences between what you guessed and what you hear.**

Now listen again and complete the gaps in these sentences.

1. I work as . . . . I'm self-employed.
2. I'm a student at the moment, but I'd like to work for a big publishing company as . . . . when I graduate.
3. I work for a small clothes company as . . . .
4. I'm a housewife now, but I used to work . . . . as a cashier.
5. I . . . . in a local hospital as a nurse.
6. I'm a student, but I work part-time in a restaurant as . . . .
7. I work part-time in . . . . as a teacher.
8. I'm unemployed at the moment, but I used to work for a dotcom company as . . . .

2 Free practice

Talk about yourself and your family using some of the patterns in Exercise 1. For example:

My dad's retired now, but he used to work for a building company as a civil engineer.

I'm a student, but I work part-time in a clothes shop as a sales assistant.

3 Speaking

Discuss these questions with a partner.

1. Why do you think the speaker in number 8 in Exercise 1 is unemployed now?
2. Do you know anybody who is unemployed at the moment? Why?
3. Why do you think the woman in number 4 in Exercise 1 left her job?
4. Do you know anybody who has left their job? Why?

4 | Do you like it?

Do these comments show that the person likes their job or doesn't like it?

1. I have to travel a lot.
2. I get to travel a lot.
3. The money's terrible. I only get about five pounds an hour.
4. The money's great. I get over forty thousand a year.
5. The hours are great. Most days I can leave by three.
6. The hours are awful. I often have to work late.
7. I don't have to come in to work if the kids are ill.
8. I have to deal with some really difficult customers sometimes.
9. I have to take work home with me sometimes.
10. I can work from home on my laptop, if I want.
11. I don't have to wear a suit or get dressed up for work.
12. I have to wear a bright orange uniform.
13. I don't get on very well with my boss.
14. I get on well with the other people at work.

Go back and underline all the expressions which use these verbs:

- have to
- don't have to
- can

Complete these explanations with have to, don't have to or can.

a. We use . . . . to show that we have no choice about doing something.
b. We use . . . . and . . . . to show that we have a choice about whether to do something or not.

Very often we don't like things about which we have no choice – things we have to do – but we like things we don't have to do or can do if we want. Complete these sentences with the correct form of have to, don't have to or can.

15. I . . . . get up really early. I hate it!
16. I . . . . work at weekends if I don't want to. It's optional.
17. I . . . . deal with some very rude people sometimes.
18. I . . . . go to lots of boring meetings.
19. I . . . . deal with a lot of complaints.
20. I . . . . go on lots of interesting courses if I want to.
21. I . . . . work nights. It depends if I feel like it or not.
22. I . . . . wear what I like to work. Nobody minds.
23. I . . . . do much paperwork. Thank goodness!
24. I . . . . start and finish when I like. It's really flexible.

Real English: thank goodness

We use thank goodness to show we are happy or relieved that we don't have to do something or that something terrible has stopped or not happened.
Thank goodness they've stopped making that terrible noise.
Thank goodness you're here! I thought you'd had an accident.
I don't have to get up early tomorrow. Thank goodness!

Thank goodness is polite and for some people a bit old-fashioned. Many people use stronger versions.

5 | Free practice

Work in groups of three. Each person should choose one of the jobs in the pictures. Don't tell anyone else which job you have chosen. The others should ask questions to try to find out which job it is. Use these structures to help you:

Do you have to … ?
Can you … if you want to?
What's the money like?
What're the hours like?

Using grammar

1 | A good job?

Do you think being an accountant would be a good job? Why/why not? Read this text and see if it makes you change your mind.

Marika from Denmark: Accountant

Don't let your parents push you into becoming an accountant, like I did. Yes, the money's good and yes, there's job security, but honestly, it must be the worst job in the world! I spend ten hours a day looking at figures and reading the most dry, boring reports you can imagine. It really drives me mad! Most nights I have to stay in the office really late, not because there's any real work to do; it's just that it doesn't look good if you're the first person to leave. When I started, my parents said, 'Don't worry. You'll get used to it,' but I never have – and I never will.

2 | Get used to/be used to

In the text, Marika says she has never got used to being an accountant – and she never will! Things that feel strange to begin with often start feeling normal after a while. If we had to, we could get used to lots of things – being in a different country, different weather, terrible jobs, having a broken leg! However, some things are so strange or annoying that we believe we could never get used to them!

Tell a partner which of the following you could get used to – and which you could never get used to. Why?

I could (never) get used to … because …

* having a woman as a boss
* working from nine to five
* being a boss
* being self-employed
* working a six-day week
* being unemployed
* working a twelve-hour day
* working in an office
* working shifts
* working outside
* working from home
* working with computers
* working in a factory
* working with my hands

3 | Matching

Match the statements 1–6 to the follow-up comments a–f.

1. I'm so used to getting up early
2. I'm still trying to get used to working in such a big office.
3. I still haven't got used to working nights yet.
4. It took me a long time to get used to working from home,
5. I don't think I'll ever get used to working a six-day week.
6. I'm sure you'll get used to having a woman boss.

a. It's really hard getting up when everyone else is going to bed!
b. but now I really enjoy the freedom it gives me.
c. I'm so used to having my weekends free that it's driving me mad!
d. I keep getting lost and forgetting where I am.
e. I don't even think about it any more.
f. I mean, it *is* the twenty-first century, isn't it!

4 | Speaking

Which statements are true for you? If some statements are *not* true, can you change them using some of the other get used to expressions from Exercise 3 above so that they are true?

1. It took me a long time to get used to the different sounds of English.
2. I'm slowly getting used to hearing spoken English.
3. I'm sure I'll get used to English grammar.
4. I still haven't got used to English spelling.
5. I don't think I'll ever get used to the difference between American and British English.

Compare your answers with a partner and explain your choices.

5 | Word order

Complete these short dialogues by putting the words in brackets in the correct order.

1. A: So, how're you finding your new job? Is it going OK?
    B: Yeah, it's OK, but I .... working from nine to five yet.
    (haven't / got / to / still / used)

2. A: So, how're you finding the computer course you're doing so far?
    B: It's OK. I'm .... things.
    (used / to / getting / slowly)

3. A: How do you find working nights? It must be quite hard, isn't it?
    B: No, it's OK. You .... after a while.
    (it / used / to / get / just)

4. A: How're you finding working in the bank? Is it going OK?
    B: Not really. I .... being stuck behind a desk all day! I'm thinking of leaving.
    (I'll / used / don't / ever / get / to / think)

5. A: How do you find working from home? Do you enjoy it?
    B: Yeah, it's nice, but it .... being on my own all day!
    (time / me / used / a / long / get / took / to / to)

6. A: How're you finding your new boss? Is she OK?
    B: Yeah, not bad. She's a bit bossy, but I'm .... her.
    (sure / to / get / I'll / used)

Real English: stuck behind a desk all day

We often use (be) stuck to show we can't change our situation and we don't like it. Notice it often goes with a time expression.
I'm stuck in front of a computer all day.
I'm stuck inside all day.
I'm stuck outside all day.
I was stuck on the motorway for about three hours.

---

6 | Role play

You have gone to live in a foreign country. Spend two minutes thinking about which country you are in and what living there is like. Your partner is going to phone you. Your partner is a friend of yours from home. He/she will ask about how things are going using some of these questions.

So, how're you finding | the language?
the people there?
the food?
the weather?
being away from your family?
the culture?

Try to use these sentences to explain how you're finding things.

I'm already used to it.
It took me a long time to get used to it.
I'm slowly getting used to it.
I'm sure I'll get used to it.
I still haven't got used to it.
I don't think I'll ever get used to it.

Now change roles and have another phone conversation.

For more information on how to use *get used to / be used to*, see G5.

Listening

1 | Before you listen

You are going to hear Maria and Ken, who have recently met, talking about their jobs. All the words below are connected with their work. Try to decide what each person does. Use a dictionary to help you if you need to.

Maria: AIDS   depressed   needles   rewarding
             rehabilitation centre

Ken: currency   boring   long hours   office

2 | While you listen

Cover the conversation below. Listen to the conversation and try to answer these questions.

1. What jobs do Maria and Ken do?
2. What do their jobs involve exactly?

Now listen again and complete the gaps.

So, what do you do?

Ken: So, what do you do, Maria?

Maria: Oh, I'm a drugs worker.

Ken: Right, so what does that (1) . . . . ? Do you work in a rehabilitation centre or what?

Maria: No, no. I work in an area of Bristol where there are a lot of (2) . . . . We go out in a van and give out clean needles, food and things like that. We also give them information about how to stay (3) . . . ., or give them help if they need to see a doctor.

Ken: So you don't try to make them stop?

Maria: No, not if they don't want to. If we tried to make them stop, they wouldn't want to know us. I mean, if they want to stop, sure, we help them (4) . . . . in a rehabilitation centre, but we don't try to persuade them or anything. We try not to make judgements.

Ken: (5) . . . . ? So what's the point? Aren't you making things worse? You know, encouraging them to take more drugs?

Maria: No, I don't think so. You can't really persuade them. They have to want to give up. What we do is make sure they stay as healthy as possible so they don't (6) . . . . like AIDS and they don't leave dirty needles lying around.

Ken: Mm, maybe. You must get a bit depressed, though, seeing all those people wasting their lives.

Maria: Yeah, I do sometimes, but it can also be (7) . . . . when you help people sort out a problem. And the money's quite good as well.

Ken: So you like it, then?

Maria: Yeah, it's OK. There's lots of good things about it. I mean, I work in the afternoons and evenings, so I (8) . . . . get up early, and the people I work with are really nice, so you know …

Ken: Well, that's the main thing, isn't it?

Maria: What do you do, then?

Ken: Oh, I work for Barclays Bank.

Maria: (9) . . . . ?

Ken: Buying and selling currency.

Maria: Yeah? I have to say, that sounds a bit boring.

Ken: It can be, and I (10) . . . . really long hours, but then again, the money's really good.

Maria: Mm, right.

Ken: And I (11) . . . . quite a lot. We've got an office in New York that I go to every month.

Maria: That must be good.

Ken: Yeah, it is.

Real English: get to

Ken said: I get to travel quite a lot. We often use get to + verb to talk about good things we have the opportunity to do.
I get to travel a lot in my work – so I get to meet lots of interesting people. My company pays for all my flights – so I get to fly business class. I stay in a lot of big hotels and get to eat in a lot of nice restaurants.

Can you say anything really good about yourself like this?

3 | Speaking

Discuss these questions with a partner.

1. Do you have drugs workers in your country?
2. Does it involve the same kind of work as Maria described in the conversation in Exercise 2 on page 40?
3. Do they get paid or is it voluntary work?
4. Do you think Maria's is the best way of dealing with the drug problem? If not, what is?
5. Is money the most important thing about a job? If not, what is?

4 | Opinions with *must*

Read these short bits of the conversation from Exercise 2 on page 40. Underline the two expressions with must.

Ken: You must get a bit depressed, though, seeing all those people wasting their lives.
Maria: Yeah, I do sometimes, but it can also be very rewarding.
Ken: And I get to travel quite a lot. We've got an office in New York that I go to every month or so.
Maria: That must be good.
Ken: Yeah, it is.

We often use *that must be* or *you must get* + adjective to say how we would feel if we were doing the job we are being told about. For example:

You must get depressed. = if I did your job, I would often feel depressed.

That must be good. = I think your job is good.

**We respond to That must be ... by saying Yeah, it is or Yeah, it can be.
We respond to You must get ... by saying Yeah, I do or Yeah, I do sometimes.**

Complete these short conversations with you must get or that must be and an appropriate response.

1. A: I have to get up at six every morning and I don't get back till seven or eight in the evening.
   B: .... really tiring.
   A: ....

2. A: I spend most of the day just sitting in front of a TV screen.
   B: .... quite bored.
   A: ....

3. A: People often shout at me when I give them a ticket. Some have even threatened to hit me.
   B: .... quite difficult to deal with.
   A: ....

4. A: I get to see people develop and really improve their English.
   B: .... quite rewarding.
   A: ....

5. A: I often want to do more for patients, but I can't because we don't have the money.
   B: .... really frustrated.
   A: ....

6. I have to do a lot of paperwork and a lot of the time no-one ever reads it.
   B: .... really fed up with it.
   A: ....

With a partner, practise the conversations you wrote. What kinds of jobs do you think the speakers in 1–6 have?

> For more information on how to give opinions with *must*, see G6.

5 | Pronunciation: sentence stress

Listen to these sentences. Then practise saying them, giving the underlined parts the heaviest stress.

1. You must get quite <u>tired</u>.
2. That must be quite de<u>press</u>ing.
3. That must be quite <u>stressful</u>.
4. You must get quite de<u>pressed</u>.
5. You must get quite <u>stressed-out</u>.
6. That must be <u>really</u> <u>hard</u> <u>work</u>.
7. That must be <u>really</u> frus<u>trating</u>.
8. You must get <u>really</u> <u>well-paid</u>.

With a partner, practise reading out the dialogues in Exercise 4 above.

6 | Further practice

With a partner, have conversations similar to the ones in Exercise 4 above, but starting in these ways.

1. I get to go all over the world.
2. I'm on my feet all day.
3. I'm in charge of twenty other people.
4. I often can't explain what I want to say.
5. I often have to tell people that their relatives have died.
6. I'm a fireman.

I think I'm a small. • I'm only window shopping. • How much is it? • No, I'm just looking, thank you. • Sho
till you drop. • Have you got it in medium? • Can I try it on? • Do you like Benetton? • They're chea
and cheerful. • I wouldn't be seen dead shopping there. • I'm a nine. • Do you take Amex? • Have yo
got the 15p? • Have you got it in red? • Do you think it suits me? • It doesn't fit me. • Try Gap. • Wher
did you get it? • It's not really me, is it? • Cool glasses! • They're secon
hand. • Can I get change for this?

6 Shopping

Reading

1 | Speaking

Match the places 1–6 to the pictures A–F.

1. a branch of a global chain ☐
2. a second-hand shop ☐
3. a car-boot sale ☐
4. a small designer boutique ☐
5. a shopping mall ☐
6. a street market ☐

With a partner, try to think of one good thing and one bad thing about going shopping in each of the places in the pictures. Use these sentence starters:

One good thing about shopping in … is the fact that …
One problem with … is the fact that …

Change partners and discuss these questions.

7. Which of the places in 1–6 above do you enjoy going to? Why?

8. Are there any places you would never go to? Why not?

2 | While you read

Read the article about shopping, then answer these questions.

1. Which places does the author enjoy shopping in? Why?

2. Which places does the author hate shopping in? Why?

I'm a **car-boot sale addict** and *proud of it!*

Let's face it, it's not much fun shopping in most shops anymore, is it? The thing is, cities all over the world are starting to look more and more similar. In almost every one, you find branches of the same global chains of shops and fast food restaurants – Gap, Niketown, Benetton, McDonald's, the Body Shop and Starbucks. As the chains corner the market, lots of little shops go out of business, and with every one that goes bankrupt, the world becomes a little bit duller and more predictable. Chains will never surprise you in any way. You know exactly what you'll get before you even walk through their doors. It's getting harder and harder to find unusual, interesting, or even just different things out there … and that's really why I'm a car-boot sale addict.

Every weekend, in fields, car parks and school yards all over Britain, thousands of people unload the contents of their car boots onto little tables and sell off all the old junk they've been meaning to get rid of for ages. The prices are usually made up on the spot, and haggling over them is part of the fun. If you get there early enough, you can pick up some amazing bargains – old records, out of print books, vintage clothes, incredibly cheap antiques. On top of all that, there's lots of other strange bits and pieces to make you think: old photograph albums, collections of old love letters, second-hand glass eyes. You can find anything and everything at these places!

So next time you get fed up with being ripped off by a big chain which thinks three pounds is a fair price for a cup of coffee, say goodbye to big business and hello to the world of car boot sales!

Real English: old junk

Old junk is all the old, broken, useless stuff you don't want any more and that you need to get rid of. In Britain, people often call cheap second-hand shops junk shops. Junk mail is all the post you get from companies advertising their products. Most people just throw it in the rubbish bin.

Do you usually delete all your junk e-mails or do you sometimes read some?

3 | Speaking

Discuss these questions with a partner.

1. Has the article made you want to go to a car-boot sale? Why/why not?
2. Do you have them in your country? If not, what do you do with things you no longer need?
3. Is there anything you agree or disagree with in the article?

4 | *Thing* – an important word in English

In the article, the writer says: 'It's getting harder and harder to find unusual, interesting, or even just different things out there.' What's the most unusual or interesting thing you've ever seen while shopping?

Thing(s) is a very common word in English. Match each sentence 1–8 to the phrase a–h that expresses the meaning of the word thing in the sentence.

1. I've got to pack my things tonight.
2. Sorry, but I've left my swimming things at home.
3. Can you give me five minutes to sort my things out?
4. I've got to get a few things for my flat.
5. That's the thing I really love about her.
6. That's the thing I really hate about him.
7. That was a stupid thing to do!
8. I've got to do a few things in town this afternoon.

a. my paperwork
b. my clothes
c. my trunks
d. he's always late
e. go to the bank, pay my phone bill, gas bill, etc.
f. her sense of humour
g. losing my car keys
h. washing-up liquid, soap, washing powder

What else do you think thing(s) could refer to in the sentences 3–8 above? Did you notice that sentences 1–4 referred to concrete things and 5–8 referred to abstract things?

What's the most stupid thing you've ever done? Start your story like this:

A: You'll never believe what I once did. I …
B: How did you manage to do that, then?
A: Well, what happened was …

The writer said he likes car-boot sales because you find things like old photograph albums, collections of old love letters and second-hand glass eyes. Would you buy things like that? Why/why not?

Have you got things at home which you would like to sell at a car-boot sale?

5 | Matching

Make complete sentences by matching 1–8 to a–h.

I bought …

1. a great pair
2. a really nice leather
3. a big box
4. a lovely bunch
5. the latest
6. some cheap clothes
7. a ticket
8. a present

a. in a sale.
b. for a friend.
c. for a musical next week.
d. jacket.
e. Red Rat CD.
f. of chocolates.
g. of flowers.
h. of jeans.

Using vocabulary

1 | Different shops

Complete these short dialogues 1–7 with the name of one of the places A–G in the pictures.

1. A: I want to get a paper. Is there a . . . . near here?
   B: Yeah, there's one a couple of hundred metres down the road, opposite the school.

2. A: I need to get some petrol. Is there a . . . . near here?
   B: Yeah, there's one five minutes' drive down the road, just past the station.

3. A: I need to get some nappies. Is there a . . . . near here?
   B: No, but you could try the supermarket in Skipton. It's on the main road.

4. A: I need to get some stamps. Is there a . . . . near here?
   B: No, but you could try the newsagent's just down there, opposite the park.

5. A: I need to post this letter. Is there a . . . . near here?
   B: Yeah, there's one just round the corner outside the newsagent's.

6. A: I need to change some money. Is there a . . . . near here?
   B: No, you'll have to go into Peasmarsh. There's one on the main road, opposite the car park.

7. A: I want to go and get something to eat. Is there a . . . . or café near here?
   B: Yeah, there's a sandwich bar just round the corner.

Real English: down the road, round the corner
We often use down the road or round the corner to show that a place is near. We often follow it with a more specific place expression.

There's a cinema just round the corner on Gower Street.

There's a newsagent's just down the road past the traffic lights.

There's a nice café just round the corner from where I live.

2 | Speaking

With a partner, have conversations like the ones in Exercise 1, but change the directions you give in each one. For example:

A: I want to get a paper. Is there a newsagent's near here?
B: Yeah, there's one about four hundred metres down the road, opposite the school.

Is there anywhere near your school where you can …

1. send a fax?
2. get some photos developed?
3. send an e-mail?
4. do some photocopying?
5. get a photo taken for a passport application?
6. buy an English–English dictionary?
7. hire a video?
8. buy a film for your camera?
9. have your hair cut?
10. pick up a prescription?

Discuss these questions in groups of two or three.

- What shops and facilities are there near your house?
- Who lives in the most convenient place?
- What are your favourite shops? Why?
- Are there any shops you really don't like? Why?

3 Matching

Match the comments 1–5 to the responses a–e.

1. I always wear Wrangler jeans.
2. I always shop at Tower Records.
3. I always buy Sony hi-fi equipment.
4. I always drive German cars.
5. I always have lunch at Al Forno.

a. So do I. They're so reliable.
b. So do I. Their pizzas are so brilliant!
c. So do I. They've got such a wide range.
d. So do I. It's such good quality.
e. So do I. They always fit me really well.

Now match the comments 6–10 to the responses f–j.

6. I never buy English cars.
7. I never drink English beer.
8. I never eat at Pizza Marco.
9. I never shop at Tesco's.
10. I never wear clothes from Gap.

f. Neither do I. It tastes like water.
g. Neither do I. They're so unreliable.
h. Neither do I. They don't really suit me.
i. Neither do I. The food there tastes disgusting.
j. Neither do I, but my mother never shops anywhere else!

A very natural way to agree with someone instead of using so do I is me too. Instead of neither do I, you can say me neither. Try reading the responses above again using these forms.

4 Speaking

Discuss these questions with a partner.

1. Are there any places you always go to or never go to? Why?
2. Are there any brands you always buy or never buy? How do you feel about the following?

- Gap
- McDonald's
- Calvin Klein
- Nike
- Levi's
- Body Shop
- Benetton
- French Connection

3. How much money do you spend shopping in a normal week? What on?

5 Money collocations

Here are six verbs which collocate with money. Make sentences by matching the phrases 1–6 to the phrases a–f and i–vi.

1. I earn
2. I won
3. I was left
4. I found
5. I took
6. I save

a. a ten-pound note
b. four hundred pounds a week
c. ten thousand pounds
d. thirty pounds out of my account
e. five pounds a day
f. a million pounds

i. by taking a packed lunch to work.
ii. when my aunt died.
iii. in the street.
iv. plus overtime.
v. on the lottery.
vi. this morning and I've spent it all already!

Discuss these questions with a partner.

- Have you ever been left any money or won any money on the lottery?
- Have you ever found any money? How much? Where?
- Are you good at saving? Do you save money by doing any of the following?
  - buying second-hand clothes
  - never carrying cash with you
  - walking instead of driving
  - shopping in cheap shops

Using grammar

1 | Must/mustn't

We use I must when talking about something which is important for us to do. We use I mustn't when talking about something which is important not to do. Look at these examples from a conversation in a supermarket:

I must get some shampoo.
I mustn't forget to go to the bank later.

We often use you must to recommend something like a restaurant, a film, or a shop. For example:

You really must go and see *The Circle*. It's a really great film.
You must go to Marks and Spencer. They've got a great sale on at the moment.

Complete these sentences with must or mustn't.

1. Listen, I . . . . go. I'm meeting a friend of mine at six. See you later.

2. Listen, I've got a meeting and I . . . . be late. I'll ring you later. See you.

3. You . . . . try some octopus before you go back. It's a typical dish from this region.

4. Listen, I . . . . just go to the toilet. I'll be back in a moment.

5. We've run out of milk. I . . . . remember to get some when I go out later.

6. They've sent us the final bill for the phone. I . . . . forget to pay it today or we'll be cut off.

7. That reminds me. I . . . . forget to phone my Mum when I get home. It's her birthday.

8. Have you been to the British Museum yet? You really . . . .! It's great.

9. You . . . . come and visit us when you come to Munich. We'd love to see you.

10. Anyway, I . . . . stop now as I'm going out in a minute. Write soon. Lots of love, Andrew.

▶ For more information on using *must* and *mustn't*, see G7.

2 | Alternatives to *must* and *mustn't*

Must and mustn't can sound quite rude if you use them to tell other people what to do. For example, these two sentences are too direct and aggressive:

You mustn't go there. It's very expensive.
You must wear a suit. It's going to be a formal meeting.

There are several ways to express these ideas more politely. Here is one very common way:

I wouldn't go there if I were you. It's very expensive.
I'd wear a suit if I were you. It's going to be a formal meeting.

Sentences 1–6 are too direct. Match each one to a more acceptable alternative a–f.

1. I'm sorry, you mustn't smoke here.
2. You must pay in cash.
3. You must get your ticket in advance.
4. You must take out travel insurance.
5. You mustn't send any private e-mails.
6. You must change some money before leaving.

a. I'd get my ticket in advance if I were you.
b. I'd change some money before leaving if I were you.
c. I'm sorry, smoking's not allowed in here.
d. I'd take out travel insurance if I were you.
e. You have to pay in cash, I'm afraid.
f. You're not supposed to send private e-mails.

Parents sometimes use must and mustn't with young children. Among adults, speakers normally use alternatives a–f above. Now underline the less direct ways of saying must and mustn't.

3 | Speaking

Make a list of four things you must remember to do or mustn't forget to do this week.

I must remember to …
. . . .
. . . .
. . . .
. . . .

I mustn't forget to …
. . . .
. . . .
. . . .
. . . .

In groups, compare your lists and find out who has the busiest week ahead. Then discuss these questions.

1. How do you remember what things you have to do?
2. Do you often forget things you need to do?
3. Have you ever forgotten someone's birthday or forgotten to pay a bill? What happened?

4 | Speaking

With a partner, decide what you would say to these people.

With a partner, decide what advice to give to someone who …

• is going to come and spend a year living in your country.
• is thinking of buying a laptop.
• is going to buy a new car.
• is thinking of becoming a vegetarian.

5 | Focus on *must* and *have to*

Remember we use must for something which we think is important for us to do.

I must leave early tomorrow or I'll miss my plane.

We use have to for something which is necessary because of rules.

I have to send in my tax return by Friday at the latest.

Sorry, but you have to wear your visitor's badge. I can't let you in without one.

It says in the letter you have to pay a deposit of 10% when you book the holiday.

However, mustn't and don't have to have very different meanings.

I don't have to get up early tomorrow. I'm taking the day off. = It's not necessary for me to get up early, but I could if I wanted to.

I mustn't be late or my girlfriend will kill me. = It is essential that I'm not late.

6 | Practice

Complete these sentences with must, mustn't, have to, or don't have to.

1. There's a funny noise coming from my car. I really .... take it in to the garage.
2. You really .... be late again. If you are, you might find yourself looking for another job!
3. Thank goodness I .... write in English at work! My spelling is awful.
4. The flight's at ten, and we .... check-in at least ninety minutes before.
5. If you get the chance, you really .... go and see the Van Gogh museum while you're in Amsterdam.
6. We're having a leaving party for Anne-Marie and we want it to be a surprise, so you .... tell her, whatever you do.
7. We .... be at the hotel by 9.30. Otherwise, the coach will leave without us.
8. I really .... make an appointment at the dentist's. It's over six months since I last went.
9. You can come round whenever you like. You .... ring first. Just turn up.
10. If you want to make sure you get a seat, you'll .... get there really early. They usually sell out really quickly.

Who do you think is talking in number two? Why don't they sound rude in this situation?

7 | Speaking

Discuss these questions with a partner.

1. Have you ever been to the Van Gogh museum? Would you like to?
2. Do you enjoy going round museums? Why/why not?
3. What's your spelling like? Which words do you have most problems with?
4. How often do you go to the dentist's?

8 | Practice

Make statements that are true for you.

1. I'm glad I don't have to ....
2. I'm glad I don't have to ....
3. I'm glad I don't have to ....
4. I'm glad I don't have to ....
5. I'm glad I don't have to ....

Now explain what you have written to a partner.

7 Complaints

Is everything all right, sir? • Why do people spit out their chewing gum on the pavement? • I can't star[t] people who complain. • I'm afraid it's cold. • Excuse me, I ordered the chicken, not the fish. • What was [it] like? • Don't even ask! • It wasn't very warm. • Do you have a complaints form? • Can I speak to th[e] manager, please? • I've never eaten in a worse place in my life! • I wouldn't feed this to my dog! • It was to[o] expensive. • But it's stale. • It's shocking, really. • We had a love[ly] time. • Could you bring us fresh towels, please? • Never again!

Listening

1 Speaking

Discuss these questions with a partner.

1. Do you ever stay in hotels? When? Why?
2. What's the best/worst hotel you've ever stayed in? You can use this pattern:
   I once stayed in this hotel in … and it was amazing/ terrible. …

With a partner, make a list of all the problems you can think of that you could have when you go to a hotel. Which pair has the most?

2 While you listen

🎧 **You are going to hear someone talking about a weekend away at a hotel. As you listen, decide if you think she will stay in that hotel again. Why/why not?**

The speakers used all of the adjectives 1–8. Match the adjectives to the person or thing they describe a–h.

1. efficient ☐
2. sweaty ☐
3. apologetic ☐
4. inedible ☐
5. spotless ☐
6. disgusting ☐
7. reasonable ☐
8. ignorant ☐

a. the steak in the hotel restaurant
b. the way Gill smelt on her first night in the hotel
c. the fact that the towels had not been changed
d. the rooms
e. the staff when Gill complained to them
f. Veronica – according to the chef!
g. the prices in the hotel restaurant
h. the check-in staff at the hotel

Listen again and check your answers. Look at the tapescript on page 149 if you need help.

Real English: that seems a bit odd

We often use odd to describe someone or something that is strange.

That's odd. Ken's not answering his telephone. He said he'd be in now.

That's odd. There's no one here. Have we come to the right room?

He's really odd. He keeps looking at me in a funny way.

3 Speaking

Tell your partner whether you agree or disagree with these statements and why.

1. I wouldn't have waited so long for the maid. I would've gone down to reception and asked to speak to the manager.
2. I wouldn't have gone out without a shower.
3. I wouldn't have complained about the towels.
4. I wouldn't have sent the steak back. I just wouldn't have eaten it.
5. I would've walked out if the chef had spoken to me like that.

4 | Softening complaints

Look at these common ways of complaining.

a. I'm sorry, but my room's rather small.
   (*rather* + negative adjective)

b. I'm sorry, but my room isn't very big.
   (*not very* + positive adjective)

Which way would *you* use to complain? Why?

Now rewrite these sentences so that they sound less strong.

1. I'm sorry, but this coffee is absolutely tasteless.
   . . . . strong.

2. I'm sorry, but my room is absolutely freezing.
   . . . . cold.

3. I'm sorry, but my room is absolutely filthy.
   . . . . clean.

4. I'm sorry, but the noise outside my room is absolutely appalling.
   . . . . noisy
   outside my room.

5. I'm sorry, but my room is unbearably hot.
   . . . . cool.

6. I'm sorry, but I've been waiting for absolutely ages.
   . . . . a long time.

7. I'm sorry, but this chicken is only half-cooked.
   . . . . well-done.

8. I'm sorry, but this wine is absolutely disgusting.
   . . . . nice.

9. I'm sorry, but I think the service here has been absolutely awful.
   . . . . poor.

Notice that if you really want to make a strong complaint, use *absolutely* + negative adjective. For example:

I'm sorry, but my room's absolutely tiny.

Now match the complaints 1–9 to the follow-up requests a–i below.

a. Do you think you could turn the heating up, please? ☐

b. Do you think you could give me a room away from the road, please? ☐

c. Do you think you could hurry up with my order, please? ☐

d. Do you think you could bring me a stronger one, please? ☐

e. Do you think I could speak to the manager, please? ☐

f. Do you think you could turn on the air conditioning, please? ☐

g. Do you think you could bring us another bottle, please? ☐

h. Do you think you could send someone up to clean it, please? ☐

i. Do you think you could take it back to the kitchen and cook it properly, please? ☐

5 | Practice

Now try to remember the complaints and requests. Work with a partner. One of you is the person who is complaining. The other should reply: 'Of course, I'm terribly sorry about that. I'll sort it out straightaway.'

Change roles. This time, the person who is replying should be as unhelpful as possible. You think everything is basically the complainer's fault!

Would you like to stay in any of the hotels in the pictures? Why/why not?

Using grammar

1 Had to

In Unit 6 we looked at must and have to. We saw that in the present there is often very little difference in meaning. For example:

I have to get some milk on my way home.
(Possibly, my wife asked me to get some.)

I must get some milk on my way home.
(Possibly, I've just remembered I don't have any left.)

Must is a modal verb and has no past tense. Instead, we use had to. For example:

I had to get some milk on my way home.

Here are some more examples with must, have to and had to.

Oh, I really must get my hair cut this week.
I had to get my hair cut last week. It was getting too long.

I have to stay at work till eight tonight.
I had to stay at work till eight last night.

The past form of don't have to is didn't have to.

You don't have to pay.
We didn't have to pay.

In the listening on page 48, Gill said, 'We just had to get out of there and escape.' Can you remember what place she was talking about and why she felt like that?

2 Practice

Make sentences by matching the beginnings 1–10 to the endings a–j.

1. We were on our way to the airport when I suddenly realised I'd forgotten my passport, so
2. We arrived ten minutes late for our flight, and there wasn't another one till the evening, so
3. When we went camping last summer, the tent got full of water, so
4. I'm really short of money because
5. My plane landed at two in the morning, and there were no buses, so
6. We ran out of petrol on the motorway, so
7. I'd left my wallet at home, and didn't have any money, so
8. My computer at work crashed, so
9. They rang me to say the meeting had been cancelled, so
10. He rang me to tell me he'd missed his flight, so

a. I had to pay my credit card bill last week.
b. I had to write my report from the beginning again.
c. I had to borrow some from a friend at work.
d. I didn't have to go and pick him up.
e. I had to get a taxi to my hotel.
f. we had to go back home and get it.
g. I didn't have to go in to work.
h. I had to walk two miles to get some.
i. we had to sleep in the car.
j. we had to spend the afternoon at the airport.

Remember that you borrow money from someone, but you lend money to someone.

Spend two minutes trying to memorise the sentence endings a–j above. Then cover them. Now read out the sentence beginnings 1–10 while your partner adds the ending.

Now swap roles. Who has a better memory – you or your partner?

3 Speaking

Have you ever had to...

- **spend a long time in an airport?**
- **sleep in a car/on someone's sofa?**
- **get a taxi?**
- **walk a long way?**

What happened?

4 | Had to/didn't have to

Put these sentences into the past.

1. I must be at the station by 6.30 tomorrow morning.
   I . . . . this morning.
2. I don't have to be home early today.
   I . . . . yesterday.
3. I have to have a word with my boss later.
   I . . . . last week.
4. We must get our passports renewed.
   We . . . . last summer.
5. We have to get a taxi.
   We . . . . last night.
6. I must e-mail the report by twelve.
   I . . . . this morning.
7. We don't have to stay till the end.
   The meeting didn't finish until eleven, but we
   . . . .
8. I must pay my phone bill this week or I'll be cut off.
   I . . . . last week before
   they cut me off.

5 | More ways of expressing obligation

Match the statements 1–7 with the explanations a–g.

1. I had to borrow a tie to get into the club. ☐
2. My grandfather had to fight during the war. ☐
3. I had to spend a year in the army when I was eighteen. ☐
4. We didn't have to study French at school. ☐
5. We had to study Maths, Physics, English and PE. ☐
6. I had to do five different courses in English Literature. ☐
7. You didn't have to wear a seat belt in those days. ☐

a. We used to have military service in our country.
b. They were compulsory for all students until the age of sixteen.
c. That's what I did my degree in.
d. He was conscripted into the army.
e. It wasn't against the law.
f. It was an optional subject.
g. They had a strict dress code.

6 | Speaking

Discuss these questions with a partner.

1. Have you ever been somewhere where there was a dress code? What did you have to wear? Did they let you in if you were not dressed properly?
2. Do you know anyone who's had to spend time in the army? Did they enjoy it?
3. What subjects were compulsory and which ones were optional when you studied at school/university?
4. Have any laws changed in your country since you were a child?

7 | Excuses

We often use had to when we are giving excuses. Here are four common situations. With a partner, think up a good excuse for each one. Use the ideas in the pictures if you need to.

1. A: Why were you late this morning?
   B: Sorry, but I had to . . . .
2. A: Why didn't you come to my party?
   B: Well, I had to . . . .
3. A: Why didn't you ring me back?
   B: Sorry, but I had to . . . .
4. A: Why didn't you do your homework?
   B: Well, I had to . . . .

Now decide who thought of the best (and the worst) excuse.

8 | Free practice

Here are the endings of three stories. With a partner, choose one of the endings, and make up the whole story.

1. Well, I had to wear my boyfriend's trousers. It was so embarrassing!
2. Well, I had to rewrite the whole thing. It was so annoying!
3. Well, in the end, I had to go and apologise. I've never felt so silly in all my life!

When you've finished your story, try to remember as much of it as you can and then tell it to some other students. Who has the best story?

▶ For more information on using *had to/didn't have to*, see G8.

Reading

1 │ While you read

Read all the complaints on the website below. Decide which ones you agree with and which ones you think are stupid. Explain your decisions to your partner.

Shout_at_us.com — The website that helps you get things off your chest!

From Donna
I can't understand people who invite you round to their house, but don't mean it. They say: 'Oh, you must come round and have dinner some time.' When you ask them when, they say: 'Oh, I'm very busy at the moment.' When someone says to you: 'We must have lunch sometime,' or 'We must get together, or go swimming,' forget it. They never mean it!

From Marie, ex-waitress
I can't stand people who complain about the service in restaurants. I mean, don't they understand that waiters and waitresses get tired, worry about their credit card bills and have children who are causing them trouble. They are real people with emotions! They're not machines.

From Mark Forbes
I don't understand people who like country music. A typical song goes like this: 'I've lost my job. My girlfriend has left me. I'm an alcoholic and now my dog has died.' I like music which makes me feel happy. Country music lovers are weird!

From Ron
I hate the way society treats old people. We lock them away in old people's homes and forget about them. We feel guilty and visit them for an hour on a Sunday once a month. It's sick!

From Shane
Older drivers drive me mad. They drive around town doing ten miles an hour in huge old cars they can't park. Why don't we just take away their driving licences when they turn seventy?

From Butch
I'm a vegetarian. When I tell people, they say, 'So you don't eat ANY meat?' I am patient with them and say, 'No, no meat.' They then drive me mad by asking, 'Not even chicken?' Don't they realise that birds aren't vegetables! They've got flesh and blood just like you and me!

From Jim G
I can't stand people with body odour. Nowadays shops are full of deodorants. There's no excuse for B.O.

From Sue
I was in my local supermarket recently and saw a child taking a bite out of an apple. He then put the apple back so that his bite could not be seen. I told his mother. She told me to mind my own business. I then told one of the staff, who said there was nothing they could do about it. She said it happens all the time. Why do parents allow their children to do that kind of thing?

If you want to get something off your chest, just SHOUT_AT_US.COM!

Real English: sick and tired

Sick and tired is a common expression to show we really, really don't like something anymore because we feel it has been going on too long.
I'm sick and tired of him shouting at me. He's always doing it.
I'm sick and tired of my job. It's just the same problems day after day.
I'm sick and tired of the mess in our house. They're always leaving things lying around and I'm always tidying them up.

2 | Speaking

Tell a partner some of your complaints. Use these sentence starters.

1. I can't stand people who …
2. I don't understand people who …
3. I'm sick and tired of people who …
4. It drives me mad when people …
5. I get really upset with people who …

If you want to read more complaints, use a search engine to search the Web for 'Complaints'. Bring your favourites to class and share them.

3 | Problems

Listen to these conversations and complete the gaps. Then practise the conversations in pairs.

1. You are eating in an expensive restaurant.

Waiter:	Is everything all right, sir?
You:	(1) .... there's a fly in my soup.
Waiter:	Oh, you're right. Is it dead?
You:	I don't care if it's dead or alive. Just take it away, please, and (2) .... – but (3) .... a fly!
Waiter:	I'm very sorry, sir.

2. You have just bought a book which costs £9.99.

Assistant:	Thank you. 1p change.
You:	I'm sorry, but (1) .... a £20 note.
Assistant:	No, I think it was a £10 note.
You:	(2) .... I think if you check, you'll see it was a twenty.
Assistant:	You're absolutely right. Sorry about that. There you are.
You:	That's quite all right. Thank you.

3. You are paying for a shirt in a shop.

Assistant:	That's £49.99, sir.
You:	Wait a minute. (1) .... £49? The label says £29.99.
Assistant:	Mm. Let me see. You're absolutely right, but my screen says it's £49.99. There (2) .... a mistake. Just a moment. I'll check … Yes, you're right. I'm very sorry.

4 | Speaking

With a partner, have similar conversations in these situations.

1. You are in a restaurant and the waiter has just brought you a ham and mushroom pizza. You ordered a seafood pizza.
2. You gave the assistant a £50 note for a book which cost £18.50. She has given you £1.50p change.
3. The label on the pullover says £17.50, but the woman at the cash desk has asked you for £27.50.

If a shop assistant gave you more change than they should have, what would you say?

5 | Role play

Are you the sort of person who complains? With a partner, decide what you would do in these situations.

1. You have just got home after a meal at your favourite restaurant. You look again at your bill and realise they charged you twice for the wine – an extra £9.50. Would you ring them and tell them or just forget it?
2. You have just put on a new shirt which your father bought you for Christmas. Two buttons came off immediately. Your father paid £75 for it. Would you take it in the next day and demand your money back or would you sew the buttons back on and forget it? Your father has kept the receipt.

In pairs, write the two conversations you would have if you rang the restaurant or went into the shop to complain. Try to use some of the expressions from this unit.

Begin the first conversation like this:
Hello, I wonder if you can help me? I was in earlier this evening and …

Begin the second conversation like this:
Hello, I wonder if you can help me? My father bought a shirt from you just before Christmas and …

Do you live in a house or a flat? • Are you renting? • What's it like? • It's in a really nice part of town. We live in a small village out in the country. • Have you thought of moving? • Have you got a garden? We're on the ground floor. • It's a converted warehouse. • I wish I lived in a cottage in the country. Have you got mice? • We've got gas central heating. • Have you got double glazing? • We prefer the suburbs. • Do you own it? • How much a month? • W live on the top floor. • He's a real laugh.

8 House and home

Reading

1 Different kinds of homes

Match the descriptions of places 1–8 to the pictures A–H.

1. I live in a tiny little studio flat in the city centre.

2. I live on the tenth floor of a big block of flats.

3. I live in a nice cottage out in the country.

4. My partner and I live in a converted flat in an old warehouse down by the docks.

5. He lives in a huge detached house out in the suburbs.

6. They're living in a run-down little place in a slum area.

7. They live in a little bungalow.

8. We live in a ground-floor flat in a four-storey building.

2 Speaking

Which of the places in Exercise 1 would be the best/worst to live in if …

1. you're quite elderly and not very mobile?

2. you've got two young children?

3. you're a student and you don't have much money?

4. you work in the middle of town?

Have you ever lived in any places like those described in Exercise 1? Where? What were they like?

3 Speaking

Discuss these questions with a partner.

1. What's the normal age to leave home in your country? Is it the same for men and women?

2. What do you think is the best age to leave home?

3. What are the advantages/disadvantages of living at home with your parents? These structures might help:

   One good/bad thing about it is that … .

   Another good/bad thing is that … .

4 While you read

Read this article about two brothers who are still living at home. Then discuss these questions.

1. Why are Dave and Steve still living at home?

2. What do they like about it? Are there any disadvantages?

Home - but not alone

Dave and Steve Briggs share a bedroom in their parents' house. You might think that's quite normal for brothers, but Dave and Steve aren't teenagers. They're both in their mid-thirties and their parents are now retired. They are part of a growing number of children who are being forced to live with their parents well into adulthood, simply because they can't afford to rent or buy a place of their own. Steve has lived in the two-bedroom terraced house in the London suburb of Walthamstow nearly all his life, apart from two years when he was studying nursing in Derby. While he was there, he suffered a nervous breakdown and came home before completing his course.

'It was a difficult time,' he said. 'It was the first time I'd really been away from my family and I was finding the course quite stressful. In the end, I just couldn't cope and my life just went to pieces. I've suffered from depression ever since, which has meant I've been in and out of work a lot, but I've always been able to come home and know I'll be looked after, that I won't end up on the streets because I couldn't afford to pay the rent. And until two years ago, I had the bedroom to myself, so that was all right. I had the TV and PlayStation in there, so I had my privacy.'

All that changed when Dave got divorced and had to leave his large four-bedroom house to his wife and two kids. He had originally left home at seventeen, when he joined the army, and now works as a mechanical engineer for Ford Motors. 'When Lisa and I divorced, I thought I would just rent somewhere close by so I could just drop in and see the kids easily, but when I started looking, I just couldn't believe how expensive everything was. I'd never actually had to rent a flat before, being in the army, and most landlords wanted something like a hundred and fifty pounds a week just for a tiny studio flat. I thought about buying, but over the ten years Lisa and I had lived in our place, prices had just rocketed. I mean, for the money we paid for our house ten years ago, we could probably only get a one or two-bedroom flat in a large block now. It's ridiculous! There were cheaper places, but they were in really rough parts of town, where I wouldn't want my kids walking around. And the trouble is, it's not stopping. Prices have almost doubled just in the two years I've been staying with my parents. You know, the other day I saw a parking space being sold for £73,000! £73,000! For a parking space! The world's gone mad!'

So how does he find living at home again? 'It was quite weird for a long time, but you get used to it. It has its advantages. I still get my meals cooked and my clothes washed, but of course, it's difficult to have any privacy. Steve snores really badly. And he's always smoking. It's really disgusting! I sometimes stay over at my girlfriend's flat, and I'm trying to persuade her to let me move in, but she's not keen at the moment. So what else can I do?'

As many people know, the answer is 'Not much'. Unless, of course, you're prepared to move to a poor industrial town in the north or a tiny little village right out in the countryside, where you can buy a house for a tenth of the price it would be in London. I did suggest this to Steve. 'Yeah, right! So I could live in a slum or in the middle of nowhere. It's not much of an alternative, is it? No, in the end, my family and job are here, and that's what's most important.'

Real English: a rough part of town

We often talk about somewhere being rough rather than dangerous. Rough areas are usually poor areas where there is some crime and sometimes violence.

It's quite a rough area. My house has been burgled three times since I've been here.

I went to quite a rough school. I often got into fights.

It's quite a rough bar. I wouldn't go in there, if I were you.

5 | Speaking

Discuss these questions with a partner.

1. Is this kind of situation common in your country?

2. Do you know anybody who's still living at home even though they're in their late twenties or early thirties? Why?

3. Do house prices vary much in your country? Where's the most expensive place to live? Where's the cheapest? What are the areas like? How much would you have to pay to live there?

The writer didn't interview Steve's parents. With a partner, write a paragraph saying what you think they would say about their sons living back at home with them.

Using vocabulary

1 | Cities and areas

Go round the class and ask: 'Whereabouts exactly are you living?' Who do you think lives in the nicest area? Why?

Here are ten sentences describing areas. With a partner, discuss which are positive and which are negative. Then use them to describe the pictures.

1. It's dead.
2. It's really noisy.
3. It's very lively.
4. It's quite rough.
5. It's very green.
6. It's a very safe area.
7. It's quite a posh area.
8. It's quite dirty.
9. It's very convenient for the shops.
10. It's nice and quiet.

Now match the descriptions 1–10 to the follow-up comments a–j.

a. There are lots of parks and trees, which is nice.
b. There's a really good supermarket round the corner.
c. There's a big main road running through it.
d. There's not much traffic round there.
e. There's absolutely nothing to do.
f. There's a lot of crime and prostitution round there.
g. There's a lot of rubbish, litter and dog dirt everywhere.
h. There's hardly any crime.
i. There are a lot of bars and clubs. It's got a great nightlife.
j. There are lots of big, expensive houses round there.

Now cover the follow-up comments a–j above. You can read the descriptions 1–10 to help you, but try to remember the follow-up comments a–j without looking at them. Try to have conversations like this with your partner:

A: What's it like round there?
B: It's quite dirty. There's a lot of rubbish, litter and dog dirt everywhere.

2 | Further practice

Do the sentences in Exercise 1 describe any areas you know? Tell your partner.

Can you use any of the comments above to talk about a big city you know or any of the following?

| Moscow | Naples | Oslo | Paris | São Paulo | Vienna |

3 | Always doing/never does

When we complain about things people do, we often use:

*   *always* **+ present continuous**
*   *never* **+ present simple**

I hate it. They're always gossiping.
He's so lazy. He never does the washing-up.

Make sentences using always or never and the correct tense.

1. he / do / anything round the house
2. she / leave / her things lying around everywhere
3. he / use / the phone
4. he / leave / the lights on
5. she / tidy up / after herself
6. she / leave / her hairs in the bath after she's had a shower
7. they / let / me watch what I want to watch on TV
8. he / take / things from my bedroom without asking
9. he / interrupt / me when I'm talking

Which of the people in 1–9 above do you think are ...

*   selfish?
*   messy?
*   disgusting?
*   lazy?
*   rude?
*   thoughtless?

> For more information on how to use the present continuous to talk about habits, see G9.

4 | Pronunciation: sentence stress

When we complain about something, we usually place an extra stress on always and never.

They're <u>always</u> gossiping.
He <u>never</u> does the washing-up.

Practise saying the complaints 1–9 in Exercise 3 above.

5 | Speaking

Discuss these questions with a partner.

1. Do the people/relatives you live with do any of the things above?
2. Do they have any other annoying habits or are there things they never do?

Go round the class and see if you can find anyone who has the same problems as you.

6 | How do you get on with them?

Complete the sentences below with the pairs of phrases in the box.

> your brother / OK
> your flatmate / really well
> your mum / not very well
> your mum / really well

1. A: How do you get on with ....?
    B: ...., I suppose. We're quite different in lots of ways, but I've never really argued with him.
2. A: How do you get on with ....?
    B: .... Ever since I first moved in, we've got on like a house on fire.
3. A: How do you get on with ....?
    B: .... She's really strict and she stops me from doing a lot of things I want.
4. A: How do you get on with ....?
    B: .... We're very close. I can talk to her about anything.

Now complete the sentences below with the pairs of phrases in the box.

> your brother / not very well
> the people you work with / OK
> the people you work with / really well
> your flatmate / not very well

5. A: How do you get on with ....?
    B: .... She's just really boring and she never does the washing-up.
6. A: How do you get on with ....?
    B: .... We've just got absolutely nothing in common. I can't talk to him at all.
7. A: How do you get on with ....?
    B: ...., I suppose. We chat in the lunch breaks, but I never see them outside work.
8. A: How do you get on with ....?
    B: .... We always have a real laugh together in the office and we've become really good friends outside of it.

Now ask your partner how they get on with some of the people above. Can you think of any other people you can ask them about?

> **Real English:** we always have a real laugh
> We say something is a laugh or that we have a laugh to mean it is good fun or that we have a good time.
> *We had a good laugh at the party last night.*
> *We should all go out together as a class. It'll be a laugh.*
> *We always have a good laugh together when we go out.*

Listening

1 | Speaking

Do you know what an au pair is? Read this short description of what an au pair does.

My name's Ulrika and I'm from Sweden. I'm living and working with a family in Exeter for a year. I have to get the children up every day and make them breakfast. I take them to school and then I usually have the morning off so I can go to English classes. In the afternoon, I sometimes have to do some things around the house – the vacuuming, the washing-up, the washing, that kind of thing. I'm lucky because my family doesn't make me work evenings, which is great, because a lot of other au pairs have to do baby-sitting most nights. I have my own room in the house and I get £40 a week spending money too.

Does it sound like the kind of thing you'd like to do? Why/why not?

2 | While you listen

You are going to hear a conversation between an au pair and her new employers. She has just arrived at the house of the people she is going to work for, Paul and Angela. Paul has just brought her from the airport. With a partner, predict how you think they will use these words.

bed	show
coat	bags
breakfast	alarm clock
eat	journey

Listen and answer these questions.

1. How's the au pair feeling?
2. Does she meet the children?
3. When does she start work?
4. Who wears the trousers – Angela or Paul? How do you know?

Now complete these sentences with the eight words in the box. Were you right about how they were used?

5. You can leave your .... in the hall.
6. Take your .... off.
7. Can I get you something to ....?
8. Did you have a good ....?
9. Do you want me to .... you around the house now or shall we do it in the morning?
10. Is it OK if I just go to ....?
11. Have you got a(n) ....?
12. The children really do need to have their .... by seven thirty.
13. I'll .... you where your bedroom is.

3 | Speaking

Do you think it's fair that the au pair has to start work on her first full day with the family? Why/why not?

Get into two groups. One group should make a list of the problems au pairs might have with their employers. The other group should make a list of the problems employers might have with their au pairs.

Get together with a partner from the other group and compare your lists. Who do you think has the best side of the deal – the employers or the au pairs? Why?

4 | *Make* and *let*

Read this conversation between two au pairs. Who has the better employer? Why?

Katrin: I can't believe your family let you take the morning off! Mine make me work a twelve-hour day!

Anna: That's outrageous! But they let you have weekends off, don't they?

Katrin: Well, sometimes, but they often make me take the kids to their ballet classes on Saturday mornings.

Anna: So, no sleeping in with your boyfriend, then?

Katrin: You must be joking! They don't even let me have friends round for coffee!

Anna: That's terrible! Mine even let me have a little birthday party a couple of weeks ago.

Read the conversation again and underline the six expressions with make and let.

Now complete these sentences with make or let.

1. When I was younger, my dad always used to . . . . me wash the car every weekend!

2. My parents never used to . . . . me stay over at my friends' houses.

3. My parents used to . . . . me pick up my little sister from school every day.

4. My parents used to . . . . me help with the washing-up after dinner every day.

5. Once I reached eighteen, my parents used to . . . . my girlfriend spend the night at our house sometimes.

6. My parents always used to . . . . me eat my greens.

7. Once I reached eighteen, my parents used to . . . . me have a beer with dinner if I wanted to.

8. My parents used to . . . . me and my friends go off camping for the weekend on our own.

9. My parents used to . . . . me keep my bedroom neat and tidy.

10. My parents used to . . . . me stay up as late as I wanted.

> For more information on how to use *make* and *let*, see G10.

5 | Speaking

In which of the sentences 1–10 in Exercise 4 do the parents sound:

1. strict and authoritarian?
2. open-minded, progressive and liberal?

Tick the sentences above that are or were true for you.

Can you think of anything else your parents used to make you do or let you do? Compare experiences with a partner. Whose parents were stricter? Who had the strictest upbringing in the class?

6 | Role play

With a partner, you are going to role-play a conversation between someone renting out a room in their house and someone looking for a room. Spend three minutes planning what you are going to say and then role-play the conversation.

Student A
Imagine you are going to rent out a room in your flat/house. Think about what you would tell the person who wants to rent it about these things:

1. the room
2. the house
3. the area you live in
4. the rules you would make them follow (I'm afraid you'll have to …/I'm afraid you won't be able to …)
5. what you would let them do

Student B
Imagine you are looking for a room to rent. What questions would you ask about the following?

1. the room
2. the house
3. the area the house is in
4. the rules you will have to follow (Will I have to … ?)
5. the things you can do (Is it OK if I … ?)

Now talk to a different partner and role-play the conversation again. Repeat this two or three times. Tell the class which room you would most like to rent and why.

7 | Speaking

What would your dream house be like? Where would it be? Work out the details in pairs. Then vote for the best one in the class.

Review: Units 5–8

1 | Grammar review

Choose the correct form.

1. Listen, I must / I mustn't just make a quick phone call. I'll be back in five minutes.

2. The contract for my flat says I mustn't / I don't have to have parties.

3. I didn't really like that book. You mustn't read it / I wouldn't read it if I were you.

4. Sorry I didn't come to the lesson yesterday. I must / I had to pick up a friend from the airport.

5. I wouldn't go there again. The rooms weren't very clean / dirty.

6. I was lucky, because my parents never used to make / let me go to extra classes after school.

7. Is it OK if I / Do you think you could borrow this for a minute? I won't need it for long.

8. A: How long was your flight?
   B: Nine hours.
   A: Oh, no. You must be / You are exhausted!

9. I hate it! He's always interrupting / He never interrupts me when I'm talking!

10. When I first left home, it took me a long time to be / get used to living on my own.

Compare your answers with a partner and explain your choices.

2 | Follow-up comments

Match the statements 1–6 to the follow-up comments a–f.

1. I'm still finding the weather here a bit depressing,

2. I still haven't got used to living on my own yet.

3. It took me a long time to get used to working shifts,

4. I'm slowly getting used to the food here.

5. I don't think I'll ever get used to living here.

6. I'm so used to travelling with my job,

a. This place just feels like a different planet!

b. but it's OK now. I don't mind working nights.

c. At least the bread's good.

d. but I'm sure I'll get used to all the snow in the end.

e. I don't even think about it any more.

f. It still feels really strange cooking for myself.

3 | Have to, don't have to, can

Complete these sentences with have to/has to, don't have to or can.

1. It's great where I work, because I . . . . start whenever I like.

2. I . . . . wear a suit or anything like that, but I do . . . . dress quite smartly.

3. In the kitchen, everyone . . . . wear this horrible hair net and hat.

4. We . . . . work late, but I do sometimes if I need the overtime.

5. There's a work canteen and I . . . . get cheap food there if I want to.

6. I hate working in a fast food restaurant because I . . . . wash my hands every ten minutes!

7. One nice thing about my job is the fact that I . . . . work weekends. It's nice having plenty of free time.

8. There's a machine on the first floor where you . . . . get free tea and coffee.

Rewrite these sentences using the words in brackets.

9. I'm sorry, but smoking's forbidden in here. (allowed)
   I'm sorry, but you . . . . in here.

10. I wouldn't leave before six if I were you. (supposed)
    You . . . .

11. You'd better phone first to see if they still have tickets left. (if I)
    . . . .

12. Why don't you talk to him and see what he says. (if I)
    . . . .

13. No one's supposed to go into that part of the building. (allowed)
    You . . . .

4 | Look back and check

Look back at Exercise 4 Softening complaints on page 49. Remember, you can emphasise an adjective by placing absolutely before it.

Think about some place you've been to that was absolutely freezing/filthy/magical, or about something you've eaten that was absolutely disgusting/tasteless/delicious. Tell a partner about these experiences.

5 | Verb collocations

Match the verbs 1–10 to the groups of phrases they collocate with a–j.

1. be stuck
2. wear
3. work
4. buy
5. try
6. show
7. complain
8. earn
9. live
10. do

a. behind a desk all day / in front of a computer all day

b. the garage up the road / the newsagent's round the corner

c. about the service / to the manager

d. three pounds fifty an hour / thirty thousand a year

e. from home / with computers

f. in a nice little cottage out in the country / on the thirty-fifth floor

g. the vacuuming / the washing-up

h. you round the house / you where everything is

i. a uniform at work / a suit to work

j. it in a sale / her latest CD

You have one minute to memorise the collocations a–j. Now cover the exercise above. Your partner will read out the verbs 1–10. How many collocations can you remember?

With a partner, try to think of one more common collocation for each of the verbs 1–10.

6 | Adjectives

Complete the sentences below with the adjectives in the box.

bright	dead	flexible	ignorant	latest
optional	posh	rewarding	strict	wide

1. I can't believe he'd never heard of Latvia! He's so . . . . !

2. The dishes they have are quite tasty and good value, and they've got a very . . . . choice.

3. It's a typical tourist resort, so it's really busy in the summer and then . . . . in the winter!

4. Why do you always do everything the same old way? You need to be a bit more . . . . in the way you do things.

5. Listen, you don't have to do it if you don't want to. It's . . . .

6. I had a very . . . . upbringing. My parents didn't really let me do anything.

7. It must be very . . . . working with kids, watching them learn and develop.

8. Have you read Ian McEwan's . . . . book? It's brilliant!

9. I don't really like the colour. It's a bit too . . . . for me. Couldn't we get something a bit darker?

10. The rent's quite cheap even though its quite a(n) . . . . area.

7 | Questions and answers

Match the questions 1–10 to the answers a–j.

1. What does your job involve?
2. How are you finding your new job?
3. So how was New York?
4. Is everything all right?
5. What's the money like?
6. Is it OK if I have people stay over?
7. How do you get on with him?
8. Why didn't you ring me back?
9. Do you think you could hurry up with it?
10. Do you have to?

a. I'm afraid not, actually.

b. Yeah, of course, if you want to.

c. I design books for architectural companies.

d. Not very well, actually.

e. Sorry, but I had to go out and pick up my dad from work.

f. It's OK. I'm slowly getting used to it.

g. Yes, of course. I'm sorry. I'll sort it out at once.

h. It's OK, but it could always be better.

i. No, not really. I just want to.

j. Brilliant. I had a great time.

8 | What can you remember?

With a partner, note down as much as you can remember about the texts you read in Units 6 and 8.

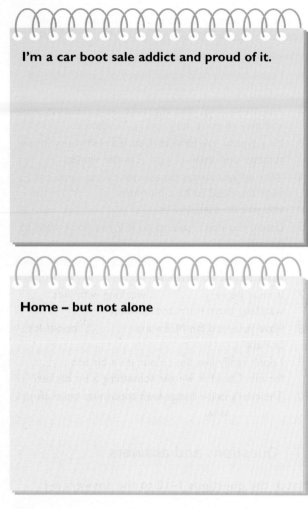

I'm a car boot sale addict and proud of it.

Home – but not alone

Now compare what you remember with another pair of students. Who remembered more?

Which text did you enjoy more? Why?

9 | Common expressions

Complete the sentences below with the words in the box.

can	common	don't have to	drives	journey
mustn't	run out of	something	used	wonder

1. It took me a long time to get . . . . to it.
2. Can I get you . . . . to eat?
3. Did you have a good . . . . ?
4. I . . . . if you can help me.
5. We've got absolutely nothing in . . . .
6. You . . . . if you want to.
7. You . . . . if you don't want to.

8. I . . . . forget to call her.
9. We've . . . . toilet paper.
10. It . . . . me mad.

Discuss these questions with a partner.

11. Can you think of anything that took you a long time to get used to?
12. Do you know anybody you have absolutely nothing in common with?
13. When was the last time you had to ask someone: 'I wonder if you can help me.' Why?

10 | Revision quiz

Discuss these questions in groups of three.

1. What's the difference between working shifts and working nights?
2. If a coat is too big for you, does it mean it doesn't suit you or it doesn't fit you?
3. What happens if your car is unreliable? And if a friend of yours is unreliable?
4. Can you think of three ways you can save money?
5. If you are sick and tired of your job, are you really ill or really bored?
6. Can you think of three things strict, authoritarian parents might make you do?
7. Can you think of three things open-minded, progressive parents might let you do?
8. What's the difference between a compulsory subject and an optional subject at school?
9. If an area is dead, is it dangerous to live there?
10. What do au pairs do?
11. How many rooms does a studio flat have?
12. What do you do when you do up a run-down house?
13. If your job is rewarding, does it mean it's well-paid?
14. Can you think of three places you could pick someone up from?
15. Can you think of four different kinds of bills you sometimes have to pay?
16. If you're self-employed, who's the boss?
17. What's the difference between 'you're not supposed to' and 'you don't have to'?
18. What's a dotcom company?
19. What's the most famous department store in the town/city you're studying in?
20. Can you think of two ways you could you answer the comment: 'That must be very stressful'?

Learner advice: Recording and revising vocabulary

It's hard trying to remember all the vocabulary you meet in class.

What do you think of the way this student is trying to revise new language?
Which notes do you like best? Why?

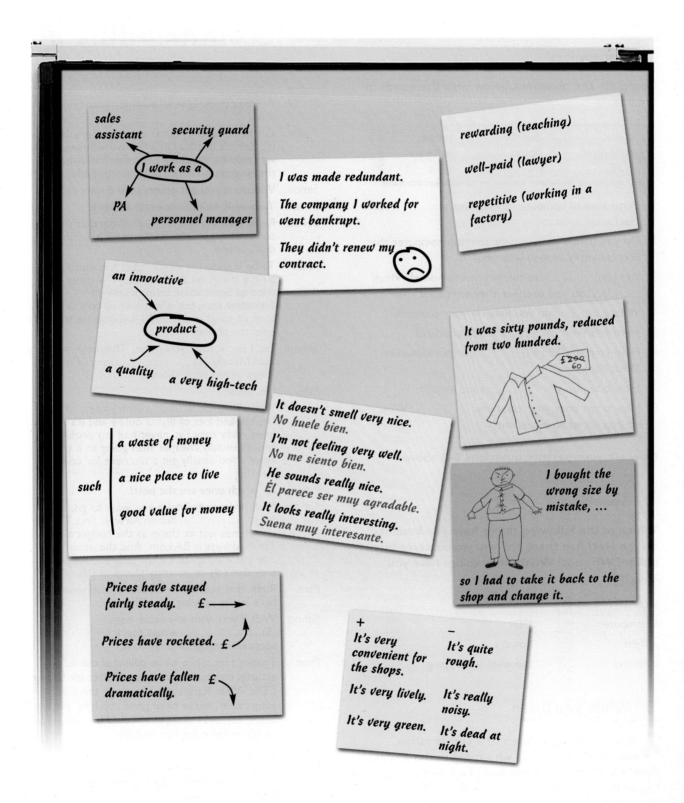

Where else do you think you could stick notes like this?

Why not try it with some of the expressions you've learned this week?

Do you work on a PC or a Mac? • I usually work on my laptop. • I've got too much software. • Do y
use Microsoft Office? • Pictures use up so much memory, don't they? • I'm thinking of getting mo
memory. • I deleted the lot! • I get about fifty e-mails a day. • I use Express. • Are you with AOL?
I hope you back your work up every day. • I lost everything. • Log on for free. • Have you heard abo
this new virus? • Know any good sites? • We met in a chat room
You should phone the help desk. • I'll e-mail it over now.

9 Computers

Listening

1 | Vocabulary

Complete the questions below with the words in the box.

check	deleted	server
connected	laptop	software
crash	PC	virus

1. What kind of computer do you use, a .... or Mac?

2. Do you have a .... or palmtop computer that you can carry around with you?

3. Are you .... to the Internet at home? Which .... do you use? Are they any good?

4. What .... do you have on your computer?

5. Have you ever .... a file by accident?

6. Have you ever had a .... on your computer? What happened?

7. How often do you .... your e-mail?

8. How often does your computer ....? What do you do when it happens?

Now ask your partner questions 1–8 above.

2 | Speaking

Which of the following things have you bought on the Net? Are there any you would never buy online? Why not? What other things have you bought?

a car	☐	books	☐
a computer	☐	CDs	☐
a flight	☐	flowers	☐
a holiday	☐	the weekly shopping	☐

3 | While you listen

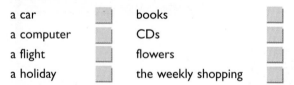 **You are going to listen to a conversation between two friends who meet in the street. Pete is looking in the window of a travel agent's. Cover the conversation. As you listen, try to answer these questions.**

1. What things from the list in Exersice 2 above do they talk about buying?

2. Why does Pete want to buy them?

Now listen again and compete the gaps.

Recommending a website

Simon:	Are you booking your summer holiday already, then?
Pete:	Oh, hello, Simon. I didn't see you there. No, no. It's Karen's birthday in a few weeks' time and I was thinking of taking her away somewhere for the weekend. There's not much on offer, though.
Simon:	Well, have you got access to the Internet?
Pete:	Yeah, well, we're connected at work.
Simon:	Right. Well, (1) .... try that? You can sometimes get some really good last-minute deals online.
Pete:	To be honest, I've never really had much luck buying things on the Internet. The other day, I tried to book some train tickets on Ticketline.com, but it was just so complicated. It took so long! In the end, I just gave up and did it over the phone.
Simon:	Yes, I know what you mean. That site's not very user-friendly. (2) .... any of the cheap airline sites, though?
Pete:	No, never.
Simon:	Well, (3) ...., I'd try some of them. I've booked lots of flights online and it's always been really easy. I've never had any problems and it's usually cheaper than going to a travel agent's. You usually get a discount for online booking.
Pete:	So, which ones are the best?
Simon:	Well, it depends where you want to go. You (4) .... British Airways first. They're sometimes just as cheap as the budget airlines. Their address is BA.com. And the other one I've used quite a lot is easyJet.com, but they don't fly to as many places as BA.
Pete:	Right, that sounds much better than standing here in the pouring rain. Thanks.
Simon:	Well, if you want any more help, (5) .... e-mail me. It's spencersimon@shotmail.com.
Pete:	Thanks. Hey, while we're talking about it, actually, do you know any good sites for buying CDs? When Karen and I first met there was a song called 'You've been gone too long' playing in the bar and I thought it would be really nice to try to get it for her birthday.
Simon:	Very romantic!
Pete:	Yeah, well, I do my best. The only problem is I'm not sure who it's by and I've never seen it in any record shop.
Simon:	I'm not sure. You (6) .... dustygroove.com. My brother's always talking about them. Otherwise, (7) ...., I'd go to one of those music chat sites and see if anyone there can help you.
Pete:	Right, OK.

Complete the time expressions in these sentences with words from the conversation on page 64.

a. We're going on holiday in a few weeks' . . . .

b. I'm going to Dublin . . . . the weekend.

c. I met John the . . . . day.

d. . . . . the end, we decided not to go abroad.

4 | E-mails and website addresses

When saying website addresses:

@   is said 'at'.

.   is said 'dot'.

_   is said 'underscore'.

/   is said 'forward slash'.

Listen to these e-mail and website addresses and repeat.

1. bill.macdonald@amac.com
2. www.soccernet.com
3. tigerlilly17_08@wowzer.com
4. pete_smith@shotmail.com
5. reo@sb4-so-net.ne.jp
6. www.intosomethin.com/barracuda

Now listen and write down the addresses you hear.

7. . . . .
8. . . . .
9. . . . .
10. . . . .

Who do you e-mail regularly? How often do you check your e-mails?

5 | Speaking

Discuss these questions with a partner.

1. Do you have any favourite websites? Why do you like them so much?
2. Pete wants to do something romantic for his girlfriend's birthday. What's the most romantic thing you've ever done? Have you ever done any of the things in the pictures?
3. Which songs remind you of special times or people in your life? Why?
4. Do you know anyone who's obsessed with computers?

6 | Speaking

Go round the class and see if anyone knows the following:

1. a good search engine
2. a good chat room
3. a useful site to learn English
4. a good site for jokes

Before your next class, try out these addresses. Then agree on the best sites.

Using grammar

1 | Three classic mistakes

Here is the opening paragraph of an article from a computer magazine. The article is called 'Three Classic Mistakes'. Read about the first classic mistake and then discuss with a partner what you think the other two are.

> There are three classic mistakes to avoid if you work on computers and I've made them all! The first was to load on all the free software I could get my hands on. I loaded on everything I got free with every computer magazine. I downloaded lots of free software from the Internet. My hard drive was full of stuff I never used. This slowed my machine down to the point where I wanted to throw it out of the window! The solution is simple. Don't keep any programs which you don't use. Bin them!

Ask your teacher if your predictions were right or read the rest of the article on page 175.

2 | Present perfect and past simple

Look at these examples from the article in Exercise 1 above:

Present perfect
I've made all the classic mistakes.

Past simple
I downloaded free software.
I lost a whole morning's work.
I got a computer virus.

When do we use these two different tenses? Compare your ideas with a partner. Now read the explanations below and see if you were right.

1. We use the present perfect to look back from the present on an event or a period in the past. We do this when there is some kind of present result.

   I've just pressed the wrong button and lost everything!
   I've made lots of mistakes in my life, but I'm all right now.

2. We use the past simple for simple factual events or periods in the past.

   We lived in Spain for six years.
   We moved back to the UK last year.

3. We can use both forms to talk about similar things, but from different perspectives.
   I've been to Cairo. I went there first in 1992.
   I've known Pete for ten years. We first met when we were at college together.

   When we use the past simple, we often mention a particular time: this morning, last night, when we were at university, in 1985, when I was young.

In each of the following pairs of sentences, one sounds more natural. Which is it? Why?

1a. I did history at university.
1b. I've done history at university.

2a. Hello, I think we met before, didn't we?
2b. Hello, I think we've met before, haven't we?

3a. Oh, you've had a haircut!
3b. Oh, you had a haircut!

Read 'Three Classic Mistakes' again. Underline all the examples of the present perfect and the past simple.

3 | Practice

Look at this pair of sentences:

I won £100,000 in the Lottery last year.
I've spent it all already.

Make similar pairs of sentences with these ideas.

1. start reading the new Harry Potter book last week / almost finish it
   ....
2. buy some grapes this morning / eat them all already
   ....
3. get my new car yesterday / just have an accident
   ....
4. study English at school / forget most of it already
   ....
5. sit my exams in May / just hear that I've passed!
   ....

4 | Linked questions

Look at this short dialogue. The first question uses the present perfect and the second uses the past simple.

A: Have you ever been to London?
B: Yeah, I have, actually. I went a couple of years ago.
A: Did you go to the Tower of London?
B: No, we didn't get round to it.

Make questions in a similar way.

1. been to Rome? / see the Sistine Chapel?
2. been to Greece? / go to Delphi?
3. been to America? / go to New York?
4. been to Asia? / go to Thailand?

Now make similar questions about computers.

5. load on too much software? / manage to remove most of it?
6. forget to save your work? / lose all of it?
7. get a virus? / manage to get rid of it?

With a partner, have similar conversations to the ones above.

5 Time expressions

Look at these two sentences:

a. I've known John (since 1985).
b. I met John (in 1985).

Do these time expressions fit sentence a or sentence b?

1. for a long time
2. when I was in Japan
3. for over twenty years
4. three years ago
5. all my life
6. last Christmas
7. for ages
8. since we were at school
9. last week
10. this morning

6 Always/never

We often use a more general time expression with the present perfect. For example:

I've never been to South America.
I've always liked my coffee black.
I've been to Paris before.
I haven't finished yet.

Complete these sentences with always or never.

1. I've . . . . had any problems with my job.
2. I've . . . . loved Belgian chocolates.
3. I've . . . . won anything on the National Lottery.
4. I've . . . . been quite good at sport.
5. I've . . . . been any good at ball games.
6. I've . . . . had a terrible memory.
7. I've . . . . been on a plane.
8. I haven't . . . . got on with my brother. It's quite a recent thing.

Are any of the sentences 1–8 true for you?

Can you finish these sentences about yourself?

I've always …
I've never …
I haven't always … . It's quite a recent thing for me.

7 How long? When?

Look at the questions in this dialogue:

A: How long have you lived here?
B: Since 1997.
A: When did you move here?
B: A few years ago.

Make questions in a similar way.

1. know your girlfriend? / meet her?
2. be married? / get married?
3. be a vegetarian? / decide to stop eating meat?
4. work for IBM? / leave Compugraphics?
5. have this job? / get it?
6. have a car? / buy it?

8 Further practice

Complete this text with the correct form of the verbs in brackets.

Even though I like England, I (1) . . . . (always / want) to work abroad, but until recently, I (2) . . . . (never / think) I really would. A couple of months ago, though, I (3) . . . . (see) an advert on the Internet for a job in a bank in Switzerland, which (4) . . . . (look) really interesting. I (5) . . . . (fill in) the application form online and (6) . . . . (send) it off. I (7) . . . . (not hear) back from them for quite a while, but yesterday they (8) . . . . (e-mail) me, telling me they want me to go to Zurich for an interview. I (9) . . . . (spend) the last twenty-four hours in a real panic, arranging flights and hotels and that sort of thing.

> For more information on how to use the present perfect and the past simple, see G11.

Real English: a real panic

We often use a real + noun for strong emphasis.
It was a real disaster. Everything that could go wrong, did.
It was a real rip-off. It cost 25 euros to get into the club and it was really boring.
He's a real idiot. He's always saying really stupid things, which he thinks are funny, but just aren't.

We often use right and complete in the same way.

Using vocabulary

1 | General advice

In the conversation on page 64, Simon gives Pete several pieces of advice:

Why don't you try the Internet?
Have you tried any of the cheap airline sites?
You could try British Airways first.
If I were you, I'd try some of them.

🎧 **Listen and practise saying the four sentences giving advice from the conversation. Then complete the dialogues below with the phrases in the box.**

> doing a search
> nicotine patches
> pressing Alt, Control, Delete
> taking it next year
> the petrol station down the road
> turn it off and switch it back on again
> wait and improve your English a bit more

1. A: Do you know any good sites for learning English?
   B: No, not really. Have you tried
      . . . .?
   A: Yes, but there were so many I didn't know where to start.

2. A: Do you know where I can buy some milk?
   B: No, not at this time of night. I guess you could try
      . . . .
   A: OK, thanks. I hadn't thought of that.

3. A: I really want to give up smoking, but I just can't.
   B: I know. It's so difficult, isn't it. Have you tried
      . . . .?
   A: No, I haven't, actually. Maybe I'll give them a try.

4. A: Do you think I should take the First Certificate exam?
   B: If I were you, I'd . . . . You
      could try . . . .
   A: Yeah, you're probably right.

5. A: There's something wrong with this computer. The screen has just frozen.
   B: Oh, that keeps happening to me. Have you tried
      . . . .?
   A: No.
   B: Well, try that. Otherwise, I'd just
      . . . .

Underline the sentences giving advice in 1–5 above. Then practise the dialogues with a partner.

2 | Giving computer advice

Here are six common computer problems. With a partner, ask for and give advice. Use the four structures from Exercise 1.

1. I've never had a home computer, but everyone tells me I should get one. I don't know anything about them. I don't want to spend more than £1,000.

2. I keep having trouble whenever I try to send e-mails. I can receive e-mails, but can't send any.

3. I keep getting cut off when I'm online – usually after only about two minutes.

4. Whenever I print a document, it seems to take ages and I can't do anything until the printer has stopped. I'm wasting hours and hours just sitting waiting.

5. My mouse isn't working properly. Someone told me I should clean it, but I don't know how to.

6. My computer doesn't seem to be as fast as it was when I bought it two years ago. It takes much longer to open files than it should.

> **Real English: not working properly**
>
> If something is not working properly, you can still use it, but it isn't working well or as it should be.
> *The TV's not working properly. I can't get channel two or three.*
> *The computer's not working properly. It's much slower than it should be.*
> *The air-conditioning's not working properly. It's not very cool in my room.*

3 | Keep + -ing

If something keeps happening, it happens too often and is usually annoying. Do you remember these examples?

I keep having trouble whenever I try to send e-mails.
I keep getting cut off when I'm online.

Make sentences by matching the beginnings 1–4 to the endings a–d.

1. The screen keeps
2. My computer keeps
3. My car keeps
4. Our dog keeps

a. getting lost.
b. crashing.
c. breaking down.
d. freezing.

Complete the sentences below with the correct form of the verbs in the box.

crash	get (x2)	lose	say
forget	give	phone	

5. I don't know why, but the computer just keeps
. . . .

6. My teacher keeps . . . . us lots and lots of homework to do.

7. I keep . . . . really terrible headaches.

8. A boy from my class keeps . . . . me up and asking me if I want to go out with him!

9. My mum keeps . . . . I should get married soon and settle down and start a family. I'm only twenty-four!

10. I keep . . . . sent lots of junk e-mails! It's driving me mad!

11. I keep . . . . people's birthdays. It's terrible, because they never forget mine!

12. I don't know why, but I keep . . . . things. Yesterday I spent an hour looking for my keys!

4 Further practice

With a partner, decide what advice you would give to the speakers in Exercise 3 above. Try to start:

Have you tried ... -ing?
Why don't you ... ?
If I were you, I'd ... .

Do you keep doing stupid things? What?

Do any of your friends or relatives keep doing things that annoy you? What?

> For more information on giving advice, see G10.

5 Speaking

Read these three reports of embarrassing computer mistakes. Which is the most embarrassing?

1. A British bank advertised a new credit card on their website. They offered an interest rate of 0.5% for six months to customers who changed to their card. It should have been 10.5%, but the programmer missed out the number '1'. Nobody in the bank noticed the mistake for two weeks. The mistake cost the bank over £100,000!

2. A customer called the helpline to say she couldn't get her new computer to switch on. The technician asked her what happened when she pushed the power button. The woman told him that she pushed and pushed on the foot pedal and nothing happened. She had put the mouse on the floor, thinking it was the foot pedal!

3. A computer engineer was invited to a friend's party, but it turned out to be a real disaster! The friend had just bought a new PC, but she couldn't get music CDs to play in the CD-ROM drive. She said she was going to send it back. The engineer thought he knew what was wrong, and said it would only take him a couple of minutes to fix it. He removed the outside case, connected up the sound card, put in a CD and it played. Everyone at the party cheered! The engineer felt great. He then forgot to switch it off. As he was putting the case back on, the metal of the case touched something live. There was a flash, a smell of burning, and he knew he had just ruined the whole thing. It cost him hundreds of pounds. He lost a friend and his professional reputation!

Have you ever heard any other stories like the three above? Have you ever had any embarrassing experiences with a computer or any other piece of machinery? When? What happened?

6 Opposites

Find words in the three reports in Exercise 5 which mean the opposite of these words.

1. include . . . .
2. disconnect . . . .
3. take out . . . .
4. dreadful . . . .
5. remember . . . .
6. switch on . . . .
7. take off . . . .
8. amateur . . . .

7 Advantages and disadvantages

With a partner, make a list of all the good things about computers that you can think of. Then make a list of all the negative things. Compare your lists with another pair of students. Do they have any ideas you didn't think of?

Sorry I'm late. • Shall we meet after work? • See you later, then. • I'm easy. • Why don't I pick you u after work? • Where shall we meet, then? • I'll be wearing a blue skirt. • Can we make it nine? • I'll under the clock. • Do you fancy going for a pizza? • I never thought I'd meet you here! • I'll meet you the foyer. • See you in the bar. • We could meet at your place, if that's all right. • Ring him on his mob • Maybe some other time, then? • I've heard a lot abo you. • I had dinner with my in-laws. • It's been ages!

10 Meeting people

Using vocabulary

1 | Speaking

Look at the people in the four photographs below. Where do you think they usually meet the people they know? The following structure may help you:

This man/woman would probably meet his/her … in/at …

2 | Waiting for ages!

Discuss these questions with a partner.

1. Do you usually get to places early, just on time, or do you often turn up late? Does it depend on who you're going to meet?

2. What excuses do you give if you're late?

3. Do you get angry with people if they are late?

Read this article and decide if you are more like the writer now, the writer when he was younger, or his friend Jane.

I know it might sound strange, but recently I've started thinking about what the places you arrange to meet say about you. Let me give you an example of what I mean. The other day, I arranged to meet a friend of mine outside the post office in Moss Side, a particularly rough area of Manchester. My friend was late – as usual. I had to wait for half an hour in the street, watching the police drive by and the rain come down. While I was there, two people asked me for money and a big guy came up to me and said: 'What are you looking at?' I suddenly thought: 'What am I doing here? This is a terrible place to meet!'

When I was younger, I used to meet people at bus stops because I didn't want my parents to see who I was going out with. I didn't want to meet in a bar because if I was the first one there, I'd look lonely and the manager might ask me my age. Now that I'm older and don't live with my parents, I don't care if I have to sit in a café or somewhere like that by myself. I'd rather look a bit lonely than be outside, getting cold and wet.

The friend I met the other day is always worried about being left on her own in a bar, so I had to wait in the street. When she finally turned up, we had our typical opening conversation. 'Jane. There you are. I was beginning to worry.' 'Sorry, I'm late. The traffic was awful.' The excuse can vary, but it's never: 'I'm sorry, I'm completely hopeless. I was basically just wasting time window shopping because I wanted to make sure you were here first so that I didn't have to wait around for you.' And then I say: 'Oh well, never mind. At least you're here now.' 'Have you been waiting long?' she asks. 'No, only five minutes.' And off we go. I suppose I should get angry, but I don't want to spoil the evening. I guess it's a sign that I must be getting old.

Now tell your partner who you are most like and why.

Real English: Have you been waiting long?

We often just add long to questions instead of a long time.

You're very good at this. Have you been doing it long?

You speak English very well. Have you been in Australia long?

A: *I'm just going out to the shops.*

B: *Are you going to be long?*

---

3 | Speaking

Discuss these questions with a partner.

1. What do you think of the writer of the article on page 70? Do you think he's stupid or nice or what? Why?

2. What do you think of his friend, Jane? Why do you think she doesn't want to meet in a bar?

3. Have you ever had any good/bad/funny experiences while waiting for people?

4. What's the worst place you've ever had to meet someone?

4 | Prepositional phrases

Make sentences by matching the sentence beginnings 1–7 to the groups of typical prepositional phrases a–g.

1. I'll meet you at the hotel
2. I'll meet you at the cinema
3. I'll meet you at the station
4. I'll pick you up
5. I'll meet you at the airport
6. I'll meet you at the bus stop
7. I'll meet you in the bar

a. on the platform / by the main exit / by the ticket barriers.

b. from the airport / from your place / from your room.

c. in the foyer / I'll come up to your room / in the bar.

d. at the check-in desk / just outside International Arrivals / at the front, by the taxi rank.

e. halfway along Baker Street / just in front of the post office / in front of McDonald's.

f. in the main bit / in the upstairs bit / at the tables outside.

g. by the ticket office / in the foyer / just outside the main entrance.

5 | Speaking

Now describe where the people in the pictures below are, using some of the phrases from Exersice 4 above.

6 | Pronunciation: weak forms

In prepositional phrases containing the words from, of and at, the vowels are nearly always unstressed.

 **Listen to these prepositional phrases. Then practise saying them.**

1. from the airport
2. from the station
3. from work
4. in front of the school
5. in front of the station
6. in front of your hotel
7. the other side of the ticket barriers
8. at the front by the taxi rank
9. at the end of your road
10. at the check-in desk

Put these short dialogues into the correct order.

1. a. Yeah. Whereabouts?
    b. Oh, I'll meet you at the check-in desk. OK?
    c. Shall I meet you at the airport, then?

2. a. Do you know Bar Q4, the one on Sorrento Street?
    b. Yeah.
    c. Where shall we meet, then?
    d. Well, I'll meet you there in the upstairs bit.

3. a. Yeah.
    b. Where shall we meet, then?
    c. Well, I'll meet you there – just the other side of the ticket barriers.
    d. Oh, right. Well, do you know New Street Station, then?
    e. Do you know my hotel?
    f. No.

Listen and check your answers. Then practise the dialogues with a partner.

Change partners. Have similar conversations using places you know and some of the prepositional phrases above.

7 | Speaking

Discuss these questions with a partner.

1. Where do you normally meet your friends?

2. What are the most popular meeting places in your town?

3. Is there any special place where teenagers usually meet? Old people? Tourists? Lovers?

Listening

1 | Speaking

Discuss these questions with a partner.

1. What did you do on your last birthday?
2. Did you enjoy it?
3. Did you get any presents?

What would you like to do on your next birthday? Rank the activities below from 1 (you would really love it) to 6 (you would really hate it).

- have a big party at home
- go out clubbing
- ignore it and pretend it isn't happening!
- go to the cinema with some friends
- go to a musical, a play or a concert
- have a quiet meal in your favourite restaurant with your close friends and family

In groups of three, compare your decisions and explain the order you chose.

2 | While you listen

You are going to listen to three friends – Jamie, Martin and Rachel – talking about what they're going to do for Rachel's birthday. Cover the conversation. As you listen, try to decide what arrangements they make.

Now listen again and complete the gaps.

Rachel's birthday

Jamie: Well, Rachel, happy birthday!

Martin: Yeah, happy birthday, Rachel!

Rachel: Oh, flowers! (1) ....! Thanks. I'll just go and put them in some water.

Jamie: So, what would you like to do tonight, then?

Rachel: To be honest, I haven't really decided yet. I've been so busy all day I haven't really thought about it. What do you (2) ....?

Jamie: (3) .... It's up to you, really. It is your birthday, after all.

Rachel: I know, but I hate (4) .... decisions.

Martin: How about going to see that musical which is on at the King's?

Rachel: We could do, I suppose.

Jamie: Oh, no, that's (5) .... awful. A friend of mine went and she left halfway through.

Martin: Oh, right. OK, well, how about Ben's café? They do jazz on a Wednesday.

Rachel: Yeah, we could do (6) .... if you want.

Jamie: Oh, Ben's! Please, no! The food in that place is so expensive, and you only get tiny little portions. Anyway, I hate jazz. I'd rather go (7) ...., if we can.

Martin: Yeah, well, it's not your birthday! Anyway, I thought you said you weren't bothered what we did.

Rachel: No, it's all right if Jamie would prefer to do something else. Listen, I've had an idea, (8) .... bowling? There's that bowling place in Moortown.

Jamie: Oh, yeah! I know the one. I've been there before. It's really good.

Martin: Yeah, sounds fine.

Rachel: OK, great. Let's do that, then.

Jamie: What time do you want to go, then? Seven? Seven thirty?

Rachel: (9) .... eight? I want to have a bath, get changed and just chill out for a bit first.

Jamie: Yeah, sure.

Martin: Whatever. I'm easy. Listen, though, I told Stella and Mike we might be doing something later.

Rachel: Oh, right, great. Do you want to (10) .... and tell them what we're doing?

Martin: Yeah. Where shall I tell them to meet us?

Rachel: You know where it is, (11) ....?

Martin: Yeah, I think so. It's just near the station, isn't it? On Otley Road.

Rachel: Yeah, that's it. Well, we'll meet them there – just inside the entrance, in the foyer.

Martin: OK. By the way, do you think we'll have to book the lanes?

Rachel: I don't know. I've never (12) .... been there. Do you know, Jamie?

Jamie: I think we should be OK. It's the (13) .... I doubt it'll be that busy.

Real English: chill out

If you chill out, you just take it easy and relax. People also often just say chill.

I'm just going to stay at home this weekend and chill out.

I need a holiday! I'd like to just lie on a beach somewhere and chill.

3 | Speaking

Discuss these questions with a partner.

1. Do you like making decisions or do you prefer someone else to make them for you?
2. What do you think of Jamie? Is he being too fussy?
3. Do you ever just go along with people's suggestions even if you don't like them? Why?
4. Is it OK to invite other people to a friend's party like Martin did?
5. Would you like to go out with these people? Why?/why not?

4 | Role play

With a partner, write one of these conversations.

1. The telephone conversation between Martin and his friends Mike and Stella as they make arrangements to meet.
2. A telephone conversation between Jamie and the bowling alley after he decides to book a lane.

Practise the conversation in pairs. Then act it out for another pair.

5 | Time expressions

When someone suggests a time to meet, we may want to suggest a different time. To do this, we say:

Can we make it (eight o'clock)?

We usually give a reason for suggesting a different time. For example:

Jamie: What time do you want to go, then? Seven? Seven thirty?
Rachel: Can we make it eight? I want to have a bath, get changed and just chill out for a bit first.

In each of the six answers below, circle the word or words that make the best response to these questions:

> When do you want to meet, then? Would tomorrow evening about seven be OK?

1. Can we make it six / eight? I don't finish work till seven.
2. Can we make it a bit earlier / later? I've got a meeting at five and it could go on for ages.
3. Can we make it a bit earlier / later? I want to get back home in time to watch the baseball match.
4. Can we make it half six / eight? The first show starts at quarter past seven and we don't want to miss it.

5. Can we make it Thursday / next week some time? I'd forgotten I'd got a meeting and then I'm away for the rest of the week.
6. Can we make it some other time / the day after? I've got this awful cold. I'm going to take the next couple of days off.

6 | Free practice

You have two minutes. Try to memorise the answers above. Then close your books and test each other in pairs.

For each of the answers above, try to think of a different reason for changing the time. Compare your answers with a partner. Did you have the same ones?

7 | I'm easy

When other people suggest doing something, you can use I'm easy to mean I don't mind. You decide. This is normal spoken English. Here are two more expressions which mean the same thing:

It's up to you.
I'm not bothered.

Look back through the conversation on page 72 and find examples of these expressions and how they are used. Do you have similar expressions in your language? Do you use them much or do you find them annoying?

Complete this conversation with appropriate words or phrases.

A: Do you want to eat out tonight or shall we eat in?
B: I'm (1) . . . .
A: OK. Well, let's eat out, then. Where shall we go?
B: I (2) . . . . mind. It's (3) . . . . to you.
A: OK. Well, let's go to that nice Italian place in Rusafa. Shall we go now or later?
B: Whenever suits you. I'm (4) . . . .
A: OK. Well, let's go now, shall we? Do you want to walk or shall I call a cab?
B: I'm not (5) . . . . It's up (6) . . . . you.

In pairs, try to have similar conversations starting:

Do you want to go the cinema tonight or shall we do something else?

How long can you keep the conversation going?

Using grammar

1 | The *-ing* form and the infinitive

What can you remember about the conversation you heard between Rachel, Martin and Jamie on page 72? Compare what you remember with a partner. Who has the better memory?

These verbal expressions were all used in the conversation. They are often used when we are making arrangements.

Do you fancy	going?	(the gerund or *-ing* form)
Would you like	to go?	(the infinitive with *to*)
Do you want	to go?	
I'd prefer	to go.	
I'd rather	go.	(the infinitive without *to*)
Shall I/we	go?	

From the examples, you can see there are three ways of following the verbal expressions. Try to remember which verbs are followed by which pattern.

2 | Practice

Complete the short conversations below using the verbs in the box in the correct form. You will need to use some verbs more than once.

do   eat   go   invite   stay   try

1. A: Do you fancy . . . . to see a movie later?
    B: To be honest, I'd rather just . . . . in and watch something on video instead. It'd be cheaper!

2. A: Do you fancy . . . . out tonight?
    B: Yeah, that'd be great. Shall we . . . . that new Moroccan place up the road? It looks quite nice.

3. A: Do you want . . . . bowling tomorrow? It might be a laugh.
    B: To be honest, I'd prefer . . . . something else instead. You always beat me – and you know I hate losing!

4. A: Do you want . . . . up to the park on Saturday for a picnic?
    B: Yeah, that'd be great. Shall we . . . . Ray and Sharon as well? We haven't seen them for ages.

5. A: Would you like . . . . up to the mountains next weekend? I thought it might be nice to get out of town.
    B: To be honest, I'd rather just . . . . in town instead. A friend of mine's having a party that Saturday.

6. A: Shall we . . . . to Croatia this summer?
    B: To be honest, I'd prefer . . . . to somewhere like Greece instead. I've been to Croatia already.

3 | Further practice

With your partner, have similar conversations to the ones in Exercise 1 on this page using these ideas.

1. A: go swimming later?
    B: to be honest / go for a run

2. A: go to visit my parents this weekend?
    B: to be honest / stay home and catch up with work

3. A: go to a concert next Friday?
    B: yeah / great / phone now and book tickets?

4. A: go to that new club tonight?
    B: go to Rock City instead

5. A: eat Chinese for dinner tonight?
    B: eat Mexican instead

6. A: go to a café for lunch?
    B: yeah / great / that new place round the corner?

Have the conversations above again with someone else. However, this time you should add a comment to your responses. For example:

A: Do you fancy going swimming later on this afternoon?
B: Well, to be honest, I'd rather go for a run. I haven't got any swimming trunks with me.

> For more information on using the *-ing* form and the infinitive, see G13.

Real English: that new club

We often use that with a noun when the person we are speaking to knows the thing we are talking about.

Shall we go to that fish place in Selva Street?

I went to that café round the corner.

Have you been to that new cinema in town yet?

What was the name of that guy we met last night?

We often use this when the person doesn't know the thing we are talking about.
I saw this really good film last night.

We're going to this Moroccan restaurant tonight. It's supposed to be great.

4 | The -ing form, infinitive with to or infinitive without to?

Choose the correct form in these sentences.

1. Have you got used to use / using this book yet?
2. Did your parents let you stay / to stay / staying out late at night when you were sixteen?
3. Did your parents make you learn / to learn a musical instrument when you were younger?
4. Is there anything you always try to avoid to do / doing?
5. Is there anything your parents warned you not to do / doing? Did you follow their advice?
6. Is there anything you regret to do / doing? Why?
7. Is there anything you should really do / to do later on this week?
8. Can you remember to go / going on a plane for the first time?

Now ask your partner the eight questions above.

5 | Do you want to ... or shall we ...?

We often give two choices when we are making suggestions. For example:

Do you want to eat now or shall we wait till later?

Make suggestions by matching the beginnings 1–8 to the endings a–h.

1. Do you want to e-mail them
2. Do you want to cook tonight
3. Do you want to get a cab there
4. Do you want to take a break now
5. Do you want to go out somewhere later
6. Do you want to do it now
7. Do you want to watch anything on TV
8. Do you want to take the camera with us

a. or shall we get a take-away?
b. or shall we carry on till we've finished?
c. or shall we give them a ring?
d. or shall we do it tomorrow?
e. or shall we just get the bus?
f. or shall I just turn it off?
g. or shall we just leave it here?
h. or shall we just stay in?

Work with a partner. One student should read the first half of the question. The other should try to remember the second part.

Now write an answer for each of the questions above, beginning with Let's ... . Try to explain the reason for your choice. For example:

A: Do you want to go out somewhere later or shall we just stay in?
B: Let's just stay in, shall we? We've been out every night this week!

> For more information on using *Let's ...* , see G14.

6 | Free practice

Using the ideas in the pictures, invite a partner to join you in these activities in the next few days. Think about:

- **where it is.**
- **where you would meet people.**
- **what time would be best to meet.**

Now invite other students. Try to use as much of the language from this unit as you can. Make a note of where and when you agree to meet other people who have invited you. Remember you can't be in two places at once!

I drive a Volvo. • I use public transport. • I can't drive. • He's passed his test. • Shall we get a cab? • flight took eleven hours. • We stopped over in Dubai. • I get seasick just thinking about ferries. • The was hardly any traffic. • We had to stand all the way! • It was a bit bumpy. • I don't mind going by coa actually. • The bus is much cheaper. • I'd fly if I were you. • He didn't indicate! • It's an accident black sp • We got lost on the way here. • We almost out of petrol.

Reading

1 | Speaking

Discuss these questions with a partner.

1. Can you drive?
2. Do you have a car? What kind? Why?
3. Do you think that the car you drive says anything about the kind of person you are?
4. Does the colour say anything about you? These structures might help you:

   People who drive … tend to be … .

   … tend to use them to … .

Look at these pictures. What kind of person do you think typically owns each vehicle? What do you think the owners might look like? How old do you think they are? What do you think they use their vehicle for?

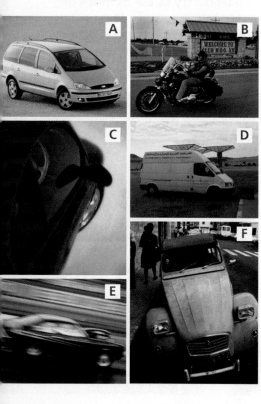

2 | While you read

Read the descriptions 1–6 and match them to the pictures A–F. Were the descriptions of typical drivers the same as you predicted?

1. The white van
The typical white van driver is usually in his twenties and makes deliveries for a living. He only ever drives in second gear because (a) he's too lazy to change it and (b) because the van makes more noise that way! He is completely antisocial, whistling at women, swearing at everyone else, and cutting in front of everybody when he drives.

2. The second-hand French car
Typical drivers of anything old and French in the UK tend to be old hippies, who have Greenpeace and Save The Whales stickers in the windows. In the back of the car, there are always piles of old papers and bottles and clothes that they always mean to take to the recycling centre, but never quite seem to get round to!

3. The customised saloon car
The typical driver of this kind of car is still in his teens, tends to have terrible spots and has only just started shaving, *but* his parents have bought him a car. It may only be a pathetic little Ford Escort or something like that, but he drives it as if it's a Formula One car, racing up and down the local high street with his friends, all of whom spend most of their time and money buying new lights and bigger wheels for their precious cars – which they call 'motors' or 'my wheels'.

4. The car with tinted windows
There are some cars that you feel before you see, as the bass from their car stereos is so unbelievably loud that your windows start to shake and things fall from your shelves as they make their way up the road towards you. When you do finally see them, they're nearly always the same – BMWs or Mercedes, which are either open-topped or have tinted windows, and are driven by macho men wearing sunglasses, gold chains and designer sportswear.

5. The big Harley Davidson
The typical Harley rider is usually in his mid-forties. He's going bald and he's getting increasingly fat. Women have stopped looking at him (if they ever did!). He wakes up one morning and suddenly realises 'I'm going to die!', but instead of spending more time with his wife and kids, he buys a twenty-thousand-pound Harley Davidson – customised, of course – and then he rides around, desperately trying to pretend he's still young. Of course, he usually only goes round town at 30 kph, just in case he gets too excited and has a heart attack!

6. The people carrier
People carriers are usually driven by middle-class mums, who use them to take their kids on their eight-minute drive to school. They tend to have a sticker in the back window saying Baby on Board!, no matter how old the children are. The funny thing is, these kinds of drivers say that the only reason they drive their kids to school is because there are so many cars on the roads these days that they're worried their children would get hit by one if they let them walk!

3 | Speaking

Discuss these questions with a partner.

1. Do you have any of the same kinds of drivers in your country?

2. Do you have any other different ones? What do they drive? What kind of people are they?

3. Are you similar to any of the drivers in the text on page 76? In what way?

4. Which kind annoys you the most? Why?

4 | Number adjectives

In the texts in Exercise 2 on page 76, you read that …

- **the typical Harley rider buys a twenty-thousand-pound Harley Davidson.**

- **middle-class mums use their people carriers to take their kids on their eight-minute drive to school.**

We don't say 'a twenty-thousand-pounds motorbike' or 'an eight-minutes drive'. We often make compound adjectives like those in the examples above to talk about price, distance, height, weight and duration. When we make compound adjectives using a number + a noun, we leave the plural -s off the nouns. Notice where the hyphens come.

Re-write these sentences with number adjectives. The first one is done for you.

1. It takes two hours by car.
   It's a *two-hour drive.*

2. The suit cost three hundred pounds.
   It's a . . . .

3. I had to wait for fifteen minutes.
   I had a . . . .

4. Her son is five years old.
   She's got a . . . .

5. I jogged four miles.
   I did a . . . .

6. It takes fifteen minutes by bus.
   It's a . . . .

7. I'm going on a cruise for two weeks.
   It's a . . . .

Now try to use number adjectives and nouns to answer these questions.

8. What's the most expensive piece of clothing you've ever bought?

9. How far do you live …
   - from the nearest station?
   - from the nearest bus stop?
   - from here?
   - from where you work?
   - from your parents?

5 | Driving vocabulary

Are you a good driver? Who do you think make better drivers – men or women? Why?

Make sentences describing bad drivers by matching the beginnings 1–5 to the endings a–e.

1. He never indicates
2. He never looks
3. He's always answering
4. He's always trying to read
5. He sometimes goes through

a. his mobile while he's driving.
b. red lights.
c. when he's turning left or right.
d. in his mirror.
e. the map while he's driving.

Now make sentences by matching the beginnings 6–10 to the endings f–j.

6. She's always driving in
7. She's always cutting
8. She sometimes overtakes
9. She's always driving too close
10. She's always driving too fast

f. on blind corners.
g. on the motorway.
h. the bus lanes.
i. in front of other people.
j. to the car in front.

Do you ever do any of the things above? Have you ever seen anyone else do any of them? Use these structures:

I was in the car with … once and he/she … . It was awful!

I was in the car with … once and we almost had an accident because he/she … .

Using grammar

1 | Comparatives and superlatives

🎧 **You are going to hear two friends trying to decide where and when to go and eat. As you listen, cover the conversation and say what they decide to do.**

Listen again and complete the gaps below. Then practise reading out the conversation with a partner.

A: When do you want to eat, then?

B: The sooner, (1) . . . . I'm starving. Where were you thinking of going? Did you have anywhere special in mind?

A: Well, I was thinking of this place just round the corner, actually. It's one of (2) . . . . to eat in town, but it depends on how much you want to spend. It *is* quite expensive.

B: Well, I'm a bit short of money at the moment, so (3) . . . . , the better, to be honest.

A: OK, well, in that case, there's a nice little café on the other side of town we could go to, but we will have to get a bus.

B: Is that going to take a long time?

A: No, it shouldn't be too bad. There's a bus that goes straight there now, almost non-stop. It's (4) . . . . than it used to be. You used to have to go a really roundabout way.

B: OK, so shall we go, then?

A: Yeah. Let me just get my things together and then we'll be off.

Real English: be off

We often use be off to mean we are leaving or going somewhere.

Listen, I must be off. I'm late for my train.

Right, I'm off. I'll see you later.

A: When are you off?

B: Tomorrow morning. My flight leaves at six.

---

2 | Speaking

Discuss these questions with a partner.

1. Do you ever go out to eat with your friends? Where do you go? Why?

2. What's the transport system like in your town/city? Has it got better over the last few years?

3 | Comparing now with the past

Complete the sentences below with the words in the box.

be	last
before	much
bigger	remember
bit	time
good	used

1. It's better than my . . . . one. It's more powerful.

2. It's better than it was . . . . There are actually more buses now.

3. It's . . . . than our old one. There's a lot more room.

4. It's more touristy than it . . . . to be. They've built several big new hotels. It's horrible now.

5. It's . . . . cheaper than it used to be. It used to cost £200 to get there.

6. It's a . . . . better than it was yesterday. It's not quite as painful.

7. It was quicker than last . . . . There was hardly any traffic.

8. It wasn't as . . . . as the last time we went. The music was terrible this time.

9. It wasn't as good as I . . . . it being. The first time I saw it, I thought the special effects were amazing.

10. It's not as good as it used to . . . . I think it's changed hands and it's gone downhill a bit.

With a partner, decide what the questions that produced the answers 1–10 above were.

Now take turns asking each other questions so that your partner can use the answers 1–10 above. For example:

A: What's your new flat like?

B: It's ... than our old one. There's a lot more room.

A: How was your journey?

B: It was quicker than last ... . There was hardly any traffic.

> For more information on comparatives and superlatives, see G15.

4 | Comparative phrases

Match the comments 1–6 to the responses with comparative phrases a–f.

1. Sorry I'm late. The traffic was awful.
2. How big do you want it?
3. When do you want it by?
4. When do you want us to come over to your house?
5. Is it OK if I bring a friend tonight?
6. How much do you want to spend?

a. The later, the better, to be honest. At least, not before eight.
b. Not too much. The cheaper, the better.
c. Sure. The more, the merrier.
d. Never mind. Better late than never.
e. The sooner, the better, to be honest. It's two days late already.
f. The bigger, the better.

Complete these sentences with a word or phrase so that they are true for you.

7. As far as .... is/are concerned, I personally think the smaller, the better.
8. As far as .... is/are concerned, I personally think the bigger, the better.
9. As far as .... is/are concerned, I personally think the cheaper, the better.
10. As far as .... is/are concerned, I personally think the stronger, the better.
11. As far as .... is/are concerned, I personally think the sweeter, the better.
12. As far as .... is/are concerned, I personally think the less you see of them, the better.
13. As far as .... is/are concerned, the less said about it/them the better.

Tell a partner your opinions and see if they agree or not. For example:

A: As far as mobile phones are concerned, I personally think the smaller, the better.
B: Me too. I really like those tiny ones. They're so light you hardly notice you've got one in your pocket.

A: As far as computers are concerned, I personally think, the smaller, the better.
B: Do you think so? Personally, I don't really like very small ones. They're really difficult to use.

Now discuss the following with a partner using patterns similar to those in the comments 7–13.

- English classes
- food
- holidays
- lie-ins
- men
- music
- women
- work

▶ For more information on comparative phrases, see G16.

5 | Superlatives

We often use superlatives to describe places. Look at these examples:

A: What's the restaurant up the road like? Is it nice?
B: Oh, it's great. It's one of the best places to eat in town.

A: What's that bar in the town square like? Is it nice?
B: I'd give it a miss if I were you. It's one of the most expensive places in town!

Complete these sentences by putting the words in brackets in the superlative form.

1. It's one of the .... (big) museums in town.
2. It's one of the .... (good) places to just go and relax in.
3. It's one of the .... (beautiful) bits of the city.
4. It's one of the .... (expensive) restaurants in town.
5. It's one of the .... (bad) clubs in town – a real tourist trap and a total rip-off!
6. It's one of the .... (old) buildings in the whole country.
7. It's one of the .... (nice) parks in the whole city.
8. It's one of the .... (interesting) bits of the city.

Write down the places in your town that you would describe using sentences 1–8 above. Compare your answers with your partner. Do you agree?

Using vocabulary

1 | Speaking

Discuss these questions with a partner.

1. How do you prefer to travel? Why? Does it depend on anything? These structures might help you:

   It depends how much time I've got.
   It depends how far I'm going.
   It depends where I'm going.
   It depends how much money I've got.
   If ... , I prefer to ... .

2. What's the longest plane journey you've ever been on? What was it like?

3. What's the longest coach journey you've ever been on? The longest car journey? The longest train journey? What were they like?

2 | How was your journey?

Here are twelve different answers to the question: 'How was your journey?' Decide if the speaker in each sentence travelled by plane, car, ferry or train. The first one is done for you.

1. It was fine. We stopped over in Dubai, so I did a bit of duty-free shopping, which was nice. ...*plane*...

2. It was terrible! We were stopped outside Metz for almost an hour! There was something on the line.
   ....

3. Terrible! The traffic outside York was horrendous, and then we broke down just outside Durham!
   ....

4. OK. We got lost coming off the motorway, but what do you expect if you ask Dave to read the map!
   ....

5. It was great. Very quick, very direct. It's a very fast line. ....

6. Awful! We got caught in this storm coming over the Alps. I thought we were going to crash. ....

7. Terrible! Both the kids got seasick! ....

8. OK, but the sea was a bit rough coming into Rotterdam! ....

9. Terrible. We got delayed in Munich for about an hour, and then they lost our luggage! ....

10. Lovely. The sea was really nice and calm and it didn't take that long, really. ....

11. Great! There was hardly any traffic. It only took us an hour to get here. ....

12. Awful! It was really crowded. The only seat I could find was in a smoking carriage. ....

Compare answers with a partner and discuss how you made your choices.

3 | Trip expressions

Complete these sentences without looking back at the sentences 1–12 in Exercise 2.

1a. We stopped .... in Moscow for a night.
1b. I .... a bit of duty-free shopping on the plane.
1c. We got .... in a storm coming in to Heathrow.
1d. We .... delayed in Rome for almost a day!

2a. The train stopped .... outside Bristol!
2b. It was so .... I couldn't find a seat.
2c. It's a very fast ....

3a. The .... was horrendous!
3b. We broke .... outside Munich!
3c. We .... lost coming off the main road.
3d. There was hardly .... traffic on the roads.

4a. My mum .... seasick on the way over.
4b. The .... was a bit rough coming in to Bilbao.
4c. The sea was really nice and ....

Tick any of the expressions above which were true for you on the longest journeys you talked about earlier. Find a new partner, and tell them about your journeys, using some of the expressions above.

4 | Listening

You are going to hear two different people talking about terrible journeys they've just had. As you listen, try to decide how each person travelled and take notes on the different problems they had. Who do you think had the worst journey? Why?

5 | Speaking

With a partner, imagine you have had a really terrible journey. Decide how you were travelling and which of the things from Exercise 3 on page 80 went wrong. Try to think of two or three other problems that you had. Ask your teacher for help if you need to.

Now go round and talk to some other students in the class. Ask each other: 'So how was your journey?' You should begin by saying: 'Terrible!' and then give more details. Who had the worst journey in the class?

6 | Learner advice: dictionaries

Which word in the box collocates with the words and phrases in each group below?

bus	car	flight	train
cab	coach	stop	

1. ....:
   call a ... , try to stop a ... , take a ...

2. ....:
   take the ... , go in the ... , take you in the ... , park the ... , lock your keys in the ... , it's ten minutes by ... , the ... won't start, the ... broke down on the motorway, a fast ... , a new ... , an old ... , a flash ...

3. ....:
   get off at the wrong ... , this is my ... , get off at the next ... , it's three ...s down the road

4. ....:
   get the ... , miss my ... , get off the ... , get on the ... , I had to change ...s twice, the ... was late getting in, my ... was delayed, my ... was cancelled, the ... stops at every station, the fast ... , a through ... , the slow ... , a long ... journey, a short ... journey

5. ....:
   get the ... , go to work by ... , run for the ... , miss the ... , wait ages for the ... , I was stuck on the ... for ages, it's twenty minutes by ... , have you got change for the ... , the ... broke down, the ... goes a really roundabout way

6. ....:
   go by ... , go on a ... tour, sit at the back of the ... , the ... was late getting in, the ... broke down on the motorway

7. ....:
   miss my ... , book my ... , get my ... , my ... was cancelled, my ... was delayed, my ... goes via Moscow, a bumpy ... , a charter ... , a cheap ... , a domestic ... , a long ... , a direct ... , my connecting ...

How many of the collocations above are new for you? Does your partner know any collocations that you don't? Which five collocations do you think you will use most often? Why?

7 | Speaking

Discuss these questions with a partner.

1. The collocations in Exercise 6 are example entries of what you can find in a collocation dictionary. Have you ever used a dictionary like this? How is it different to your normal dictionary? Which is better? Why?
2. What dictionary or dictionaries do you use? Why? In groups, look up the word 'plane' in all the dictionaries you have. Which is the best?
3. Which dictionary is laid out the best?
4. Which is the easiest to understand?
5. Which has the most examples?
6. Which gives the best information about collocates?
7. Which is the easiest to carry round?
8. Which has the most pictures?
9. Which has definitions for the most words?
10. Has any of this made you change your mind about the kind of dictionary you're using?

12 Food

I love Chinese food, don't you? • I've never tried haggis. • I'm allergic to nuts. • Do you eat fish? • [
wonder they're so fat! • It's very good for you, but I can't stand it myself. • I love spicy food. • British fo
can be very bland, can't it? • I love their desserts. • Can you use chopsticks? • I'll just have the house r
• It's off! • I'm so hungry, I could eat a horse! • Is Yorkshire pudding a dessert? • Mm, this is yummy! •
very filling. • It's a kind of soup. • I'm on a diet. • I have a sweet tooth. • It's very more
• It was so disgusting, I had to spit it out! • I'll just grate a bit of cheese on it.

Using vocabulary

1 Different food

Look at the pictures A–I below and discuss what kind of food you can see. You might need to say:

I'm not really sure what that is. What do you reckon?
I've got no idea what that is, but it looks
delicious/disgusting.

Where do you think each comes from? Have you ever tried them? What were they like?

Now listen and match the descriptions 1–9 to the pictures A–I.

1. Picture	6. Picture .....
2. Picture	7. Picture .....
3. Picture	8. Picture .....
4. Picture	9. Picture .....
5. Picture	

2 Describing food

Can you remember which pictures the following expressions were used to describe?

1. It's quite rich, quite heavy.
2. It's a kind of a salad.
3. It's a kind of traditional Spanish seafood dish.
4. You grill it.
5. It's quite fattening.
6. It's a kind of vegetable.
7. It's very filling.
8. It's got quite a strange texture.
9. It's a traditional Middle Eastern starter or side dish.

3 | Speaking

With a partner, take turns describing the food in the pictures. Begin by saying 'It's a kind of …' and add any extra information you can remember. Can your partner guess which food you are describing?

Think of five different kinds of foods from your country and spend five minutes planning how to describe them. Now tell other students as much about each food as you can.

4 | English food!

Which country do you think has the best food in the world? Why?

Which region of your country has the best food? Why?

Three people describe how they feel about English food. Complete the texts with the words in the boxes.

1. Michael Lemerre, Chef, The Royal Hotel, London

| bland | comfort | prefer | sauces |

To be honest with you, I find most English food a bit (a) .... The English don't really know how to use seasoning or spices, so everything's a bit tasteless. Having said that, England does have great (b) .... food, you know, things that make you feel better when you're down – cakes, puddings, that kind of thing. Personally, though, I (c) .... French food. It has great (d) .... and the French really know how to cook meat well!

2. Julie Tippetts, Musician, Bristol

| filling | healthy | kind | limited |

I quite like English food sometimes, though it's not very (a) .... I'm a vegetarian, so it's important to me that I eat well. I like most English soups, they're usually nice and (b) .... , great in the winter. I also really like almost any (c) .... of salad too – potato salad, green salad, fruit salad, whatever! Generally, though, I find English food a bit (d) .... , there's just not enough choice. Asian food is a lot more varied – and better if you don't eat meat!

3. Jack Jones, Builder, Birmingham

| fattening | foreign | greasy | rich | spicy |

I love English food. You can't beat a full English breakfast, although I must admit it can sometimes be a bit too (a) .... English food can be quite (b) .... as well, so it's best not to eat it all the time, unless you want to get really fat! If I have to eat (c) .... food, I prefer Indian – it's nice and (d) .... and is great after drinking. I've tried French food, but I just find it much too (e) .... , you know, all that cream and brandy and wine!

Underline any expressions or collocations in the texts above that are new for you.

Who do you agree with most? Why?

Using vocabulary

1 | Before you read

Match the descriptions 1–5 to the situations a–e.

1. Very thin teenage girls who don't eat because they think they're fat.
2. People caught in a famine in Africa.
3. A whole family, all ill after eating out.
4. People who are so fat it's very unhealthy.
5. Teenage boys who eat too much chocolate.

a. They're starving to death.
b. They're obese.
c. They've got food poisoning.
d. They can get really bad spots.
e. They're anorexic.

Are any of the problems above common in your country? Why/why not?

2 | Eat your greens!

Read this article about one of the problems in Exercise 1 above. As you read, try to answer the questions.

1. Which problem is being talked about?
2. What has caused it?
3. What solution to it has been put forward?

People in developed countries are increasingly suffering from illnesses resulting from over-eating. While starvation and famine are still big problems in many poor countries in the world, in America and other western countries, more than twenty-five percent of the population are obese. This doesn't just mean you're a little bit fat, it means you are more than twenty kilos overweight. And Dr John Colon from Ohio State University says the problem is only going to get worse. 'As more women have gone out to work, you find that parents in general have less time to spend on preparing food. That's not just the cooking, but also planning what to eat, doing the shopping and buying fresh food. Families, therefore, increasingly rely on ready-made and frozen meals, which tend to be high in fat and contain a lot of additives and sugar. The other thing is that parents seem to feel guilty about not spending so much time with their kids, so they tend to give in a lot quicker to children's demands for things like sweets and chocolate.'

Ben Brown, who is a British Member of Parliament, blames the big food companies. He wants to ban any food advertising which is aimed at children. 'The problem is that these companies spend millions of pounds selling food to children. It's all crisps in the shape of dinosaurs and chocolate in the shape of Mickey Mouse. I mean, what's going to seem more fun to an eight-year-old – an ice cream with a free toy or an apple?'

One food company thinks it has an answer to this: it has invented pizza-flavoured broccoli, baked-bean-flavoured peas, cheese and onion-flavoured cauliflower and chocolate-flavoured carrots. It developed the 'Whacky Veg' with money donated by a cancer research charity, which found that a diet containing lots of fruit and vegetables helps reduce cancer. However, today's sweet-toothed kids need to be bribed into a healthy diet, and will only eat their greens if they taste different.

3 | Speaking

Discuss these questions with a partner.

1. Who do you agree more with – Dr Colon or Ben Brown? Why?
2. How much time do you spend cooking every day?
3. Do you buy fresh food every day or do you go to the supermarket once a week?
4. Do you ever eat ready-made meals or frozen food?
5. Do you think Whacky Veg will catch on? Would you eat it?
6. What's the weirdest thing you've ever eaten?

4 | Vocabulary focus

Which words in the box collocate with the words and phrases 1–8 below?

diet	fruit	meal	salad
food	good	meat	weight

1. lose / put on a bit of / gain . . . .
2. a balanced / a healthy / a special / a poor . . . .
3. health / organic / fast / fresh / junk . . . .
4. a light / a heavy / a big / a lovely / our main . . . .
5. ripe / tropical / rotten / tinned . . . .
6. white / red / lean / fatty / raw . . . .
7. a potato / a green / a side / a fruit . . . .
8. . . . . for your health / for your heart / for your digestion / when you've got a cold

Say something about yourself using five collocations from above.

5 | It should be banned!

Ben Brown wants to ban food advertising which is aimed at children. Which of the following do you think should be banned? Why?

cars in city centres	smacking kids
female boxing	smoking in public places
golf	the teaching of grammar
karaoke	whaling

Can you think of anything else that you think should be banned? Why?

6 | I can't eat that!

Eight people say why they can't eat a particular kind of food. Match the first part of their comments 1–8 to their reasons a–h.

1. I can't eat anything with meat in it, ☐
2. I can't eat anything too fattening, ☐
3. I can't eat sushi, I'm afraid, ☐
4. I can't eat any of the fish dishes, ☐
5. I can't eat anything with chillies in, ☐
6. I can't eat anything too salty, ☐
7. I can't eat any of the pizzas, ☐
8. I can't eat hamburgers or chips or anything like that, ☐

a. because I'm supposed to be on a diet at the moment.
b. because I just don't like spicy food.
c. because my doctor said it's bad for my health.
d. because I just don't like junk food.
e. because I'm allergic to tomatoes!
f. because I'm a vegetarian.
g. because I can't stand raw fish!
h. because I can't be bothered to pick out all the bones.

7 | Who's the fussiest eater?

Look at this menu and discuss with your partner what you *can't* eat. Make sure you explain why.

Menu

Starters

Sashimi *(four different kinds of raw fish, served with soy sauce and spicy wasabi paste)*

Chicken livers

Garlic bread

Snails in garlic sauce

Duck liver paté and toast

Sheep's eye soup

Frogs' legs

Main courses

Quattro formaggi pizza *(cheese and tomato pizza topped with four different kinds of cheese, including two strong blue cheeses)*

Cheese and tomato pizza topped with anchovies and mushrooms

Pork chop, peas and rice

Chicken satay in peanut sauce

Squid *(cooked in its own ink)*

Lamb vindaloo *(very hot curry)*

Double cheeseburger with chips

Desserts

A chocolate bar deep-fried in batter

Coffee and walnut cake with cream

Vanilla or rum ice cream

Lychees

Using grammar

1 | Listening

You are going to hear two people having a conversation at the end of a meal. As you listen, try to answer these questions.

1. Did they enjoy the meal?
2. Why/why not?
3. What do you think might have happened to Steve at the end of the meal?
4. Have you ever had any similar problems? Where? When? What happened?

Real English: a bit too ... for my liking

We often use the structure a bit too ... for my liking to politely say we don't like something.
It's a bit too spicy for my liking.
It's a bit too sweet for my liking.
It was a bit too crowded for my liking.

In the examples above, it is more spicy/sweet/crowded than you like.

2 | Should've

In the conversation in the restaurant, Cathy said to Steve: 'We should've gone somewhere else' and 'You should've asked for some more soup'. Can you remember why she said these things?

We often use *should've* + past participle to talk about something in the past which was a good idea, but which we didn't do. We often use it because there is a present result that makes us regret something or that now makes us realise a mistake we made in the past. For example:

I'm really hungry because I forgot to eat breakfast. I should've had something to eat this morning.

I've got a terrible headache because I went to a really loud concert last night. I shouldn't have stood so close to the speakers!

3 | Practice

Re-write the 'Why didn't you ...?' questions using should've.

1. A: Mum, I'm hungry.
   B: Well, why didn't you eat more at dinner?
   ....

2. A: Mum, I need to go to the toilet.
   B: Why didn't you go before we came out?
   ....

3. A: I'm cold, mum.
   B: Well, why didn't you bring a coat?
   ....

4. A: I can't eat this. I'm allergic to eggs.
   B: Why didn't you tell me before? I could've cooked something else.
   ....

5. A: Actually, it's my birthday today.
   B: Really! Why didn't you say? We could've done something special.
   ....

6. A: I just stayed in last night and watched TV.
   B: Why didn't you come to the party? It was great fun.
   ....

Practise the conversations above with a partner. Use 'You should've ... .'

Now complete the sentences below using should've or shouldn't have and a correct form of the verbs in the box.

add	come	have	
bring	go	order	see

1. This stew isn't very nice, is it? I . . . .
   some wine or something. It's a bit bland as it is.

2. I don't believe it! It's raining again. I told you we
   . . . . an umbrella.

3. Ooh, I feel a bit sick. I knew I . . . . all that
   cream with the cake.

4. We had a wonderful meal last night. You
   . . . . You would've really enjoyed it.

5. At the end of the meal, James asked Kate to marry
   him. He got down on one knee, and gave her a rose.
   You . . . . it. It was so romantic. I wish I'd
   had my camera.

6. Sixty pounds! I knew I . . . . to the bank
   before I came out. I haven't got enough money now.

7. I don't know why I asked for this pasta. I'm not really
   that hungry. I . . . . something lighter.

4   Pronunciation: contractions

🎧 **Listen to these sentences using should've and
shouldn't have and then practise saying them.**

1. You shouldn't have said that.
2. We should've gone somewhere else.
3. I should've done it earlier.
4. He should've sent his application form off earlier.
5. I shouldn't have asked.
6. You should've thought about that before, shouldn't
   you?
7. You should've told me about it before.
8. I shouldn't have bothered!
9. You should've come.
10. I shouldn't have eaten so much!

**What do you think the result of each of the
mistakes above might be? For example, in
number 1:**

You shouldn't have said that because now you've hurt
her feelings and she's not talking to you any more.

> ▶ For more information on using should've and shouldn't
> have, see G17.

5   Further practice

**Read this story and say what mistakes the people
made, using should've and shouldn't have. Who
do you think was most to blame, Nick or Janet?
Why?**

Dear John,

I'm just writing to apologise for missing your wedding
last week. We left a bit late because Janet decided to
ring her mother five minutes before we were supposed
to go out. Don't ask me why! Anyway, we finally managed
to leave half an hour later. When we got to the station,
we tried to buy a ticket, but the next train was
completely full. They're usually almost empty, so I hadn't
booked seats. There was another train an hour later, but
Janet thought it would be better to go back home and
take the car, so that's what we did. When we got to the
motorway, the traffic was awful. I said I knew a short cut,
so at the next exit, we went off the motorway.
Unfortunately, it's such a long time since I've been to
your place, I got a bit lost and we ended up going thirty
miles in the wrong direction. I have to say, Janet did
suggest asking someone, but I was sure I was going in
the right direction.

We had to stop and buy a map because we had left ours
at home. Unfortunately, Janet then misread it, so we
went the wrong way again. We then changed over and I
read the map while Janet drove. We were so late that
Janet started driving much too fast and unfortunately a
policeman stopped us for speeding. When Janet tried to
give the policeman £10 to say nothing and just let us get
to the wedding, he arrested us for trying to bribe him!

So, sorry again. I hope you have a nice honeymoon and
I'll give you your present when we get out of prison
next year.

All the best,

Nick

Has anything like this ever happened to you?

> **Real English:** end up
>
> End up is very common in spoken English and it
> explains what finally happened or where we finally
> arrived, usually after something unplanned happened.
> *I missed the last bus, so I ended up walking all the way
> home.*
>
> *We took the wrong turning and we ended up in
> Scotland!*
>
> *I was just going to go out for a quick drink with Tony, but
> then we bumped into some friends and we ended up
> going clubbing.*
>
> *I only came here for a holiday, but then I met my
> husband and I've ended up staying here for fifteen
> years!*

Review: Units 9–12

1 | Grammar review

Choose the correct form.

1. When did you start / have you started cycling to work?

2. Korea was / has been one of the best places I ever went to / I've ever been to in my life.

3. If I were you, I'll / I'd try phoning the service help desk about it.

4. The trains never come / are never coming when they're supposed to!

5. You should be / You should've been here yesterday. We had a really good class.

6. It wasn't as quick as the last time we came / we've come.

7. My mobile keeps cutting out / is keeping cutting out! The reception's really bad here.

8. I like your laptop. How long did you have / have you had it?

9. I learnt French at school but I forgot / I've forgotten most of it now.

10. A: Shall we to go / go out later?
    B: To be honest, I'd rather to stay in / stay in and watch that film on TV. It's got Brad Pitt in it. He's gorgeous.

Compare your answers with a partner and explain your choices.

2 | Comparing things

Complete the sentences below with the superlative form of the adjectives in the box.

annoying	cold	nice	scary
badly-paid	depressing	painful	well-paid

1. That was lovely, one of the .... meals I've had in a long time.

2. It was freezing in Finland. It's one of the .... places I've ever been to in my life.

3. I hate the ring tone he's got on his phone. It's one of the .... things I've ever heard in my life!

4. It was horrible when I broke my leg. It's the .... thing that's ever happened to me!

5. It was great working in the bank. That was the .... job I've ever had. I really miss the money!

6. That's one of the .... films I've ever seen in my life. I felt really down for a long time after seeing it.

7. Working in that burger bar was awful. It's one of the .... jobs in the world! Only five euros an hour!

8. I couldn't sleep after watching *Nightmare 2*. It's one of the .... films I've seen in a long time.

3 | Verb forms

Complete this conversation by putting the verbs in brackets into the correct form.

Jed: What are you doing for the summer holiday?

Matt: I'm thinking of just (1) .... (stay) at home. I can't really afford (2) .... (go) anywhere at the moment.

Jed: I can imagine. I bet they don't pay very much at the bookshop.

Matt: No, they don't!

Jed: Have you tried (3) .... (ask) the bank for a loan?

Matt: No, but to be honest, I'd prefer not (4) .... (get) into debt. I've always avoided (5) .... (get) a credit card, because you can end up spending money without thinking.

Jed: Yeah, I guess so. I sometimes regret (6) .... (take out) that loan to buy my car. I'm still paying £250 a month for it after two years – and it keeps (7) .... (break down)!

Matt: Well, I did warn you not (8) .... (buy) it, didn't I?

Jed: OK, OK, there's no need to keep going on about it!

Matt: All right, sorry. Listen, why don't you come with us next weekend? We're going camping by the sea.

Jed: That's really nice of you to offer, but to be honest, I'd rather just stay here. I've never really liked (9) .... (walk) and fresh air and all that kind of thing. I'm a city boy at heart.

Matt: Yeah, well, you know I used to live in the countryside, don't you? So I love all that. In fact, I've never really got used to (10) .... (live) in Birmingham, but you have to go where the work is, don't you?

Jed: Yeah, I suppose so. Oh, no, is that the time? Look, I must get going. I'm meeting Tim in ten minutes, so I'll give you a ring later.

Matt: OK, see you.

4 | Look back and check

Look back at Exercise I General advice on page 68. Tick all the words and expressions you can remember. Ask a partner about anything you have forgotten.

Now work with a partner. One of you should read out the problems 1–6 from Exercise 2 on page 68. The other should try to give advice about each using the language from Exercise I on page 68.

5 | Verb collocations

Match the verbs 1–10 to the groups of phrases they collocate with a–j.

1. pretend
2. bribe
3. press
4. go on
5. read
6. check
7. download
8. get
9. overtake
10. book

a. a flight online / a table
b. the map / the instructions
c. my e-mail / my phone messages
d. bad food poisoning / bad spots
e. software from the Internet / music from the web
f. the car in front / on a blind corner
g. holiday / the ferry
h. a policeman / the judge
i. the wrong button / the accelerator
j. it didn't happen / you didn't see him

You have one minute to memorise the collocations a–j. Now cover the exercise above. Your partner will read out the verbs 1–10. How many collocations can you remember?

With a partner, try to think of one more common collocation for each of the verbs 1–10.

6 | Adjectives

Complete the sentences below with the adjectives in the box.

amazing	awful	bland	greasy	hopeless
obsessed	quiet	spicy	user-friendly	wrong

1. I didn't do anything special for my birthday. I just had a . . . . meal with a few friends.
2. He's a bit strange if you ask me. He's absolutely . . . . with motorbikes!
3. I don't really like potatoes very much. I find them a bit . . . . They don't really taste of anything.
4. They've got a really great website. It's very . . . ., very easy to order things from.
5. I got off at the . . . . station by mistake and ended up having to get a taxi home.
6. The traffic on the motorway was . . . . The last twenty miles took us two hours.
7. What a brilliant film! The special effects were . . . .
8. I don't really eat much fried food. I don't like . . . . stuff very much.
9. How many chillies did you put in here? It's really . . . .!
10. He's always late. He's absolutely . . . .!

7 | Questions and answers

Match the questions 1–10 to the answers a–j.

1. Are you connected to the Internet at home?
2. Have you tried talking to them about it?
3. How long have you lived here?
4. When did you move there?
5. Did you have anywhere special in mind for dinner?
6. Do you want to do it now or shall we wait till later?
7. Do you fancy doing something tonight?
8. How was your journey?
9. Why don't you try changing the batteries?
10. Could we have the bill, please?

a. It was about fifteen years ago, I think.
b. Yeah, I'd love to. What did you have in mind?
c. Let's leave it for a bit, OK?
d. Yeah, there's a nice pizzeria just up the road.
e. Terrible!
f. Yeah, but it didn't make any difference.
g. Oh, yeah. That might do it.
h. Yeah, we've just got broadband, actually.
i. Certainly, madam.
j. It's almost seven years now.

8 | What can you remember?

With a partner, note down as much as you can remember about the texts you read in Units 11 and 12.

Typical!

Eat your greens!

Now compare what you remembered with another pair. Who remembered more? Which text did you enjoy more? Why?

9 | Common expressions

Complete the sentences below with the words in the box.

banned	better	bothered	going	hardly
have	late	mind	thought	to go

1. It should be . . . . !
2. You should've . . . . of that earlier.
3. I shouldn't . . . . asked!
4. There was . . . . any traffic on the roads.
5. The sooner, the . . . .
6. Better . . . . than never.
7. Do you fancy . . . . out tonight?

8. Do you want . . . . and see a film tomorrow?
9. I'm not . . . .
10. I don't . . . .

Discuss these questions with a partner.

11. What things do you think should be banned? Why?
12. Can you think of two questions you could answer by saying: 'The sooner, the better'?
13. Can you think of two questions you could answer by saying: 'I'm not bothered' or 'I don't mind'?

10 | Revision quiz

Discuss these questions in groups of three.

1. Can you think of two places that have a foyer?
2. The answer is: 'Yeah, of course. The more, the merrier.' What was the question?
3. What do you do with a mouse?
4. What's the difference between an amateur and a professional?
5. What kind of thing is comfort food?
6. What kind of person might you ignore?
7. What's the problem if you're obese? And if you're anorexic?
8. Can you think of three endings for this sentence? It's really annoying. He keeps …-ing.
9. Can you remember three possible endings for this sentence? I'll meet you at the station … .
10. Can you think of three different kinds of salad?
11. Why might you get rid of a TV/software or your computer/staff in a business?
12. What's the difference between junk food and fast food?
13. What can a virus do to your computer?
14. Why might you need to follow a special diet?
15. When and where might you stop over?
16. Why might you say: 'I shouldn't have eaten so much'?
17. Can you remember two other ways of saying: 'I'm not bothered'?
18. Which is nicer to eat – rotten fruit or ripe fruit?
19. What foods can be too greasy? Too spicy? A bit bland? Very rich?
20. Why might your plane get delayed?

Learner advice: Recording and revising vocabulary

It is a good idea to develop some kind of system for recording vocabulary. If you just write down all the language you meet, one piece after another, it can be hard to see any connection between things. It is a better idea to try and sort the language into connected groups. For example, 'vocabulary connected to health' or 'expressions with the word *mind*' or 'typical responses', such as *Oh, right. Really?* and *That sounds good.*

Organise the expressions below into groups. Four possible groups are the topics of Units 9 to 12: *computers, meeting people, transport and travel* and *food,* but others are possible. Also, some of the expressions don't fit these groups. You will have to think about how to group them.

Decide which items you want to put in which groups and make your own new lists below.

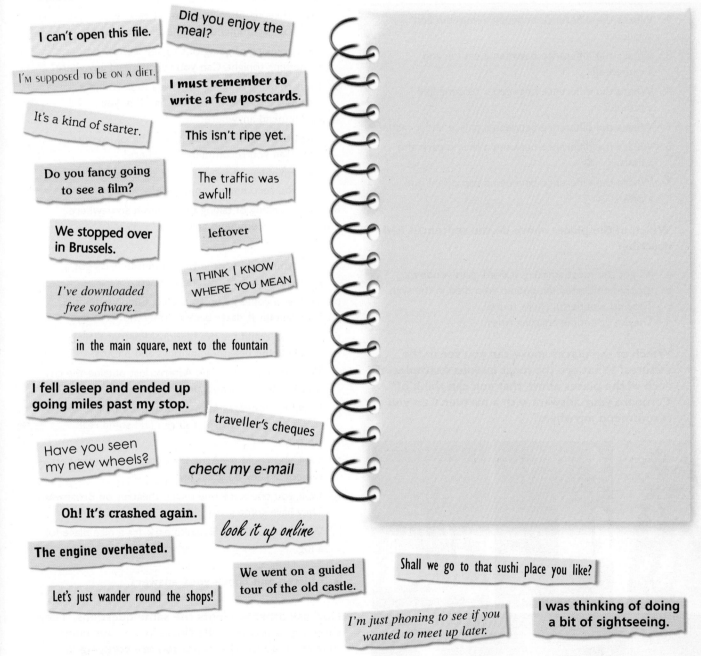

I can't open this file.

Did you enjoy the meal?

I'm supposed to be on a diet.

I must remember to write a few postcards.

It's a kind of starter.

This isn't ripe yet.

Do you fancy going to see a film?

The traffic was awful!

We stopped over in Brussels.

leftover

I've downloaded free software.

I THINK I KNOW WHERE YOU MEAN

in the main square, next to the fountain

I fell asleep and ended up going miles past my stop.

traveller's cheques

Have you seen my new wheels?

check my e-mail

Oh! It's crashed again.

look it up online

The engine overheated.

We went on a guided tour of the old castle.

Shall we go to that sushi place you like?

Let's just wander round the shops!

I'm just phoning to see if you wanted to meet up later.

I was thinking of doing a bit of sightseeing.

Compare the way you've re-organised these expressions with a partner. Who do you think had the best ideas?

Why don't you try and organise the vocabulary you learnt in class recently into groups in your notebook?

What a view! • It's well worth a visit. • Did you go to the castle? • What did you think of the Nation Gallery? • The temples are amazing. • How did they build the pyramids? • Make sure you go on t guided tour. • The weather was perfect for sightseeing. • The markets were really great. • Did you go the bazaar? • The kids loved the mummies. • I just shopped till I dropped! • It's a total rip-off. • Did yo see the Impressionists? • Don't miss the Acropolis. • Some friends ours are putting us up. • It's a bit too touristy for my liking.

Using vocabulary

1 Sightseeing words

Discuss these questions with a partner. Use your dictionary to help you if necessary.

1. What's the difference between a statue and a monument?
2. What's the difference between a museum and a gallery?
3. What's the difference between a church and a cathedral?
4. What's the difference between a mosque and a temple?
5. What's the difference between a palace and a castle?
6. What's the difference between a theme park and a funfair?
7. What's the difference between a restaurant and a café?

Which of the places above do the sentences a–d describe?

a. It's got the most amazing stained-glass windows.
b. It commemorates the people who died in the war.
c. They do wonderful paella there.
d. They've got some amazing rides.

Which of the places above can you see in the pictures? What are the most famous examples of each of the places above that you can think of? Compare your answers with a partner. Can you recommend anywhere?

2 Recommending

Match the questions 1–8 to the most suitable response a–h.

1. I was thinking of trying some of the local food. Can you recommend anywhere?
2. I was thinking of buying a few souvenirs. Can you recommend anywhere?
3. I was thinking of going to an art gallery. Can you recommend anywhere?
4. I was thinking of going out to see a show or something tonight. Can you recommend anywhere?
5. I was thinking of going to have a look round a museum or somewhere like that. Can you recommend anywhere?
6. I was thinking of maybe getting a bit of exercise later. Can you recommend anywhere?
7. I was thinking of doing a bit of sightseeing. Can you recommend anywhere?
8. I was thinking of taking the children somewhere. Can you recommend anywhere?

a. Well, you could try the British Museum. It's got a great collection of ancient artefacts.
b. Well, you could go up to the big Buddhist temple. It's beautiful. It dates back to the tenth century.
c. Well, you could try the National Portrait Gallery. It's got some beautiful paintings and photos.
d. Well, you could try Parc Asterix, just outside the city. It's a really fun theme park.
e. Well, you could try Jalan Surabaya. It's a big long street market in town. You can find some real bargains.
f. Well, you could try Agut. It's a great restaurant near the port. They do great fish.
g. Well, you could try one of the theatres off Broadway. They have some great plays on there sometimes.
h. Well, you could try Shinjuku park. It's a nice place for a jog.

 **Listen and check your answers.**

Now ask other students the same questions. They should give answers like those in a–h, but ones that are true for the place you are studying in.

3 | Collocations

Make sentences by matching the beginnings 1–10 to the endings a–j.

1. I must've taken
2. We went on
3. I must remember to book
4. The restaurant was fully
5. The concert was completely sold
6. I must remember to write
7. I managed to buy a ticket on
8. I must remember to cash
9. I've had
10. I must remember to change

a. booked.
b. a few postcards.
c. the black market from outside the stadium.
d. some travellers' cheques tomorrow.
e. a guided tour of the old castle.
f. my bag stolen!
g. about a thousand photos so far!
h. some money at the bank later.
i. some tickets for that musical.
j. out.

Your partner should cover the endings of the sentences a–j. Read out the beginnings 1–10 and see if your partner can remember how the sentences end.

4 | Speaking

Discuss these questions with a partner.

1. Have you ever bought anything on the black market? What? Why?
2. Have you ever had anything stolen while you were on holiday? What happened?
3. Have you ever been on any guided tours? When?

5 | What's it like?

Decide if the sentences 1–8 can be followed by a or b.

1. It's a bit of a rip-off.
2. It's the best place to eat in town.
3. It's a bit of a tourist trap.
4. It's a really horrible place.
5. It's a bit of a rough area.
6. You can pick up some real bargains there.
7. You get a great view of the city from up there.
8. It's a nice gallery. There's a great exhibition on there at the moment.

a. It's well worth a visit.
b. I'd give it a miss if I were you.

Now listen to the eight short dialogues and see if you were right.

Real English:
a tourist trap

A tourist trap is a common negative expression for a place where only tourists go. There is often very little to do or see there, but there may be lots of shops or cafés and they are all very expensive.

Which of the places described in sentences 1–8 can you see in the pictures below?

Think of four places you know in the town or city where you're studying that you would describe using some of the sentences 1–8. Have conversations with other students like this:

A: Have you been to the Tate Modern?
B: No, what's it like?
A: Oh, it's a great gallery. It's well worth a visit.

A: Have you been to the Bronx?
B: No, what's it like?
A: It's a bit of a rough area. I'd give it a miss if I were you.

Listening

1 | Speaking

Discuss these questions with a partner.

1. What kind of places do you usually stay in when you go on holiday?

2. Have you ever made any friends while you were on holiday?

3. Which cities can you see in the pictures below?

4. If you went on holiday to these places, how would you spend your time?

2 | While you listen

🎧 **You are going to hear a conversation between two couples who have recently met in a hotel. They meet at breakfast and talk about their plans for the day. Cover the conversation. As you listen, try to answer these questions.**

1. Which of the cities in the pictures do you think they are visiting?

2. Which couple is more organised about what they want to do? David and Victoria, or Jason and Kylie?

A day out

Kylie:	Morning, David. Victoria. Do you mind if we (1) . . . . ?
David:	Hi, Kylie. No, of course not. Go ahead.
Victoria:	Did you sleep well?
Kylie:	Yes, very well, thanks. They're lovely rooms, aren't they. Really (2) . . . .
David:	Wonderful. We've got (3) . . . . of the river from ours.
Kylie:	Have you? We can only see the car park from ours.
Victoria:	That's a shame.
David:	So, what are you planning to do today?
Kylie:	We haven't really (4) . . . . , have we Jason?
Jason:	No.
Kylie:	We'll probably just take it easy this morning, you know, go and (5) . . . . the shops.
Jason:	Yeah.
Kylie:	We might go to the Picasso exhibition at the Louvre this afternoon. It (6) . . . . what the queues are like. I've heard it (7) . . . . very busy. A friend of ours went and she said she had to wait for over an hour to get in. Isn't that right, Jason?
Jason:	Yeah.
Kylie:	So, what are you two doing today? Any (8) . . . . ?
David:	Yeah, we're going to go up the Eiffel Tower this morning and then we're going to go for a cruise down the river. We (9) . . . . art galleries and museums and things like that, do we, Victoria?
Victoria:	No.
Kylie:	Right. Well, it (10) . . . . a nice day, anyway. I hope it doesn't rain for you.
David:	Why? What's the forecast?
Kylie:	Well, they said it's going to rain this morning, but it might (11) . . . . later.
Victoria:	Well, it was OK when we got up.
David:	Are you going to eat here tonight?
Kylie:	I don't know. We might go out, it depends (12) . . . . we get back this afternoon.
Jason:	And how much money you spend shopping.
Kylie:	Hm. Why? What are you doing tonight?
David:	Well, we've (13) . . . . at a restaurant on the Champs Elysée. It's supposed to be amazing. You're welcome to join us, if you like.
Kylie:	That's very kind of you. We (14) . . . . , won't we Jason?
Jason:	Hm, It sounds a bit expensive.
Kylie:	Don't be silly, we can (15) . . . .
Jason:	As I say, it depends how much you spend when we wander round the shops.

Listen again and complete the gaps.

Who would you rather spend the day with –
Kylie and Jason or David and Victoria? Why?
These structures might help:

He/she sounds a bit + negative adjective.
He/she sounds really + positive adjective.
I'm not really into … and they sound like they are.

3 | Talking about the weather

**Our holiday plans often depend on the weather.
What did the people say about the weather in
the conversation in Exercise 2?**

**Below are ten answers to the question: So what
was the weather like while you were there?
Complete each one by adding Great!, OK or
Terrible!**

1. .... It rained the whole time.
2. .... We didn't see a cloud in the sky the whole time.
3. .... It was really hot and sticky.
4. .... It was a bit chilly, but quite bright and sunny most of the time.
5. .... It poured down a couple of times, but the rest of the time it was quite nice.
6. .... The heat was unbearable! It was something like 45° in the shade.
7. .... I thought it was going to be freezing, but it was actually quite mild.
8. .... It was quite sunny, but it was quite windy most of the time, too.
9. .... It was boiling! Haven't you noticed my tan?
10. .... We had two or three huge storms. There was thunder and lightning. It was terrifying!

**Now ask your partner these questions. Try to use
some of the language above when answering.**

1. What was the weather like the last time you went on holiday?
2. What's the best time of year to visit your country?
3. What's the weather like in the summer in your country?
4. What's the weather like in the winter?
5. What's the worst kind of weather you get in your country?

4 | Weather forecasts

**Make sentences by matching the beginnings 1–6
to the endings a–f.**

1. They said it was going to rain all night tonight, but with any luck it'll
2. They said there was going to be a huge storm today, but with any luck it'll
3. They said it's going to be cloudy this morning, but with any luck it'll
4. They said it would be dry on Saturday, but knowing our luck, it'll probably
5. They said it'll be bright and sunny today, but knowing our luck, it'll probably
6. They said there'll be lots of snow when we go skiing, but knowing our luck, it'll probably

a. pour with rain all day.
b. miss us.
c. all melt before we get there.
d. be dry by morning.
e. be all grey and cloudy.
f. brighten up a bit later on.

> **Real English: with any luck/knowing our luck**
>
> We often use with any luck to mean I hope. We use it to talk about things we want to happen.
> *With any luck, I'll get this job I applied for.*
> *I'll see you later, with any luck.*
>
> We use knowing my/our luck to show we are pessimistic about something because we often have bad luck.
> *I don't think I've ever been happier, but knowing my luck something terrible's going to happen.*
> *I've revised quite a lot for the exam, but knowing my luck, all the wrong questions will come up.*

**Have you heard the weather forecast for
today/tomorrow/this weekend? What did it say?**

Using grammar

1 | Going to, will probably, might

Do you know the difference between these three ways of talking about the future?

I'm going to visit my parents.
I'll probably visit my parents.
I might visit my parents.

Tell your partner what you think. Then read the following explanation and see if you were right: We often use either I'm going to, I'll probably, or I might + verb to answer questions about our plans for the future.

We use I'm going to + verb when we've decided before the person asks. For example:

A: What are you doing tonight?
B: I'm going to see a film with a friend of mine.

A: What are you doing tonight?
B: I'm just going to have an early night. I'm really tired.

We use I'll probably and I might when we haven't completely decided before the person asks. We often use these structures with phrases like I don't know, I'm not sure and I haven't decided yet. For example:

A: Are you doing anything at the weekend?
B: I don't know. I'll probably just stay in and take it easy.

A: Are you doing anything at the weekend?
B: I haven't decided yet. I'll probably go to the cinema, but I might stay in and watch the football instead.

We use I might to show we are less sure. It means I'll possibly. We often say I suppose I might. We often show it is only a possibility by adding a phrase with it depends. For example:

A: What are you going to do after you've finished university?
B: I don't know. I suppose I might go travelling. It depends if I've got any money.

A: What are you going to do after you've finished university?
B: I might do a postgraduate course or I might just look for a job. It depends on my exam results.

Find examples of going to, 'll, probably, and might in the conversation between David, Victoria, Kylie and Jason on page 94. Underline any other phrases that go with the structures.

2 | Practice

Complete these short dialogues by adding I'm/we're going to, I'll/we'll or I/we might.

1. A: What are you doing tonight?
    B: I don't know. . . . . probably just stay in tonight and take it easy. I suppose . . . . get a video out. It depends what's on TV.

2. A: What are you going to do while you're in New York?
    B: Basically, ... just . . . . go shopping. I've been saving up for about the last six months and I've decided . . . . go mad and spend it all. Apart from that, I've got no plans. I suppose . . . . go up the Empire State Building or something, if I have time, but I'm not that bothered one way or the other, to be honest.

3. A: Have you got any plans for tomorrow?
    B: We haven't really decided yet. It depends on the weather. If it's sunny, ... probably go to the beach and spend the whole day sunbathing, but if the weather's bad, I don't know. I suppose . . . . go and have a look round the castle.

4. A: What are you going to do for your holiday? Are you going anywhere?
    B: I'm not sure yet. My brother has rented a villa in Spain and asked if I wanted to go with him, so I suppose . . . . go and stay with him or another possibility is . . . . go and visit a friend of mine who lives in Munich. It depends. Then again, I'm so bad at making decisions, ... probably just end up staying at home and doing nothing!

5. A: What are you going to do after your English course finishes?
    B: . . . . go back to the Czech Republic. I've still got to finish my last year at university.

6. A: What are you going to do for your birthday? Anything special?
    B: I haven't really thought about it. . . . . probably just go and have a meal with my girlfriend. I suppose . . . . invite a few friends, but . . . . not . . . . have a party or anything like that.

3 | Further practice

In pairs, find out what your partner is going to do ...

*   after class today.
*   tonight.
*   tomorrow.
*   at the weekend.
*   for the summer holidays.

*   for their birthday.
*   when the course has finished.
*   when they finish school/university.

For more information on using *going to, will,* and *might*, see G18.

4 | It depends

Notice how depends is used:

It depends on the weather.
It depends what the weather's like.

We use on if the next word is a noun or a pronoun. Complete these sentences with depends or depends on.

1. It . . . . you.
2. It . . . . the price.
3. It . . . . how much you want for it.
4. It . . . . when it finishes.
5. It . . . . your parents.
6. It . . . . if I've got the time or not.
7. It . . . . a lot of things.
8. It . . . . whether it's free or not.

Now complete the sentences below with the words or phrases in the box.

how	what
how long	what time
how much	whether

9. Maybe. It depends . . . . I feel.
10. Maybe. It depends . . . . time we've got.
11. Maybe. It depends . . . . the film finishes.
12. Maybe. It depends . . . . tired I am.
13. Maybe. It depends . . . . it'll take.
14. Maybe. It depends . . . . I get home.
15. Maybe. It depends . . . . I get back in time or not.
16. Maybe. It depends . . . . kind of thing you like.
17. Maybe. It depends . . . . I've got paid or not.

5 | Pronunciation: linking

When a word ends in a consonant and the next word starts with a vowel, we join them together when speaking. For example:

It depends if I get up early.
It depends when I start in the morning.

Mark where you think the words join together in the sentences 9–17 in Exercise 4 above.

Now listen and repeat the sentences.

6 | Further practice

Ask your partner these questions. They should try to answer using the answers from Exercise 4, sentences 1–8. Sometimes more than one answer is possible.

1. Do you want to go out later?
2. Do you want to go for a drink after the film?
3. Do you want to go to see a play at the theatre?
4. Do you want to go for a run later?
5. Can you lend me some money?
6. Can you help me with my essay later?
7. Will you be able to visit us while you're here?

7 | Speaking

Which of the places in the pictures would you like to visit if you were on holiday?

Have you done your homework? • What did you do at university? • I dropped out. • I'm doing Frer at Nottingham. • I'm having a gap year. • I've got my finals in two months. • I'm in my second year. • A you going to do a Master's? • What was your degree in again? • I've got my results. • My mind we blank. • How old were you when you left school? • I got three As and a B. • I didn't get in. • Did y pass? • I hated school. • What do you call A-levels in your country? • Y swot! • I used to get bullied a lot. • He gave me a detention!

14 Studying

Reading

1 Speaking

Discuss these questions with a partner.

1. What makes a good/bad teacher? Does your partner agree?

2. Has teaching changed over the last twenty years in your country? How?

3. What teachers do you remember most from school? What were they like? These structures might help:

   I'll never forget my old History/English teacher. He/she always used to … .

2 While you read

🎧 **Read this article about schools in Britain. Mark the text with an S where you think the situation is the same in your country or the school you went to. Put a D where you think it is different. Put a question mark (?) where you are not sure or don't understand something.**

The bad old days

The other day, a teacher got sacked for tearing a boy's shirt. The boy was fighting with another child when the teacher grabbed him and pulled him away to try and stop the fight. In doing this, he tore the boy's shirt. The boy's parents complained to the headmaster and the teacher was sacked for physically abusing the boy. Many people in Britain support the teacher, saying he was only trying to do what was right and that it was the boy who was at fault. Many of these people are also probably remembering what their own teachers were like and how much stricter they were!

When I think of the teachers I had less than twenty years ago, I immediately remember ones who used to give out terrible punishments. My English teacher was known as Johnny Headbanger because if he caught two students talking in class, he used to grab their heads and bang them together. Another one called Mr Golding, who taught us Maths, used to make you hold your arms out like a cross and then he put a Maths textbook in each hand. Those books used to weigh about two kilos each and after about twenty seconds you would be sweating and your muscles would be killing you, but he would just smile and carry on teaching the class. Many teachers were quite happy to give you a smack on the back of the head if you were cheeky. That kind of thing used to be quite normal.

Nowadays, however, it sometimes seems like a teacher can't even touch a pupil without the headmaster threatening them with the sack. Many people now feel the law's gone too far. They say pupils have too much power and have learned how to push teachers to the limit. They blame the outlawing of all physical punishment for an increase in bad behaviour in children. But do we really want to go back to the bad old days when teachers were basically free to beat you up?

Unsurprisingly, those teachers didn't actually teach me very much – apart from how to hate them. However, the best teacher I ever had – my Chemistry teacher, Mr Green – never hit anyone. He controlled the class, because he obviously really liked what he was doing and could bring the subject alive. He showed us experiments and made them relevant by explaining how they related to real life. He was also very encouraging. He wouldn't just say 'Good' or 'Excellent', but he'd actually listen to our ideas and when we were wrong he would talk us through things. He's the main reason I became a pharmacist.

So, OK, maybe things have gone too far if a teacher can get sacked for stopping a fight, but personally, I don't miss those days. I think the best way to avoid bad behaviour in class is simply by being a good teacher. Most students actually want to learn. And what about when students break the rules? Well, even in those days I remember the worst punishment didn't involve any violence. I was caught smoking in the toilets and as a punishment the headmaster wrote a letter to my parents. I tell you, my life was hell for weeks afterwards!

With a partner, compare what you have marked with an S, a D, or a question mark (?). Some of these sentences or sentences starters may help:

That's exactly the same in my country.
Something similar happened in ... .
This used to be the case here, but it isn't any more.
That would never have happened here.
I don't quite understand this bit about ... . Do you?

3 | Speaking

Discuss these questions with a partner.

1. Do any of the teachers described in the text in Exercise 2 on page 98 remind you of any teachers you've ever had?

2. What happened in your school if you were caught ...
   - cheating in a test?
   - smoking?
   - talking in class?
   - skipping classes?

4 | Verb patterns

Make sentences by matching the beginnings 1–7 to the groups of endings a–g.

1. He complained
2. He was sacked
3. She was caught
4. They blamed
5. He threatened
6. She carried on
7. They made

a. teachers for poor exam results / the rise in crime on poor parenting / me for what happened.

b. us stand outside in the rain for ages / us go running even when it was snowing / us call them 'Sir' or 'Madam'.

c. drinking in school / kissing a boy in a cupboard / speeding.

d. studying after she left school / working while she was pregnant / driving even after her accident.

e. me with a knife / to take me to court / her with the sack.

f. for always being late / for hitting his students / for being incompetent.

g. to the manager about it / several times about it / to the council about the state of the roads.

Look up the verbs in 1–7 above in your dictionary. Can you find other ways of finishing the sentences?

Look back and underline these seven verbs and the words which follow them in the text in Exercise 2 on page 98. Underline whole expressions.

> **Real English:** get sacked / get the sack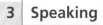
>
> If you get sacked / get the sack, you are told by your boss that you are no longer wanted at work. It's usually because you haven't been doing your job very well. In American English, you can say get fired.
> *I got the sack because I was always late for meetings.*
> *I got sacked because my boss said I hadn't met my sales targets!*

5 | Speaking

Discuss these questions with a partner.

1. Have you ever been blamed for something you didn't do? When? What happened?

2. What did your teachers use to make you do?

3. Do you know anyone who's been sacked? What for?

4. Have you ever been caught doing something wrong? What happened?

5. Has anyone ever threatened you? What happened?

6 | Teachers and students

Decide if the sentences 1–12 refer to teachers or students. Then discuss with a partner if each sentence is positive or negative.

1. He never pays attention in class.
2. He always pays attention to what we say.
3. She never does any homework.
4. He was caught hitting a pupil.
5. He's always getting detentions.
6. He never marks the homework.
7. She's top of the class.
8. She's very encouraging.
9. He was caught copying in an exam.
10. He's always making mistakes on the board.
11. She's the teacher's pet.
12. She's very strict.

Which three sentences above are most connected to your life? In what way? Tell your partner something about your experiences.

Listening

1 | Test, exam, degree, etc.

Complete the sentences below with the words in the box.

certificate	examinations
degree	qualifications
diploma	

1. We have regular tests, but we sit our final .... at the end of the three-year course.

2. Sometimes I wish I had a .... from a good university, but I'm afraid I've only got a .... in Hotel Management from my local college of education. Still, I am the manager of the Hilton and I earn a lot more than most graduates! I think personality is more important than ....

3. The web design course I want to do is only two weeks long, but I do get a .... at the end of it.

What qualifications have you got?

2 | Speaking

Do you like taking exams or do you prefer a system of continuous assessment? Why?

Are you good at exams and tests? Put the following in the order you think they would happen.

a. I failed.

b. I managed to pass.

c. I had a Maths exam.

d. I messed up a question.

e. I got my results.

f. I had to re-take it.

g. I did a lot of revision for the exam.

h. I got the results of my re-take.

Compare your order with a partner's.

3 | Listening

You are going to hear three conversations between students and their English teachers. They are all talking about exams. Here are summaries of the three conversations you will hear. Before you listen, discuss with a partner how you think these sentences could be completed.

1. Sergei's teacher thinks he will .... the exam. Sergei's needs to pass the exam to ....

2. Blanca messed up the exam because ....
....

3. Antonio failed his exam even though he .... Antonio will now have to ....

Now listen and try to complete the summaries above.

4 | Matching

Make sentences by matching the beginnings 1–6 to the endings a–f.

1. I messed up one
2. All of the questions I was
3. It was really
4. My mind went
5. I should've revised
6. I just about

a. scraped through it.
b. of the questions.
c. harder.
d. easy.
e. expecting came up.
f. completely blank.

Now decide if the sentences above mean that the person did well in the exam or not so well.

5 | Pronunciation: intonation

In Conversation 3 in Exercise 3, when Antonio tells Frances he has failed, she sympathises by saying: 'I'm sorry'. Listen to these short dialogues. Then practise reading them with a partner. Try to sound sympathetic.

1. A: I've just heard that I've failed my First Certificate.
   B: Oh, no! I'm really sorry to hear that.

2. A: I was expecting an A, but I only got a C.
   B: Oh, no! I'm sorry. That's a shame.

3. A: I'm sorry I'm so late, but I had an accident in the car on the way here.
   B: Oh, no! I'm sorry to hear that. Are you all right?

4. A: My father's not very well. In fact, he's just been taken into hospital.
   B: Oh, no! I'm really sorry to hear that.

5. A: We've just had a terrible weekend. When we got home on Saturday, we found the house had been broken into.
   B: Oh, I'm really sorry to hear that.

6. A: We had a fire in the kitchen on Sunday. It was awful!
   B: Oh, no! I'm so sorry.

Real English: I'm sorry

We use I'm sorry a lot in English for things which are very unimportant – if we accidentally touch someone, for example. We use I'm *really* sorry or I'm *so* sorry for more important things like failing an exam. It's important to stress really or so.

We use I *am* sorry for really important things – if a relative or friend dies, for example.

What would you say in your language in these situations?

6 | I messed up badly!

Here are three stories about people failing exams. Complete them with the words in the boxes.

Story I

failed	last	notes	revision

A friend of mine always left his (a) . . . . for his exams till the (b) . . . . minute. Most of the time it worked fine, but one time, the night before a Chemistry exam, he stayed up all night reading through his (c) . . . . He took several caffeine tablets to keep himself awake. Unfortunately, in the middle of the exam, the effects of the tablets wore off and he just fell asleep. Needless to say, he (d) . . . . !

Story 2

enough	failed	pass	test

I (a) . . . . my driving (b) . . . . five times. The last time I took it, I was sure I would (c) . . . . , but halfway through, I saw a friend of mine that I hadn't seen for ages and she started waving at me. I didn't look at her for long, but it was long (d) . . . . for me not to see the car in front of me pull out. I crashed straight into the back of it. Needless to say, I failed!

Story 3

cheating	confident	copied	well

A friend of mine once tried to get through a test by copying the answers of the girl next to her. She was sure the teacher couldn't see her (a) . . . . and, as the girl she was sitting next to was one of the best students in the school, she was fairly (b) . . . . she would pass. Unfortunately, without thinking, she (c) . . . . the name of the girl as (d) . . . . as the answers! Needless to say, she failed!

🎧 **Listen and check your answers.**

Now discuss these questions with a partner.

1. Which story did you find the funniest?
2. Do you believe they're all true? Why/why not?
3. Have you ever failed an exam? Why?
4. Have you ever heard any other stories like the ones above?

7 | Speaking

Work with a partner. Decide where, when and why all these tests and exams are taken.

a blood test	a written exam
a breath test	an entrance exam
a driving test	an eye test
a drug test	an intelligence test
a listening exam	an oral exam
a medical test	end-of-year exams
a mock exam	final exams
a pregnancy test	spelling tests
a screen test	weekly tests

Choose one of the above and tell your partner when you took it, why you took it, and how you got on. For example:

I once had to take an intelligence test for a job I applied for. I actually quite enjoyed it. It was like doing puzzles. Unfortunately, I didn't get the job.

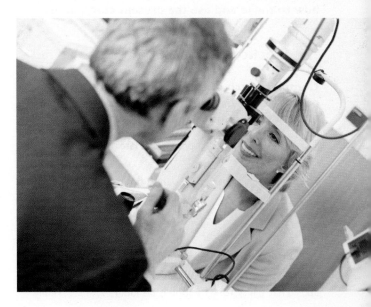

Using grammar

1 | The future: seven important verbs

Complete the dictionary definitions below with the verbs in the box.

apply	look forward to
dread	plan
expect	think
hope	

1. If you .... for something, you ask for something, officially, by writing or by sending in a form.

2. If you .... something, you feel bad or worried about something that will happen in the future.

3. If you .... to do something, you decide it in detail and organise it in advance.

4. If you .... to do something, you want to do it – even though you might not actually do it.

5. If you .... of doing something, you have an idea you might do it in the future at some time.

6. If you .... something, you feel happy about doing it in the future.

7. If you .... something or .... to do something, you think there's a strong possibility it will happen – even though you might not want it to.

We often talk about our hopes and plans for the future by using the verbs above in the present continuous. Look back at page 30 to remind you how to make and use the present continuous.

2 | Practice

Complete each of these pairs of sentences with one of the verbs from Exercise 1 above. Use the present continuous.

1a. I .... a phone call later from a friend of mine.

1b. I .... not .... him home until tomorrow.

2a. I .... for all kinds of different jobs in PR.

2b. I .... for a Green Card so I can go and work in America.

3a. I can't wait to go on holiday this year. I .... really .... it.

3b. That party tonight should be fun. I .... really .... it.

4a. I .... to have enough money to be able to go to America for a few months.

4b. I .... that my dad will give me a bit of money to help me through university.

5a. I .... to spend the summer working abroad.

5b. I .... not .... to stay here in Hull much longer.

6a. I .... of maybe studying Dentistry or something like that.

6b. I .... of trying to get into Oxford or Cambridge, if I can.

7a. I'm meeting his parents for the first time next weekend! I .... it!

7b. I've got to go to the dentist's tomorrow. I .... it!

Use the seven verbs in the present continuous to tell your partner seven true things about yourself.

3 | Asking for an opinion

We often ask people for their ideas about the future using a question in this form: *Do you think + (I) + will + verb.* **For example:**

A: Do you think I'll pass?
B: I doubt it.

A: What do you think they'll do about it?
B: They'll probably sack him.

Make typical questions about the future by putting the words in the correct order.

1. you / do / she / think / come / 'll / ?
....

2. you / coat / do / think / 'll / need / I / a / ?
....

3. later / think / do / 'll / you / see / you / Ken / ?
....

4. be / do / back / think / 'll / by / you / we / eight / ?
....

5. pass / do / 'll / think / you / you / ?
....

6. graduate / Master's / you / 'll / you / do / think / do / you / a / after?
....

Listen and check your answers. Then listen again and practise saying the sentences. Pay particular attention to the way you pronounce 'll.

For more information about the future and these seven important verbs, see G19.

4 | Short natural answers

When we answer questions like 1–6 in Exercise 3 on page 102, we often use short responses to show how sure we are that something will happen.

95% sure it'll happen:	It's/she's/he's/I'm bound to. *or* Definitely
95% sure it *won't* happen:	Definitely not. *or* I doubt it.
70% sure it'll happen:	Probably.
70% sure it *won't* happen:	Probably not.
50% sure it will happen:	It/he/she/I might.

Complete the three possible answers to each question with the short answers in the boxes.

1.
> It might   I doubt it   It's bound to

   A: Do you think it'll rain later?

   B: (a) .... The forecast said it was going to stay fine.

   B: (b) .... It always rains when we decide to go for a picnic.

   B: (c) .... It looks a bit grey. I'm going to take an umbrella anyway – just in case.

2.
> definitely   hopefully   probably

   A: So who do you think'll win on Wednesday?

   B: Lazio, (a) .... I'll win ten pounds if they do!

   B: Leeds, (b) .... They're playing so well at the moment, I can't see them losing.

   B: Arsenal, (c) .... I think they're just a little bit better than Man U, but I think it'll be close.

3.
> Hopefully   I doubt it   Definitely

   A: Do you think she'll pass?

   B: (a) .... She's been top of the class in every test this term.

   B: (b) .... She hasn't done any revision and she only went to half the lectures.

   B: (c) .... If she doesn't, her parents are going to kill me, but she should be OK.

We use hopefully when we want something to happen and hopefully not when we don't want it to happen.

5 | Write a conversation

Write two possible answers for each question in Exercise 3. Use the short answers in Exercise 4. Try to add a follow-up comment to each answer. For example:

A: Do you think she'll come?

B: I doubt it. You know what she's like! / Definitely. She never misses things like that!

Real English: just in case

We do something just in case to be prepared for something that may happen in the future.
I'd take an umbrella if I were you – just in case.
Why not take a sandwich – just in case.

You can also add a more detailed reason.
I'd better take a pullover with me, just in case it gets cold later.
You should take a map, just in case you get lost.

---

6 | Pronunciation: 'll

Listen and notice how 'll is pronounced in these sentences. Then practise saying them.

1. I doubt it'll help.
2. I'll definitely bring it tomorrow.
3. Hopefully, I'll see him later.
4. They'll probably win.
5. I doubt she'll be there.
6. It'll rain later.
7. I'll give you a hand with it.
8. I'll definitely think about it.
9. She'll probably call you later.
10. Hopefully, I'll get into Oxford.

7 | Free practice

Go round the class and ask other students these questions about the future. Try to answer using short natural responses.

1. What do you think the weather'll be like tomorrow?
2. Do you think you'll ever speak English like a native speaker?
3. Do you think you'll ever get married?
4. Do you think you'll ever do a PhD?
5. Do you think you'll carry on studying English after this course?
6. Do you think they'll ever find life on other planets?
7. Do you think your country will win the next World Cup?
8. Do you think you'll live to be a hundred?

Do you play any sport? • They're playing at home this weekend. • He should have been sent off
I support Kilmarnock. • He's the number one seed. • I play squash with some friends from work
I haven't played since I was at school. • She won the gold medal. • He came last! • It's a par 5. • Ev
been to the dogs? • Game, set and match! • It was out! • It's a fantastic stadium. • We need a ne
shuttlecock. • Do you fancy a game? • I climb. • I go cross-country skiing. • We g
thrashed. • He's got a great left foot. • The quarter finals are tomorrow.

15 Sport

Using vocabulary

1 | Are you any good?

Complete these sentences with go or play.

1. I .... climbing quite a lot.
2. I .... a lot of tennis in the summer.
3. I .... a bit of golf now and again.
4. I .... swimming quite a lot.
5. I .... jogging almost every day.
6. I .... a lot of football.
7. I .... a lot of basketball.
8. I .... baseball sometimes.
9. I .... cycling quite a lot.
10. I .... skiing every winter.

Now match the sports mentioned in 1–10 above to the follow-up comments a–j.

a. I'm quite good at putting, but my driving's not very good.

b. I'm quite good at serving, but my backhand's not very good.

c. I'm quite good at catching, but my batting's useless!

d. I'm quite good at turns, but not if it's too steep or too icy.

e. I'm quite good at the front crawl, but my backstroke's not very good.

f. I'm quite good at passing and tackling and I can run a lot, but I always miss the goal when I shoot!

g. I'm OK at mountain biking, but I did fall off and hurt myself last week.

h. I can do quite long distances, but I get a bit out of breath after five or six miles.

i. I go to the local climbing wall every week, but I haven't tried a real mountain yet.

j. I'm OK at dribbling, but I can only do it with my right hand.

Do you do any of the sports in 1–10? If so, have conversations with your partner like this:

A: I play a lot of football.

B: Oh really? Are you any good?

A: I'm OK. I'm quite good at dribbling and passing, but I'm not very good at crossing and shooting.

2 | Where do you play?

Match the words 1–10 to the words a–d to make ten places where you play different sports.

1. football		a. court
2. golf		b. pitch
3. tennis		c. course
4. basketball		d. centre
5. hockey		
6. volleyball		
7. squash		
8. badminton		
9. rugby		
10. sports		

With a partner, have conversations using the following pattern:

A: Do you know if there's anywhere I can play (football) round here?
B: Yeah, there's a park just down the road which has lots of pitches. You could try there.

3 | Keeping fit

Complete the text below with the words and phrases in the box.

aggressive	keep fit
fruit and vegetables	red meat
going on about	stamina
gym	team sports
have a go at	yoga

I'm not really very keen on sport in general, but I really hate (1) . . . . I'm not a very competitive person, and I don't like the way some people get (2) . . . . when they're playing football or watching baseball or whatever – you know, screaming and swearing at each other. I also get fed up with people always (3) . . . . sport all the time. It's just so boring! I do like to (4) . . . . , though, so I watch what I eat – I avoid (5) . . . . and fatty foods and I drink lots of water and eat lots of (6) . . . . I also go to my local (7) . . . . quite a lot and do a lot of (8) . . . . , which is great, because it helps keep me supple. I also use things like the running machines and the step machines quite a lot, to try to build up my (9) . . . . The one real sport I would like to (10) . . . . is rowing. I think it must be really nice being out on the water and so close to nature. I might start doing that this year sometime.

Underline all the parts of the text above which describe you. Tell a partner what you've underlined and why.

Real English: have a go

If you have a go at a new activity, you try it to see if you are good at it or like it.
That computer game looks good. Can I have a go?

This is quite a difficult exercise, but have a go and see how much you can do.

A: I've never done anything like that.
B: You should have a go. You'd probably enjoy it.

4 | Describing an event

Match the descriptions 1–8 to the extra comments a–h.

1. The conditions were perfect.
2. They're local rivals.
3. It's a big match.
4. It's an away game.
5. The fight was fixed.
6. The big downhill race was postponed.
7. It was a dirty game.
8. It was a really exciting match.

a. He was two sets down and then he came back to win three sets to two.
b. The slope was too icy. They've rescheduled it for next weekend.
c. The two teams are neighbours. Their grounds are only two miles apart.
d. Whoever wins goes through to the final.
e. One of them had been paid to deliberately lose.
f. It wasn't too hot and the greens were in great condition.
g. Three people got sent off and about nine others got yellow cards.
h. They're not playing at home this week.

Which sports do you think are being described above? How do you know?

5 | Speaking

Discuss these questions with a partner.

1. Who are the big rivals in your country in football and other sports? Who do you support when they play? Why?
2. Have you ever heard of any fights/races/matches being fixed?
3. What's the most exciting match/race/fight you've ever seen?
4. What's the dirtiest game you've ever seen?

Using grammar

1 | First conditionals

Read the question below. Then make answers by matching the beginnings 1–6 to the endings a–f.

> **Question:**
> Do you think he'll/they'll win on Sunday?

Answers:

1. It depends. If it's a fast race, he'll probably win,

2. It depends. If Owen's fit, they'll probably win,

3. It depends. If they score first, they'll have a chance,

4. It depends. If he serves well, then he could beat him,

5. It depends. If he doesn't have any mechanical problems, he should win,

6. It depends. If they play the way they normally do, they should win,

a. but if Rangers score first, I don't think they will.

b. but if he gives away as many double faults as he did last time, then he probably won't.

c. but if he's still injured, I doubt if they'll even score.

d. but if it's slow, he could possibly lose in a sprint finish.

e. but if he breaks down, he definitely won't.

f. but if they have an off day, then you never know, they might lose.

Can you guess which sports are being discussed in the answers above?

We often use first conditionals to predict the results or consequences of things we know are going to happen, or which we think will probably happen. The sentences are in two parts:

- **The if part, which shows the real or possible action: If they score first,**
- **The second part which shows the predicted result: they'll have a chance.**

Look at the sentences above again and underline the verb which follows if. What tense is it?

2 | Further practice

When we talk about the news, we often use first conditionals to comment on what might happen. Complete these short conversations with first conditionals using the words in brackets.

1. A: Did you see that they think the peace talks might break down?
   B: No, that's terrible! . . . .
   . . . .
   (if / happen – go to war)

2. A: Did you see that they're going to put up taxes on air travel by 200%?
   B: Yeah, I know, I heard. It's terrible. . . . .
   . . . .
   (if / do – be able to afford / holiday)

3. A: Have you heard about this famine in Africa?
   B: Yeah, it's awful. The government should do something to help. . . . .
   . . . .
   (if / do – millions / die)

4. A: Did Tony tell you he's thinking of going on a diet?
   B: No, but I'm glad to hear it. Honestly, ...
   . . . .
   (if / carry on eating so much – end up / heart attack)

5. A: Did you see that that woman who helped her sick mother to die went on trial yesterday?
   B: Yeah. Did you know she could be convicted of murder? . . . .
   . . . .
   (if / be found guilty – fifteen years)

6. A: Did I tell you that our company might be taken over?
   B: No. . . . .
   . . . .
   (how / affect you – if / happen?)

7. A: Did I tell you that I've got an interview for a promotion?
   B: No. That's great. . . . .
   . . . .
   (you / get / money – if / get it?)

Listen and check your answers. Practise the conversations with a partner. Try to continue them for as long as you can.

> **Real English:** going to
>
> In spoken English, we often use going to instead of will in first conditional sentences like those above.
> *If they don't do something soon, millions of people are going to die.*
> *What are you going to do if you don't get the job?*

Now practise the short conversations in Exercise 2 above using going to.

3 | Free practice

Write some questions about events which are going to happen in the future using this pattern:

Do you think (Brazil) will win (the next World Cup)?
Do you think (the Social Democrats) will win the next election?

Write your own answers using the first conditional patterns in Exercise 1 on page 106. Ask some other students their predictions for the same events. Do you agree with their answers? If not, why not?

4 | Role play

Imagine you and your partner are friends gossiping over a coffee. Discuss these pieces of news about some of your other friends. Student A thinks they are making the right decisions. Student B thinks they're not. Use first conditionals to explain why! See who can win each argument!

1. Have you heard that Andrew's thinking of going to work in China for a year?
2. And did you know that Maria's thinking of leaving her husband because he's been having an affair and she's going to take the baby with her?
3. Did Tina tell you she's thinking of becoming a teacher?
4. I heard that Sharon's thinking of dropping out of university.
5. Someone told me that Rob's thinking of forming a rock band.

You might want to start with something like this:

A: He's mad! If he goes there, he'll never be able to pick up the language.
B: He might! Lots of people do, you know!

5 | *If* clauses

Complete the common if clauses below with the verbs in the box.

can	feel	find	have	hear	see	want (x2)

1. I'll give you a hand if you . . . .
2. I'll come if I . . . .
3. We don't have to do it if you don't . . . . to.
4. I'll go if I really . . . . to, but I'd rather not.
5. If I . . . . the result, I'll give you a ring.
6. I'll let you have it if I can . . . . it.
7. I'll tell her if I . . . . her.
8. I might do it later if I . . . . like it.

Practise saying each expression. Which expression above do you think you'll use most often? Why?

For more information on first conditionals, see G20.

Listening

1 Speaking

Discuss these questions with a partner.

1. Have you ever been to watch a live match/race/fight? When? What was it like?
2. Do you ever watch things like that on TV? How often? What kinds of things?

2 People talking about sport

You are going to hear five conversations about sports events people have watched. As you listen, decide what kind of event they are talking about and how they felt about it.

Conversation 1: ....
....

Conversation 2: ....
....

Conversation 3: ....
....

Conversation 4: ....
....

Conversation 5: ....
....

Can you remember in which conversation they talked about these ideas?

a. gambling
b. a controversial decision
c. somebody getting thrashed
d. somebody having a good chance of winning, but blowing it
e. somebody embarrassing themselves

Compare your answers with a partner. Listen again and see if you were right.

> **Real English:** get thrashed, blow it
>
> If you get thrashed in a game, you are easily beaten – usually it's a heavy defeat! If you have a good chance of doing something, but you blow it, you miss the opportunity, you waste your chance.
> *We got thrashed! We lost 6–1.*
> *They thrashed us 8–2! It was awful!*
>
> *The interview went really badly. I think I've blown my chances of getting the job.*
> *We had some really good chances of winning the game, but we blew them all!*

3 I know!

Look at these ways of agreeing with this statement:

> Sportsmen get paid too much these days.

I know! They earn ridiculous amounts of money.

I know! I mean, how much does Tiger Woods earn a year?

I know! I mean, there are people starving in the world and we pay them millions of pounds for kicking a football. It's sick!

> **Real English:** it's sick
>
> If you think something is sick, you think something is morally disgusting.
>
> *He told this really sick joke about disabled people.*
>
> *He pays his workers eight euros an hour while he makes millions and millions of dollars a year. It's sick!*
>
> *He's living in a palace and most of his people are starving. It's sick!*
>
> *I walked out of the film halfway through. I just thought it was sick.*

Now look at the tapescript on page 156. Find five examples of this way of agreeing. Write replies agreeing with these statements following the same pattern.

1. There's too much sport on TV these days.
....
2. That was such a great game!
....
3. Politicians don't care about us.
....
4. Philosophy is a such a pointless subject.
....
5. I can't believe how badly doctors get paid!
....

Now use the statements above to have short conversations with a partner in which you agree with each other.

4 I don't know

In Exercise 2, Conversation 2, Lennox said: 'I just don't know how they can say Winton won on points.'

Do you think Lennox really doesn't know how Winton won? Can you remember how Lennox and Mike explained Winton's win?

We often use I don't know + question word/if + clause when we want to show we are surprised about something. For example:

I don't know what he's studying Norwegian for.
I don't know why she stays with him.

Make sentences that express opinions showing surprise by matching the beginnings 1–6 to the endings a–f.

1. I don't know why
2. I don't know how
3. I don't know who
4. I don't know if
5. I don't know what
6. I don't know where

a. I'll ever finish this book!
b. all my socks disappear to! They're all odd pairs.
c. men see in Jennifer Lopez!
d. anyone would want to read 'Hello' magazine.
e. would want to go to Iceland for their holidays.
f. anyone could eat dog.

Match the responses i –vi to the opinions above.

i. I don't know. I think she's quite sexy.
ii. I know. It's so long and boring!
iii. I don't know. It's supposed to be really beautiful.
iv. I don't know. Why is it any different to eating pork or beef?
v. I know. I think it's the washing machine. It must eat them.
vi. I don't know. I quite like to see how the rich and famous live.

🎧 **Now listen and check your answers.**

5 | Pronunciation: intonation

🎧 **Did you notice the intonation of I know and I don't know in the responses? Which ones had rising intonation? Which ones sounded flat? Listen again and practise the conversations with a partner.**

6 | Speaking

Write four sentences that are true for you like those in Exercise 4. Tell some other students what you are surprised about. They should agree or disagree as in i–vi in Exercise 4.

7 | And finally

Are all sports equal? With a partner, decide which of the following sports is best described as …

*   **a real sport?**
*   **not really a sport at all?**
*   **big business?**

ballroom dancing	golf
bowling	horse racing
boxing	ice dancing
bungee jumping	ice hockey
curling	sumo wrestling
darts	synchronised swimming
dog racing	tennis
football	windsurfing

He built it up from nothing. • It's an old family business. • They make widgets. • We're having a good y
• Profits are down. • They went bankrupt. • The housing market is booming. • They've been taken ov
• Unemployment is down one per cent. • Interest rates are very low at the moment. • How did y
raise the money? • He's got all the right contacts. • He could sell fridges to Eskimos! • It's a
multinational. • Do you deal with customers? • Prices have rocketed. • W
just have to start cutting costs. • Business is booming. • They went to the w

16 | Business

Reading

1 | Speaking

Discuss these questions with a partner.

1. Do you know anybody who runs their own business? What kind of business is it?

2. Would you like to run your own business? Why/why not?

People who run their own businesses face lots of problems. Below are eight of them. Tell a partner how good you would be at each of them, and why. Use these sentence starters:

I'd be good at …
I wouldn't be very good at …
I'd be terrible at …

1. dealing with employees
2. dealing with officials and bureaucracy
3. working very long hours
4. interviewing people for jobs
5. sacking people
6. raising the money to start the business
7. selling things
8. making contacts

2 | While you read

🎧 **You are going to read an article about a Chinese-Indonesian businessman, Darno Setiadi. While you read, tick any of the problems in Exercise 1 which he mentions. Does he mention any others not listed?**

A self-made man

Darno Setiadi is one of the top thousand richest men in Indonesia – not bad for someone who was born into a huge family in a tiny village in the middle of nowhere. Mr Setiadi runs his own business, importing machinery from Europe and selling it all over the country. He employs over three hundred people and lives in a mansion in a nice suburb of Jakarta, the capital city. However, as he will tell you, he had to travel down a long, hard road to get to where he is today. Building up a business takes a lot of hard work and effort, especially in a developing country.

'I'm a self-made man and I built this business up from nothing through my own hard work and brains,' said Darno. 'I come from a very poor family in a rural part of Indonesia and I've got thirteen brothers and sisters. My dad died when I was only fourteen and I had to go out to work to try to support the rest of my family. To begin with, I sold ice creams in the street; then I got a job selling cloth door-to-door in my town; after that, I started travelling all over the island selling things to people and slowly I started getting ideas about what kind of products the different markets wanted, and I started making contacts. When I was twenty-one, I left my wife and two children at home and moved to Jakarta to set up my own business, selling all kinds of machines, but particularly propellers for boats. There are over thirteen thousand islands in Indonesia, so there's a huge market for that kind of thing.

'It was really hard work. I didn't have any money of my own, so I lied and told the bank I had a contract, so that they'd lend me money. I told the companies I wanted to order from I had money, so that they'd sell to me. I even had to tell the companies I wanted to sell to that I had suppliers, so that they'd order from me. I was telling so many lies that it was really difficult trying to remember who I had told what! Luckily for me, I had some friends in high places and I had a word with them and they helped me get import licences, which meant I ended up cornering the market in propellers. Business was booming and I could finally afford to bring my wife and family over to join me. That wasn't the end of the story, though.

'First of all, I've had to do all the things every businessman has to do: pay taxes and wage bills, meet deadlines, deal with workers and officials. On top of all that, though, I've also had to deal with all sorts of other problems too: my shops have been attacked and burned in anti-Chinese riots and the economy hasn't been very good, either. The last ten years haven't been the most stable! We've had really high inflation and we've seen the value of our currency drop from three thousand rupiah to the dollar to eighteen thousand to the dollar! How are you supposed to run a business with things like that going on? It's madness!

'Anyway, here I am today – a wealthy man! The only real problem I've got now is who's going to take over the business when I retire. I'd like my son to run it, but he's not really tough enough to do it! I think perhaps his childhood was too easy, and that's made him a bit too soft to do work like this!'

3 | Useful collocations

Here are five verbs 1–5 from the article in Exercise 2 on page 110. Match them to the nouns they collocate with a–e.

1. runs
2. employ
3. build up
4. support
5. make

a. a business from nothing
b. contacts
c. lots of people
d. his own business
e. the rest of the family

Now match the verbs 6–10 to the nouns they collocate with f–j.

6. sell
7. corner
8. tell
9. deal with
10. take over

f. lies
g. the business
h. the market
i. problems
j. door-to-door

Can you remember what Darno said about the ten collocations above? Compare what you remember with a partner.

4 | Speaking

Discuss these questions with a partner.

1. Do you have any of the social and economic problems Darno Setiadi mentions in your country?
2. Does Darno Setiadi remind you of any other famous business people in your country? In what way?
3. Darno admits that he told lots of lies when he started his business. How do you feel about that?
4. How do you think Darno's son feels about taking over the family business?
5. Would you like to do the same job your parents do? Why/why not?

5 | Business, company

Complete these sentences with business or company.

1. I travel a lot in my job, but it's great because I get a . . . . car.
2. We do a lot of . . . . in South Korea and Taiwan.
3. I can't wear jeans at work. It's against . . . . policy.
4. We're losing a lot of . . . . because our currency is so strong at the moment.
5. I'm expecting a phone call any minute from my . . . . partner back home.
6. I work in the centre of Basle for a big insurance . . . .

The next two sentences include idiomatic uses of company and business.

7. What do you think about this . . . . in the news with the President and that woman, then?
8. I'm just going to the shops. Do you want to come along and keep me . . . . ?

Use your dictionary to see if you can find two more idiomatic uses for each word.

Using vocabulary

1 | Talking about money

Complete these common expressions with money with the words in the box.

burn got married short value waste

1. It's good . . . . for money.
2. It's a . . . . of money.
3. Have you . . . . any money on you?
4. I'm a bit . . . . of money at the moment.
5. She must have money to . . . . !
6. She must've . . . . him for his money.

When would you use the sentences above? Do you have any similar expressions in your language?

2 | Verb + *money*

Match the verbs 1–4 to the phrases a–d.

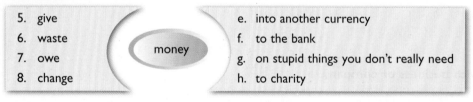

1. borrow
2. invest
3. lend
4. spend

a. to a friend
b. on new clothes and shoes
c. in research and development
d. from the bank

Now match the verbs 5–8 to the phrases e–h.

5. give
6. waste
7. owe
8. change

e. into another currency
f. to the bank
g. on stupid things you don't really need
h. to charity

Did you notice the different prepositions connected with the verbs? Go back and underline the prepositions connected to particular verbs. Remember to learn the complete expression: verb + money + preposition.

3 | Further practice

Complete these sentences with verbs from Exercise 2. You may need to change the verb form.

1. I took out a five-thousand-pound loan a few years ago, and I still . . . . twelve hundred to the bank.
2. I was left £10,000 when my grandfather died. I decided to . . . . it in the Stock Market. It's now worth over £25,000.
3. I must remember to . . . . a few hundred euros into dollars before we set off.
4. He's got more money than sense. He . . . . most of it on expensive champagne and eating out!
5. We . . . . a lot of money to charity, because we get tax breaks if we do!
6. I cycle to work, which means I don't have to . . . . any money on petrol!

Complete these sentences with the correct form of borrow or lend.

7. Can you . . . . me £5 till tomorrow?

8. You can . . . . one of these pens, if you want.

9. Have you ever . . . . a lot of money from anyone?

10. Have you ever . . . . something to a friend and never got it back?

Have you ever heard the old saying: Neither a borrower nor a lender be? Does it exist in your language? Do you agree with it? Why/why not?

4 Speaking

Discuss these questions with a partner.

1. Do you ever give money to charity/beggars/homeless people? Why/why not?

2. Do you owe anyone any money at the moment? Who? How much?

3. What do you spend most of your money on, if you don't mind me asking?

4. Have you ever had to borrow money from the bank? Why? Have you paid it all back yet?

5. When was the last time you changed money from one currency into another?

5 Collocations with *market*

In the article on page 110, Darno Setiadi said he'd been able to corner the market in propellers in Indonesia. Can you remember how he did it?

Underline the words which collocate with market in the text below. Be careful – sometimes the word market is replaced by the pronoun it.

> Twenty years ago, there was a fairly closed market in my country, but then the government decided to open it up and make it more competitive. Very quickly, big multinational companies broke into it and now it's terrible because these big companies dominate the market. A lot of small, family-run businesses have been totally squeezed out of it. On top of that, companies like McDonald's and Pizza Hut have cornered the fast food market, so we're eating more junk food and we're all getting fatter and fatter. Then there's the problem of the black market: the mafia is flooding it with fake goods and, of course, people buy them because they're cheap! Bring back the good old days, that's what I say.

How many collocations did you find? Do you know what they all mean? Compare with a partner. Does this sound like your country? In what way?

6 Talking about markets

Describe the markets below in your country using the words and phrases in the box.

bigger than it used to be	huge
booming	in decline
dead	saturated
tiny	

1. the mobile phone market
2. the English language market
3. the computer games market
4. the do-it-yourself market
5. the market in used cars
6. the market for organic food
7. the housing market

Can you think of any other markets in your country that can be described by the words and phrases in the box above?

7 Business verbs

With a partner, answer these questions. Notice the common collocations with verbs. If you need to, check any meanings in a dictionary or ask your teacher.

1. Why would a company withdraw a product from the market? Can you think of any product which was withdrawn?

2. Why would a company re-think its whole strategy? Do you remember the British Airways tailfin disaster? Why was their strategy wrong?

3. Why would a company take over another company? Can you think of a good example from your country?

4. Why would a company raise prices? Do you know any product whose prices were raised?

5. Why would a company cut prices? Have air fares been cut in your country recently?

6. What kind of things could destroy a company? Do you know any companies which have been destroyed? By what?

7. What kind of things could destroy your career? Do you know of any politicians whose careers have been destroyed? By what?

8. Why would someone take a break from their career? Do you know anyone who has?

9. Why could someone get fired from their job? Do you know anyone who was fired for the right reasons?

Compare your ideas with another pair. Did you have the same answers? Who thought of the most answers in each case?

Using grammar

1 | Listening

How do you feel about politicians? These structures might help:

If you ask me, most politicians …
Personally, I think most politicians …

🎧 **You are going to hear two people, Bob and Miriam, talking about the next election. As you listen, try to decide who they are going to vote for and why.**

2 | Second conditionals

Look at this part of the conversation and then discuss the questions below with a partner.

Bob:	We should be putting up taxes on big business and rich people, not cutting them.
Miriam:	Maybe.
Bob:	Definitely. If we did that, we could invest the money in schools and hospitals and things like that.
Miriam:	Maybe, but the government would probably just waste it. They usually do.

1. What's Bob's opinion about tax?
2. What's the government actually doing?
3. Why do Bob and Miriam use the past tense and would to explain their ideas?

Now read this explanation. Was it the same as your answer to question 3?

We use second conditionals to talk about things that we do not expect to happen. That's why we often use second conditionals to talk about what we think people should do, but we do not think they will do. Second conditional sentences have two parts:
If + past simple/past continuous → would/could/ might + infinitive

If + past simple/past continuous (= if they did that) shows us the condition – or the thing we don't expect to happen. The main clause, would/could/might + infinitive, shows the probable/possible result.

Notice that in the conversation above Miriam doesn't repeat the condition part of the sentence (the if- clause). This is because she only wants to talk about the results. This is quite normal in both conversation and writing.

Can you find two other examples of second conditionals in the tapescript on page 156?

3 | Practice

Complete the short dialogues below using the sets of words in the box.

did + wouldn't + 'd
would + 'd + wouldn't
could + wanted to + did + 'd
wouldn't + did + would + 'd
could + did + would + would
did + might + 'd

1. A: The government . . . . invest more money in schools if they . . . . , but they don't.
    B: Maybe, but if they . . . . that, they . . . . have to spend less on health or some other thing.

2. A: We should put up the minimum wage to ten pounds an hour. That way, you . . . . have people living in poverty.
    B: Yeah, but if you . . . . that, everyone . . . . want to have an increase in their wages and you . . . . get really high inflation.

3. A: They should tax all foreign goods coming into the country. That way, we . . . . protect our jobs here.
    B: Yeah, but if you . . . . that, other countries . . . . do exactly the same and then where . . . . we be?

4. A: People should be forced to vote. If you . . . . that, you . . . . get more people interested in politics.
    B: I doubt it. They . . . . probably just vote without thinking about it.

5. A: We should set up our own business. If we . . . . that, we . . . . have to listen to our bosses shouting at us all day.
    B: Maybe. But I . . . . worry all the time about losing money.

6. A: We should just ban smoking. That way, everybody . . . . be healthier.
    B: You can't do that! It . . . . start a war! People just . . . . accept it.

Which of the opinions in 1–6 above do you agree with? Why/why not? Discuss your ideas with a partner.

4 | Refusing requests and invitations

We often use second conditionals when we're refusing a request or turning down invitations. Make negative responses by matching the beginnings 1–7 to the endings a–g.

1. Listen, I'm sorry. I've got a meeting with my boss. If it was anyone else, I would say no,
2. Listen, I'm completely broke. Honestly, if I had the money, I'd love to come,
3. I'm sorry. If we didn't have this deadline we've got to meet, I'd say yes,
4. Listen, I'm sorry. It's just not my kind of thing. Maybe if I was a bit younger, I'd enjoy it,
5. I'm really sorry. If my parents weren't staying, I'd say yes straightaway,
6. Listen, if we had a bigger place, I wouldn't mind,
7. Listen, if it was mine, I'd lend it to you,

a. but I don't have the beds.
b. but as we don't, you'll have to practise somewhere else.
c. but I just don't have the time. Sorry.
d. but I really can't afford it.
e. but as Freddie's not here, I can't ask him.
f. but these days I don't.
g. but I can't – not to him.

Try to learn the endings a–g. Work with a partner and test each other.

Now write questions for the responses 1–7 above. For example:

A: Can you come round later and help me move my things out?
B: Listen, I'm sorry. I've got a meeting with my boss. If it was anyone else, I would say no, but I can't – not to him.

Go round the class and ask different people your questions. See if they can reply correctly.

> ▶ For more information on second conditionals, see G21.

Real English: not my kind of thing

We often use not my kind of thing to explain why we don't want to do something or why we don't like it.

A: *Why don't you want to go tonight?*
B: *It's just not my kind of thing. You go, I'm just going to stay here.*

A: *Do you like Dolly Parton?*
B: *Not really, it's not my kind of thing. I prefer heavy metal music.*

---

5 | Free practice

Make sentences that are true for you using these sentence starters. You will not be able to use all of the sentence starters.

1. If I had the money, I . . . .
2. If I had the time, I . . . .
3. If I were a man, I . . . .
4. If I were a woman, I . . . .
5. If I wasn't living with my parents, I . . . .
6. If I wasn't studying, I . . . .
7. If I wasn't working, I . . . .
8. If I was a bit older, I . . . .
9. If I was a bit younger, I . . . .
10. The world would be a better place if . . . .

Compare in groups and explain your endings. Did anyone have the same?

Review: Units 13–16

1 | Tenses

Complete these sentences by putting the verbs in brackets into the correct tense.

1. They said it'd be nice and hot this Saturday, but knowing our luck, it .... (probably / rain) all day!

2. If I .... (be) twenty years younger, she's exactly the kind of woman I .... (be) interested in!

3. A: What are your plans for tonight?
   B: After work, I .... (do) a bit of shopping in town and then I .... (just / go) straight home and take it easy. What about you?

4. If I .... (not live) with my parents, I .... (have) so much more freedom, but I can't afford to move out.

5. A: Do you think you .... (pass)?
   B: It depends. If they .... (ask) me about Shakespeare, I might, but if they .... (ask) me about anything else, I think I .... (probably / fail).

6. I .... (dread) this weekend. I've got to go and stay with my husband's family!

7. A: Do you think it .... (snow) this Christmas?
   B: I doubt it. It never .... (do), ... (do) it?

2 | Grammar review

Choose the correct form.

1. I was thinking / I think of going shopping for souvenirs later on today.

2. They said it was going to rain / it rains later, but it doesn't look like it will / it doesn't look like it might.

3. I really look forward to / I'm really looking forward to seeing all my old friends again at the weekend.

4. I doubt it is / I doubt it'll be that warm once we get to Istanbul.

5. It's bound to be / It's bound it'll be hot in New Zealand, don't you think?

6. I think he was sacked because he was caught buy / buying / to buy drinks for his students!

7. He was really angry. He threatened sacking / sack / to sack me on the spot if I ever did it again!

8. I might / I'll pop in and see you later. It depends on / It depends if I've got the time or not.

Compare your answers with a partner and explain your choices.

3 | Prepositions

Complete these sentences with the missing prepositions.

1. I don't like the way the government always blames things .... immigrants.

2. I'm applying .... a job with a big chemical research company.

3. Three guys came up to me in the street and threatened me .... a knife, so I just gave them my wallet.

4. I managed to buy a ticket .... the black market.

5. I had a really interesting morning. I went on a guided tour .... the big temple on the hill.

6. It was awful. Someone's bag got stolen and the teacher blamed me .... it!

7. It's really annoying because he never pays any attention .... class.

8. Basically, I think she was sacked .... being incompetent.

9. I'm applying .... three universities in Italy.

10. If you're not happy, you should complain .... the boss .... it.

11. Hi. I'd like to change three hundred dollars .... Japanese yen, please.

12. Remind me to make sure I change some money .... the bank later.

4 | Look back and check

Look back at Exercise 1 Sightseeing words and Exercise 2 Recommending on page 92. Tick all the words and expressions you can remember. Ask your partner about anything you have forgotten.

Think of a town/city that you know well. Now talk to some other students and ask each other the questions from Exercise 2 Recommending. Answer in ways that are true for the place you thought of.

5 | Verb collocations

Match the verbs 1–10 to the groups of words and phrases they collocate with a–j.

1. play ☐
2. go ☐
3. have ☐
4. get ☐
5. deal with ☐
6. skip ☐
7. lose ☐
8. revise ☐
9. save ☐
10. give ☐

a. a go at yoga this year / a day off
b. problems / bureaucracy
c. a lot of business / touch
d. money / my life
e. jogging / on a cruise
f. money to charity / it a miss
g. a video out / ripped-off
h. for an exam / the words we learned in class today
i. quite a lot of tennis / a joke on someone
j. class / lunch

You have one minute to memorise the collocations a–j. Now cover the exercise above. Your partner will read out the verbs 1–10. How many collocations can you remember?

With a partner, try to think of one more common collocation for each of the verbs 1–10.

6 | Adjectives

Complete the sentences below with the adjectives in the box.

aggressive	damaged	dead	long	physical
pointless	rough	saturated	silly	sticky

1. The school my son used to go to was really ...., so I've moved him to a better place.
2. A: Do you want me to give you some money for the dinner?
   B: Don't be ....! I'm paying for everything.
3. It gets really hot and .... in the summer. You have to take three showers a day.
4. Our roof got .... in the storm. It's going to cost us a fortune to get it repaired.
5. Things are .... at work at the moment. I've got absolutely nothing to do.
6. I don't think there's anything wrong with a bit of .... punishment every now and then.
7. I'm just going to have an early night tonight. I've had a really .... week.
8. Because of all the cheap foreign imports, the market is completely .... now.
9. She's made up her mind already. It's .... trying to persuade her to change it.
10. He's a very .... driver – always cutting in front of other people and shouting and swearing.

7 | Questions and answers

Match the questions 1–10 to the answers a–j.

1. Can you recommend anywhere? ☐
2. What's it like? ☐
3. What're you doing today? Any plans? ☐
4. What was the weather like? ☐
5. Do you mind if we join you? ☐
6. Where do you play? ☐
7. How did the exam go? ☐
8. Do you think I'll need a coat? ☐
9. Are you any good? ☐
10. Are you looking forward to it? ☐

a. OK, actually. It was quite mild most of the time.
b. No, of course not. Go ahead. Have a seat.
c. I think I probably just about scraped through.
d. Well, you could try the street market in the old town.
e. You'd better take one, just in case.
f. My speaking's OK, but my writing's not very good.
g. It's the best place to eat in town.
h. Yeah, I can't wait.
i. At the sports centre up the road from my flat.
j. I haven't decided yet. It all depends.

8 | What can you remember?

With a partner, note down as much as you can remember about the texts you read in Units 14 and 16.

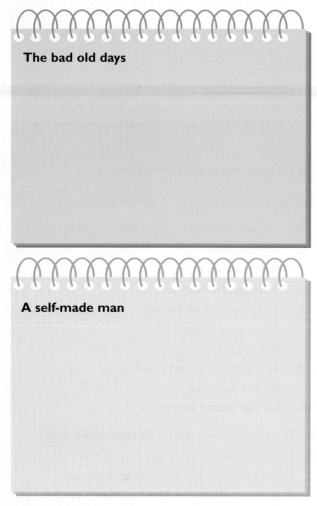

The bad old days

A self-made man

Now compare what you remember with another pair of students. Who remembered more? Which text did you enjoy more? Why?

9 | Common expressions

Complete the sentences below with the words in the box.

burn	how	rather	tell	what
difference	left	short	trap	worth

1. It's well . . . . a visit.
2. I'll . . . . him if I see him.
3. It's a bit of a tourist . . . .
4. I'm a bit . . . . of money at the moment.
5. He must have money to . . . .
6. I shouldn't have . . . . it till the last minute.
7. I will if I have to, but I'd . . . . not.
8. I doubt it'll make any . . . .
9. I don't know . . . . his problem is!
10. It depends . . . . I feel.

Discuss these questions with a partner.

11. Which places in your town/city do you think are well worth a visit?
12. And which do you think are tourist traps?
13. Do you know anybody who must have money to burn? Why do you think so?

10 | Vocabulary quiz

Discuss these questions in groups of three.

1. Can you think of three reasons why a teacher might get sacked?
2. When might you buy a souvenir?
3. How can you build up your stamina?
4. Can you think of three ways someone could cheat in an exam?
5. What happens if a race is postponed?
6. What's the difference between a temple, a mosque and a church?
7. How can a company corner the market?
8. What kind of things might a teacher's pet do?
9. What would you prefer the weather on holiday to be – boiling hot or unbearably hot?
10. If your team got thrashed, how would you feel?
11. What kinds of things could you invest money in?
12. How could you mess up an exam? How could you mess up your driving test?
13. What's happened if a fight or a race has been fixed?
14. Can you think of two sports where dribbling and passing is important?
15. If a place is a rip-off, what's wrong with it?
16. If someone has got more money than sense, what do they do with their money?
17. What's the difference between a diploma and a degree?
18. When might you ask someone if they want to come along and keep you company?
19. What kind of place might be fully booked? And what kind of event could be sold out?
20. What's the difference between 'I'll do it if I get the time' and 'I'd do it if I had the time'?

Learner advice: Recording and revising vocabulary

Some students like to draw spidergrams as a way of remembering vocabulary. The example below is composed of words and expressions from Unit 15, Sport. Check that you remember all the language there. If there's anything you have forgotten, ask your partner.

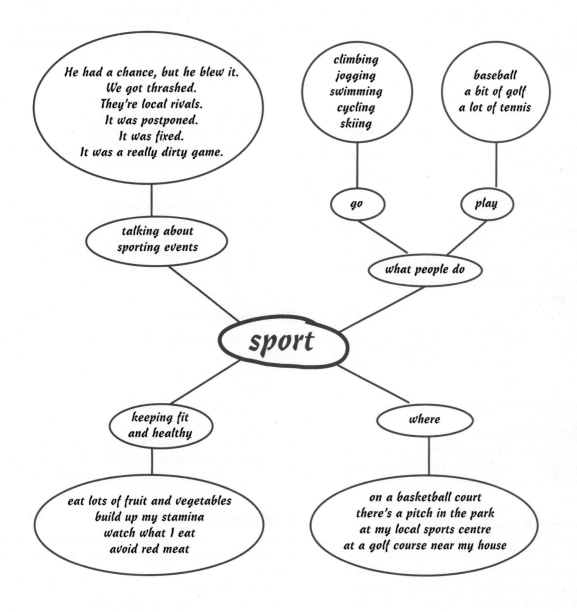

With a partner, try to make a similar spidergram for one of these topics of previous units.

* sightseeing
* studying
* food
* business

I'm one of four. • He's actually my half-brother. • How did you meet? • Mum and dad don't rea
approve of Jake. • We get on much better now. • She died in her teens. • They're very easy-going
We've known each other for ages. • It's all history now. • No, he's single, actually. • They're an item
I love hairy men. • I go for the strong silent type. • We're not speaking any more. • It's over. • Sh
got a lovely voice. • We went out for ages
We just lost touch.

17 Friends and family

Using vocabulary

1 Speaking

Find someone in your class who has got ...

1. more than three brothers and sisters
2. a brother-in-law
3. a mother-in-law
4. a niece
5. a nephew
6. more than five cousins
7. a stepbrother or sister
8. a half brother or sister

2 Adjectives

 **Complete the short conversations below with the adjectives in the box. Then listen and check your answers.**

big-headed	easy-going	fussy
generous	gorgeous	independent
liberal	mean	out-going
quiet	religious	sporty
strict		

1. A: What's your dad like?
   B: He's all right, but he can be quite .... He always wants to know where I am and he makes me come home before nine o'clock – even on a Saturday.

2. A: What's your brother like? Do you get on?
   B: Not really. He's so .... about everything! For example, he won't eat any vegetables except peas. If you suggest going somewhere, he never wants to. He's just so difficult to please. I'm the exact opposite. I'm really ....

3. A: What's your gran like? Do you get on?
   B: Yeah, I suppose so. She's OK. She's very .... She's eighty-five and she still lives on her own, but she's very .... and I'm not. She's always saying I should go to church or I'll end up in hell, but then at the same time, she can be really .... She bought me a piano for my birthday once.

4. A: What are your parents like?
   B: They're great. I'm quite lucky because they're quite .... They let me do more or less whatever I want.

5. A: What's her new boyfriend like?
   B: He's ...., really good-looking. He looks like a film star, but he's quite .... He doesn't really say anything.

6. A: What's her boyfriend like?
   B: He's awful! I don't know what she sees in him. He's really ...., he's always showing off and saying how good he is at everything, and he's so ....! Do you know what he bought her for her birthday? A bar of chocolate!

7. A: What's his girlfriend like?
   B: Really nice. She's very chatty and .... She's very easy to get on with. She's also really .... She plays football and hockey. She's really fit. Honestly, I don't know what she sees in that slob. She should be with me!

> **Real English: a slob**
>
> A slob is someone who is very lazy and/or untidy.
> *He's such a slob. He always looks as if he's just got out of bed.*
> *He's a total slob. He just spends all night watching videos and eating pizza.*
> *She's a real slob. She's always leaving her stuff lying around and she never tidies up after herself.*

> **Real English: fussy**
>
> If you are fussy, you are only happy if things are exactly the way you want them to be. It's a negative word.
> *He's a very fussy eater.*
> *She's very fussy about the way she looks.*

Ask a partner some of the questions from 1–7.

How many adjectives can you use to describe the people you know?

3 Speaking

Have any of your friends ever had girlfriends/boyfriends that made you think: I don't know what she/he sees in him/her? Why? What was wrong with them?

4 | How did you meet?

Read the question below. Then respond by matching the answers 1–4 to the follow-up statements a–d.

Question: How did you meet?

Answers:

1. I've known her since I was a child. ☐
2. I've known him since I was eight. ☐
3. I've known him since I was sixteen. ☐
4. I've known him since I was nineteen. ☐

a. We used to be in the same class at school for History.
b. My mum and her mum were friends, and they were pregnant at the same time.
c. We used to live in the same student hall of residence when we first went to university.
d. We used to live next door to each other when we were growing up.

Now match the answers 5–8 to the follow-up statements e–h.

5. I met her when I was twenty-four. ☐
6. We met them two years ago while we were on holiday. ☐
7. I've only known him for a few months. ☐
8. I met her when I was around thirty. ☐

e. He joined the company I work for quite recently.
f. We were staying in the same hotel.
g. We'd both just finished university and we used to work in the same office together.
h. A friend of mine introduced us at a party.

Discuss these questions with a partner.

9. Who's your oldest friend? How long have you known them? How did you meet? ☐
10. Who do you go out with most often? How long have you known them? How did you meet? ☐

In groups, tell other students about your friends. Who's got the oldest friend?

5 | A pathetic story

Put this sad story into the correct order.

a. I started seeing her behind Anna's back. It started getting serious. ☐
b. I tried to get back together with Anna, but she told me to get lost! ☐
c. I'd fancied Anna for ages. I finally asked her out on a date and we started going out together. ☐
d. I finally decided to leave Anna for this other woman, but it didn't work out. ☐
e. I met someone else at a party when Anna was away. ☐

Real English: I really fancy her/him

If you fancy someone, you find them physically attractive.

I think she fancies you. Have you seen the way she looks at you?

Discuss these questions with a partner.

1. What do you talk about doing if a relationship starts getting serious?
2. Why do you think the man in the story dumped Anna?
3. Why do you think the new relationship didn't work out?
4. Do you think Anna was right to tell him to get lost? Why/why not?

6 | Pronunciation: linking

What's the difference in meaning between these two sentences?

I went with a friend of mine from work.
I went with my friend from work.

Look at the words that are linked in the following replies to the question: Did you go on your own?

1. No, I went with a friend of mine.
2. No, I went with some friends of Andrew's.
3. No, I went with a friend from university.
4. No, I went with a couple of friends of mine.
5. No, I went with a couple of friends from work.
6. No, I went with my flatmate.
7. No, I went with my girlfriend.
8. No, I went with an old friend of mine.

🎧 **Now listen and practise saying the sentences above.**

7 | Speaking

Think of three places you have been to recently and tell your partner about them. You can start by saying:
I went to … the other day.

Your partner should ask you:
Oh really? Did you go on your own?

Give answers that are true for you. Pay attention to the way you link your words together.

Reading

1 | Speaking

Which of the people in the pictures below do you find attractive? Why?

2 | While you read

🎧 **Read what the six people say about the kind of people they're attracted to. Do you think you would make a good partner for any of them? Why/why not?**

Are you similar to any of these people? In what way?

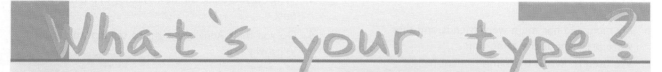

Alfonso (Mexico)

I'm really attracted to Scandinavian girls – tall, blonde, sporty, out-going, the complete opposite of me! I used to like older girls, but I've had a few bad experiences, so now I'm looking for something different. My ideal partner now would be five or six years younger than me. I also want somebody who is independent, who doesn't always need to be near me, and I think that the girls I've met from Sweden or Norway or Denmark tend to be very strong-willed. The only thing I'm worried about is that perhaps they would find me a bit quiet and shy. I'm not very confident about myself, so that could be a problem.

Rie (Japan)

I don't really have a type. The most important thing for me is that my partner is nice and sensitive and caring. I'd never go out with someone who was selfish or big-headed. It doesn't really matter to me whether somebody is good-looking or not, so long as they're not too ugly! I'd never go out with a man who didn't look after himself, though. It's important that he's healthy, that he watches what he eats and that he's fairly fit!

Chiara (Italy)

I want someone who likes clothes. I work in the fashion industry in Milan, so the way someone dresses is really important to me. I'd never go out with someone who didn't care about the way they looked. I used to like really good-looking men, but I've changed my mind about that, because they tend to be so big-headed! I also really love music, so I'd never go out with someone who didn't like music. If I'm honest, I'm also attracted to younger men, so I'm looking for someone who's maybe in their early twenties.

Lauren (Cameroon)

I'm a married man, so I'm the wrong person to ask a question like this to, really. When I was single, I used to think I wanted somebody who was easy to talk to, somebody who understood me and how I was feeling, somebody who was serious and religious, like I am – and then I met my wife, and she was everything I was looking for, and more! I can't believe how lucky I've been, but then I have to say that, or she'll kill me!

Thorsten (Germany)

To be honest, I'm too old now to be fussy, really. I want anybody who will have me! I used to worry about the kind of person that was right for me and I used to think I wanted somebody who was slim and sexy and intelligent and who had her own money and her own job and things like that, but now I've reached my forties and I'm still single, I've lowered my standards! It's taken me a long time, but I've realised that I'm not the best-looking man in the world, or the richest, and so I'd be happy just meeting someone who liked me! Sad, isn't it!

Seon-Hee (Korea)

I know this sounds strange, but all I really want is

someone with nice hands! I used to go out with this man who played the piano, and he had really beautiful hands – long, slim fingers, but really strong as well. Mm! I'd never go out with somebody who had short, fat, little fingers. I just couldn't.

3 | Language focus

Explain to a partner which of the six people you read about you could describe using the following adjectives and why.

a bit of an introvert	health-conscious
a bit strange	less fussy than he/she used to be
content	
desperate	quite fussy
fashion-conscious	unlucky in love
fit	

Now complete each sentence 1–3 in four different ways by adding an ending a–l.

1. I'd never go out with someone who was
2. I'd never go out with someone who
3. I'd never go out with someone with

a. couldn't cook.
b. a tattoo.
c. messy.
d. didn't like cats.
e. piercings.
f. a lot shorter than me.
g. had a different religion from me.
h. more intelligent than me.
i. strong political views.
j. kids from a previous relationship.
k. a lot younger than me.
l. thought work was the most important thing in life.

Why do some sentences use the past tense in the second part of the sentence, not a present tense?

Are any of the sentences above true for you? Make three more that are true using the same patterns.

4 | How old are they?

Read the question below. Then respond, matching the answers 1–8 to the follow-up comments a–h.

Question: How old are they?

Answers

1. I don't know, but he can't be older than eighteen.
2. I'm not sure, but he must be in his eighties.
3. Twenty-four, twenty-five?
4. I don't know, but he can't be more than ten or twelve months.
5. I'm not sure, but he must be in his mid-thirties.
6. I don't know, but she must be in her late forties or early fifties.
7. I'm not sure, but she can't be that far from retirement.
8. He can't be more than about thirty.

Follow-up comments

a. He's still not walking yet.
b. He's got a ten-year-old son.
c. He told me he fought in the Second World War.
d. He still hasn't left school.
e. She taught me when I was in primary school and I'm twenty-two now, so that was sixteen years ago.
f. Someone told me he was only just older than her son and he's twenty-seven.
g. I know she graduated last year.
h. She told me she'd been working here for thirty years.

Write down the names of five famous people and then ask a partner: 'How old do you think he/she is?' When you answer, try to use the following patterns:

She/he must be in his thirties.
She/he can't be more than forty.

Try to explain why you think so.

5 | Speaking

What's the difference between in his forties and in the forties?

What things happened in the world/your country during …

1. the early forties?
2. the fifties?
3. the sixties?
4. the late seventies?
5. the mid-nineties?

When do you think was the best period for fashion? Music? Life?

 For more information on expressing opinions with *can't* see G22.

Using grammar

1 | Used to, would

Do you think you've changed much since you were young? In what way?

🎧 You are going to hear the man in Picture 1 talking about how he has changed over the last fifteen years. For example, when he was younger, he used to play in the rock band in the Picture 2. Listen for the differences between the man now and his younger self. Compare with a partner and see who remembers more.

Complete the sentences below using **used to** and the verbs in the box.

be (x2)   dress   play   smoke

1. I .... quite differently.
2. I .... bass in a band.
3. I .... a lot wilder than I am now.
4. I .... around twenty a day, but I stopped a few years ago.
5. I .... a bit of a ladies' man before I met my wife.

Listen again and check your answers.

2 | Grammar study

Read the explanations and underline anything you didn't know already. Tell a partner what you learned.

We use **used to + verb** when we talk about something that we did a lot in the past but that we don't do any more, or to talk about a state that lasted for some time in the past. We often use it with a time phrase which makes it clear when these things happened.

I used to go windsurfing a lot when I was younger. (an action that happened a lot)

When I was at school, I always used to get into fights. (an action that happened a lot)

I used to have really bad skin when I was a teenager. (a state that lasted for a long time)

We often emphasise the fact that the habits/ states happened/lasted over a long period of time by adding **always** or **never**. For example:

I always used to want to stay up late on Fridays, but my mum never used to let me.

I always used to have curly hair, but then when I was eight or nine, it suddenly all went straight.

I never used to like spicy food, but I've grown to like it over the years.

I never used to worry about what I eat, but since I turned thirty, I've started thinking about it a lot.

Used to + verb is only used to talk about habits/states in the past. We don't use it to talk about the present. Also, it has nothing to do with **get used to** or **be used to**. It's best to try to learn these completely different structures separately.

3 | Practice

Make sentences which introduce a topic by matching the beginnings 1–9 to the endings a–i.

1. When I was a kid, I used to play
2. When I was younger, I used to go
3. When I was about twelve or thirteen, I used to collect
4. When I was at primary school, I used to love
5. When I was about eight or nine, I used to have this
6. When I was at school, I used to get into
7. When I was a boy, I used to spend a lot of
8. I used to be a lot more impatient
9. I used to make

a. lots of mistakes when I first started learning Spanish.
b. than I am now.
c. time down on the beach near my house.
d. the piano.
e. stamps.
f. trouble all the time.
g. fishing at the weekends in this river near my house.
h. painting.
i. great friend called Matt.

4 | Follow-up comments

Look again at the sentences in Exercise 3 above. We often add follow-up comments by talking about other actions that were related to the action we are talking about. We often do this by using (I) + would + verb. For example:

I used to go windsurfing a lot when I was younger. We lived near a lake, so we'd often go after school in the summer. My mum would drive us there and she'd help us get the boards off the car and into the lake. We'd spend hours out there. It was great.

When I was at school, I always used to get into fights. I'd usually end up in the headmaster's office, which would really annoy my parents.

Now match the follow-up comments i–ix to the sentences 1–9 in Exercise 3 on page 124.

i.   I'd be rude to teachers or I'd be late, and I'd end up having to go and see the headmaster!

ii. I'd lose my temper at the smallest thing and I'd get really annoyed if I ever had to wait for things! I was horrible!

iii. I'd have lessons every week, and I'd practise at home, but eventually I got bored with it.

iv. I'd try to catch crabs and collect shells and I'd sometimes go swimming as well. It was great!

v.   I'd get words mixed up and speak bits of French by mistake and forget things! It was awful!

vi. We'd spend all our time together and we'd go skate-boarding, climb trees and things like that.

vii. I'd buy them from a shop near my house and steam them off old envelopes.

viii.I'd do funny little portraits and trees and landscapes and things like that. It was fun.

ix. A friend of mine and I would get up early and then we'd go and sit by the river all day. Sometimes we'd catch things, sometimes we wouldn't!

5 | Free practice

Now think of three things you used to do when you were younger. Write a bit about them.

1. When I was . . . . , I used to . . . .
    I'd . . . . and I'd . . . .

2. When I was . . . . , I used to . . . .
    I'd . . . . and I'd . . . .

3. When I was . . . . , I used to . . . .
    I'd . . . . and I'd . . . .

Now tell some other students about what you have written. Can you find some other students who used to do the same things as you?

6 | Situations

Choose two questions from the box that you could use to continue these conversations below. You can use some questions more than once.

> How many a day?
>
> Were you any good?
>
> What kind of thing? Poetry?
>
> What were you doing there?
>
> When did you cut down?
>
> Whereabouts exactly?
>
> Why did you leave?
>
> Why did you stop?

1. A: I used to live in Spain.
    B: Oh, really? . . . .
    And . . . .

2. A: I used to play the violin.
    B: Oh, really? . . . .
    And . . . .

3. A: I used to smoke a lot more than I do now.
    B: Oh, really? . . . .
    And . . . .

4. A: I used to write quite a lot.
    B: Oh, really? . . . .
    And . . . .

5. A: I used to play tennis.
    B: Oh, really? . . . .
    And . . . .

6. A: I used to work at Hamleys, the toy shop.
    B: Oh, really? . . . .
    And . . . .

In pairs, try to continue each conversation for as long as you can. You will need to invent answers to the questions above.

7 | Speaking

Discuss these questions with a partner.

1. Can you think of anything you used to love, but then went off? Why did you go off it?

2. Did you ever use to want to be something, but then later went off the idea? Why did you go off it?

3. Can you think of anything you never used to worry about, but that you've started thinking about a lot more?

4. Did you ever use to have friends you were close to, but who you don't see any more? What happened?

> ▶ For more information on *used to* and *would*, see G23.

It's a big festival of the Arts. • Does anyone speak Swiss? • Scandinavians are usually blond, aren't th
• It's right on the border. • Have you been to the Canaries? • It's a very cosmopolitan place. •
commemorates our first President. • It's a kind of temple
What's the English for fiesta? • How do you celebrate New Ye
in your country? • Are y
bilingual, then?

18 Nationalities, festivals and languages

Reading

1 | Vocabulary

Match the sentences 1–8 to the pictures A–H.

1. There's a big parade through the town every spring.
2. There's a big film festival there every autumn.
3. There's a huge beer festival there every October.
4. There's a big music festival there every summer.
5. There's a big religious festival at the temple there at the start of every spring.
6. There's a huge street party with techno music and dancing every August Bank Holiday.
7. There's a big fireworks display and a big bonfire at the end of the festival.
8. There are hundreds of people throwing water all over each other there.

2 | Speaking

Discuss these questions with a partner.

1. Do you have any festivals like the ones described in Exercise 1 above in your town/country?
2. Have you been to any of them? Why/why not?
3. Where do you think the pictures in A–H in Exercise 1 are?
4. Do you know anything about any of these festivals?

3 | While you read

Read what four people have to say about the festivals they've been to.

1. Which pictures are they describing?
2. Were you right about where the festivals were held?
3. Did you learn anything new or surprising about these festivals?

FOUR EXPERIENCES

QUENTIN

Back in 1989, I went on holiday to London to visit some friends. The second day I was there, the Notting Hill Carnival was on, so I went to see what it was all about. It was amazing! It's like a huge street party right in the middle of London. It's basically a celebration of Afro-Caribbean culture, but all kinds of different people go there. There are literally hundreds of thousands of people there. Anyway, everyone dresses up in outrageous costumes and dances and has a great time. I met some really nice people that day and it really helped broaden my mind. I've been back every other year since then, and always look forward to it.

BARNABY

I've been going to the Glastonbury festival in the west of England for years. It used to be really great, but it's become a bit commercial now. It's got too big. Ten years ago, it was much smaller and it was easier to make friends and everyone was there for the music. Nowadays, everything is much more expensive and it's become a place people go in order to drink and take drugs. It's got more aggressive too. Things get stolen from your tent. There are more fights and there are so many people that you can't even see the bands. The stages seem to be miles away! I only go out of habit now, I suppose.

RICARDO

Fallas is a big annual festival they hold in my home town, Valencia. It's held every spring and it commemorates the patron saint of the city. Lots of people spend the whole year preparing for it. Each area raises money to build their own fallas – huge papier-mâché models – and they all spend ages making them look great. We make funny models of famous politicians, footballers, local celebrities, that kind of thing. The festival runs all through the beginning of March, and it's pretty crazy – lots of drinking, hundreds of people all throwing fireworks at each other, street performers and so on. Anyway, on March 19th, there's a huge fireworks display and then everyone burns all their models! It's mad, but really good fun.

YASUKO

Hounen Matsuri is a fairly strange festival. I don't really know much about it. It still happens every year, in March, but it's mainly for older people. Most young people just find it a bit embarrassing, I think. I suppose it's a celebration of spring and the end of winter and that kind of thing. People get really drunk on rice wine and parade this big wooden thing through the streets. Don't ask me why! Then they take it to the temple and pray and that's it, really. It's odd, though, because it's really popular with tourists. I guess it attracts the kind of person who likes to think they're seeing the 'real' Japan, whatever that means.

4 | Comprehension

Answer these questions.

1. How often does Quentin go to the Notting Hill Carnival?
2. How does Barnaby feel about the size of Glastonbury now?
3. Why do most people go to Glastonbury now?
4. Why does Barnaby still go there?
5. Why do they hold Fallas?
6. What is a falla?
7. Why do they hold Hounen Matsuri?

5 | Speaking

Discuss these questions with a partner.

1. Would you like to go to any of the four festivals described in Exercise 3? Why/why not?
2. Can you think of any festivals or events you know which …
   * you always really look forward to?
   * used to be really good, but have become a bit too commercial now?
   * people spend all year preparing for?
   * most young people just find a bit embarrassing nowadays?

6 | Vocabulary focus

Complete these definitions with commemorate or celebrate.

We . . . . special occasions. We also . . . . when something good has happened by doing something nice and fun.

We usually . . . . people or things from the past by doing something more serious or by building monuments to show we remember them with respect.

Make sentences by matching the beginnings 1–6 with the endings a–f.

1. Are you going to do anything
2. On August 8th, they hold a special ceremony which
3. My dad got promoted, so he took us out
4. Every July, there's a two-day national holiday to
5. There's a big monument in the main square
6. After the exams, we celebrated

a. commemorates all the people who died in the war.
b. by going clubbing.
c. commemorating the victory in the war.
d. to celebrate your birthday?
e. commemorate our patron saint, Saint Andrew.
f. to this fancy restaurant to celebrate.

Discuss these questions with a partner.

7. Think of some public holidays or monuments in your country. What do they commemorate or celebrate?
8. Do you have any local festivals? What do they celebrate?
9. What have you celebrated over the last year? How did you celebrate?

Using grammar

1 | Relative clauses

Barnaby said Glastonbury has become 'a place people go in order to drink and take drugs.' He could have said: 'a place that people go to in order to drink and take drugs.'

In sentences like this, we can choose to use that or not. Some years ago, it was more common to use that in this structure, but today most people do not use it in everyday spoken English. The clause which follows the noun gives an extra piece of information about it and is called a relative clause.

Make sentences with relative clauses by matching the beginnings 1–8 to the endings a–h.

1. I didn't get that job
2. Hey, there's that girl
3. You should try that restaurant
4. I couldn't do that homework
5. Hey, I went and saw that film
6. Do you sell those things
7. We had a good holiday, but the car
8. Have you seen those new mobile phones

a. I was talking to in the canteen yesterday. She's really nice.
b. you can cut wire with?
c. we were given yesterday. It was impossible.
d. you told me about. It's good, isn't it?
e. I applied for. I'm really disappointed about it!
f. we rented broke down twice! It was terrible!
g. we went to the other night. It was great.
h. you can send photos with? They're amazing!

Now in pairs, try to agree on an alternative relative clause for each of the examples 1–8 above. For example:

I didn't get that job I had an interview for last week.

For more information on relative clauses, see G24.

2 | Practice

Work in pairs. Student A should look at the twelve pictures on page 176 and try to describe them to Student B. Student B should then try to draw the things being described. Use the following structures to help you explain what these things are:

Number 1 is one of those things you use to open tins.

Number 2 is one of those things you put golf balls/put hot cups/cut food on.

When you have finished, compare the two sets of pictures. Did you understand all the descriptions?

Now think of five things like those in the pictures that you'd like to know the English words for and then walk around the classroom asking the other students: 'Do you know what you call those things you … with/on?'

If you understand the other students, but don't know the English word for what they're describing, use this expression:

I know what you mean, but I don't know what it's/they're called.

If nobody in the class can help you, ask your teacher at the end of the activity.

3 | Questions with relative clauses

We often use relative clauses in questions. For example, you know your friend went to a party last week. You want to know what it was like, so you ask:

What was that party you went to last week like?

Look at these three similar questions:

a. What's it like? ('it' is a pronoun)
b. What's the house like? ('the house' is a noun)
c. What's the house you're moving to like? ('the house you're moving to' is a noun + relative clause)

What is the question in the following situations?

1. You know your friend shares a flat with two other people. You want to know what they're like. You ask:

....

....

2. You know your friend stayed in a hotel in Paris. You want to know what it was like. You ask:

....

....

3. You know your friend went to a club on Friday. You want to know what it was like. You ask:

....

....

4. You know your friend works with several other people. You want to know what they're like. You ask:

....

....

5. You know your friend went to a restaurant for his birthday. You want to know what it was like. You ask:

....

....

6. You know your friend did an English course in Australia. You want to know what it was like. You ask:

....

....

7. You know your friend went to a class you missed last week. You want to know what they did. You ask:

....

....

8. You know your friend studied at a school in Sydney. You want to know what it was called. You ask:

....

....

9. You know your friend applied for a job. You want to know if they got it. You ask:

....

....

With a partner, have conversations using the questions above. You will need to use your imagination when responding. How long can you keep each conversation going?

4 | Defining people

Yasuko said that the Hounen Matsuri attracts 'the kind of person who likes to think they're seeing the "real" Japan'. If we want to explain what kind of person we're describing, we often use the pattern person + who- clause.

Try to answer these questions in pairs. Use your dictionary if you need to.

1. What do you call a person who can't stop drinking and who's always drunk?
2. What do you call a person who's always working, even at the weekend?
3. What do you call a person who organises funerals for a living?
4. What do you call a person who performs operations in a hospital?
5. What do you call a person who writes for a newspaper?
6. What do you call a person who can throw lots of things up in the air and then catch them all again?

Write four more similar questions to find out the names of other kinds of people. Use the pictures for ideas if you need to. Go round the class or ask your teacher if they know the word.

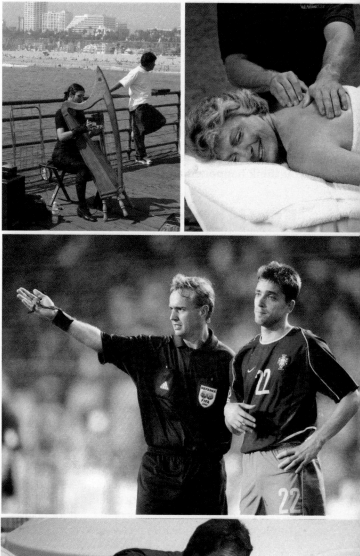

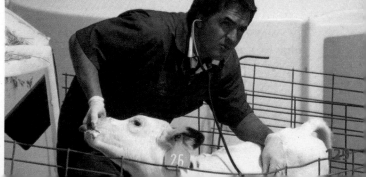

Listening

1 | Speaking

With a partner, discuss the difference between …

- an accent and a dialect.
- your mother tongue and a lingua franca.
- slang and swearing.
- being bilingual and speaking a foreign language.
- having a slight accent and having a strong accent.

Change partners and discuss these questions.

1. What's the main language in your country?
2. What minority languages are there? How many people speak them? Do some have higher status than others?
3. What languages did you grow up speaking? When did you speak each one? Why?
4. Do you have to study any special languages at school?
5. Do you think you will need any special languages to help you get a job in the future?
6. Do you use slang or swear much in your mother tongue? What about in English?

2 | Reading

Look at this headline from a newspaper. What do you think happened and why?

English teacher sacked for speaking English!

Now read the short article and see if you were right.

Gareth Davies, an English teacher in North Wales, has lost his job because he failed a test in Welsh. The 35-year-old teacher, who was actually born in Wales, recently won an award for teaching excellence, but the local education department requires all teachers to pass a spoken and written exam in Welsh. Two years ago, when Gareth moved to Wales from London, where he grew up, the school gave him a job on a temporary basis while he had Welsh lessons. After he failed the exam for the second time, the school decided to sack him. Mr Davies tried to take the school to court for unfair dismissal, but yesterday he finally lost his case.

Do you feel sorry for Gareth Davies or do you think he deserved to lose his job? Why?

3 | Radio interview

🎧 **You are now going to listen to a radio programme. One of the speakers is Gareth Davies himself. The other is a Professor of Modern Languages. Listen and note down the arguments they come up with in support of and against being forced to learn a local language.**

Arguments for
....
....
....
....

Arguments against
....
....
....
....

4 | Disagreeing

Complete the conversation below with the phrases in the box.

> Come on! That's a bit of an exaggeration!
> Do you honestly believe that?
> How can you say that?
> Let's just agree to disagree.
> Listen, we're obviously never going to agree
> So what you're saying is

A: You can't get a good job if you don't speak English.
B: (1) ....
A: No, it's not. All the best jobs these days ask you to be fluent in English.
B: (2) ....
I could be a brilliant medical student, say, and I couldn't get a job as a doctor because I can't speak English.
A: Yeah, more or less.
B: (3) ....
A: Yeah. If you don't speak English, you're nothing.
B: (4) ....
A: Because it's true.
B: That's crazy.
A: (5) ....,
so let's just talk about something else, shall we?
B: OK, but you do realise you're wrong!
A: OK, whatever. I don't want to argue.
(6) ....

🎧 **Listen and check your answers. Then in pairs, discuss the statements in Exercise 5 below. Student A should agree with the statement and student B should disagree. Try and use some of the phrases in Exercise 4 on page 130.**

Now change partners and discuss what you really think.

5 | Speaking

In groups of three, tell each other if you agree with these statements or not.

1. Everyone should learn English.
2. American English is more useful than British English.
3. People should be forced to learn a minority language from their own country.
4. It's impossible to stop foreign words coming into a language.
5. Language is part of a culture. You think differently when you speak a foreign language.
6. Foreign words that come into a language make that language poorer.
7. In a hundred years' time, everybody will speak English as a global language.

6 | Stereotypes and reality

What's your stereotype of British people? Does your teacher agree with you?

Have you met many British people? Did they fit the stereotype?

Complete the short dialogues below with the words in the box.

distant	dull	generous	nice
open-minded	out-going	quiet	two-faced

1. A: He's a typical Scot – really mean!
   B: Oh, come on! Every Scot I've ever met was really . . . .

2. A: He's a typical Italian – really loud!
   B: Oh, come on! I've got a really good friend who's from Rome and he's quite . . . .

3. A: She's a typical Japanese – really quiet and shy!
   B: Oh, come on! That's such a stereotype! Lots of Japanese people are really . . . .

4. A: She's a typical small town girl – really conservative.
   B: Oh, come on! Just because you don't come from the city doesn't mean you can't be . . . .

5. A: She's a typical Parisian – arrogant and snobbish!
   B: Oh, come on! I've got a friend from Paris and she's really . . . .

6. A: The Spanish are much more friendly than most people.
   B: Some of them, maybe! I've met some Spaniards who were really cold and . . . .

7. A: People from Osaka are usually really funny.
   B: Oh, come on! They can't *all* be funny! There must be some who are as . . . . as the rest of us!

8. A: People from the north are much more open and honest than southerners.
   B: Oh, come on! Just because you're a southerner doesn't mean you have to be . . . .

🎧 **Listen and check your answers. Then practise the conversations above with a partner.**

Can you think of any other stereotypes that are common in your country? Have conversations like the ones above using your ideas.

> **Real English:** Just because ... it doesn't mean ...
> We often use this structure in spoken English to contradict assumptions.
> *Just because I'm a man, it doesn't mean I can't cook.*
> *Just because I'm sixteen, it doesn't mean I'm stupid.*
> *Just because he's rich, it doesn't mean he's a snob.*
>
> *'Just because you're a black boy, just because he's a white It doesn't mean he has to hate you, it doesn't mean you have to fight.' (J. Dammers)*

He got life. • The jury found her not guilty. • He got what he deserved. • He mugged an old lady in [the] park. • They got away with millions! • Our house was broken into while we were on holiday. • The pol[ice] dropped the charges. • It's against the law to go topless. • He was a dealer. • They should lock him [up] and throw away the key. • I was fined £250! • It's my first offence. • Three strikes and you're out! • S[he] was just over the limit. • Call the police. • They turn a bl[ind] eye to it. • They say they're going to legalise it.

19 Law and order

Reading

1 Speaking

If you commit a crime and are arrested, you go to court. You are tried and found guilty or innocent. If you are found guilty, you are sentenced by a judge. Maybe you only get a £300 fine or maybe you get six months or even life, depending on the crime. In Britain, you usually get life if you are guilty of murder. What sentence would each of the following usually get in your country?

1. murder	6. possession of drugs
2. vandalism	7. burglary
3. tax evasion	8. rape
4. drink-driving	9. lying in court
5. speeding	

Is there a difference in your country between **murder** and **manslaughter**?

Look at the nine famous people on this page. Each person has been connected to one of the crimes 1–9 in the box. Discuss with your partner what kind of crime you think each was connected to.

2 While you read

The class should now split into two groups. One group should read the texts below and the other group should read those on page 175.

Read your texts and find out if you were right. Once you have finished reading, compare your findings with someone from the other group. Find out as much as you can about each person.

Rich and Famous or Rich and Dangerous?

They say that in the end we're all the same. You can have money and fame, but in the end you still have to do the same kind of things as everyone else – sleep, eat, fall in and out of love, and, apparently, commit crimes! Yes, when you look at the world of celebrities, it's amazing how many have had trouble with the law. Here's just a few of the ones we could remember, but the Internet has lots more!

O.J. Simpson

O.J. was involved in perhaps the most famous celebrity trial of them all. He was accused of killing his ex-wife, Nicole Brown, and her lover, Ronald Goldman, and he was allegedly filmed driving away from the scene in a truck. At first, the evidence suggesting he was guilty seemed to many people to be very clear, but the trial, which was televised around the world, found him innocent. Lots of people think the jury got it wrong and that he was lucky to get away with it. He had to pay several million dollars in damages to the victims' relatives when they took him to court afterward. However, as one American comedian said, 'Have you ever heard of a millionaire murdering someone with their own hands? These people employ someone just to answer the telephone!'

Johnny Depp

He may look sweet and innocent, but Johnny Depp has been found guilty of vandalism more than once in his life. On one occasion, he smashed up a hotel room in New York. He was charged, but it didn't go to court because he agreed to pay $2,000 to the hotel to repair the damage.

Mike Tyson

Mike Tyson continued to earn millions of dollars as a boxer even after he had been to prison for rape. He took a nineteen-year-old contestant in the Miss America beauty contest to his hotel room and forced her to have sex with him. He was later found guilty and was sentenced to six years in prison, but he got out just three years later for 'good behaviour'. He hasn't exactly shown much good behaviour since then, though!

Jean-Claude van Damme

After admitting he had been drink-driving, the so-called 'Muscles from Brussels' was ordered to pay a $1,200 fine, was banned from driving for ninety days, and was forced to go to an anti-drink-driving course. Let's hope the course was more effective than the acting lessons he took!

David Beckham

Another bad driver is David Beckham. He was convicted of driving at over ninety miles an hour when he was on his way to a training session for his former football club, Manchester United. His excuse was that he was being chased by a photographer. He was also banned from driving, but shortly afterwards the judge agreed to give him back his driving licence, because he said that, as a celebrity, it was safer for Beckham to travel in his own car than on public transport. Safer for David, perhaps, but not for everyone else on the road.

Real English: celebrity

Celebrities are famous people, especially in the world of sport or entertainment.
Jamie Oliver is the latest celebrity chef to get his own TV show.

David Beckham is such an international celebrity that it's easy to forget he's basically just a footballer!

3 | Common expressions

Here are six things often said about criminals. Which sentences would you use to talk about the people you read about?

1. He was lucky. He got off lightly.
2. He was unlucky. It was a bit harsh.
3. He should've got life for that.
4. If that had happened in my country, he would've got the death penalty.
5. He got what he deserved.
6. Typical! There's one law for the rich and another one for the poor!

Real English: got off

If someone gets off a criminal charge, it means they weren't convicted, but you think they should've been, or if they got off lightly, they got a punishment, but it should've been worse.
He got off because his father was the judge!
He got off just because he was rich.
He got off lightly. He should've got life.

4 | Speaking

Discuss these questions with a partner.

1. Do you know any other famous people who have been found guilty of crimes? Who? What happened? What punishment did they get?
2. Do you know any other cases like O.J. Simpson's where someone got off even though most people thought the person was guilty?
3. Do you know any cases of people going to prison when they were innocent?

5 | Numbers

When we say numbers, we often approximate. In the article, it said that Pavarotti has about $300 million and that he agreed to pay around $4.5 million in tax. Beckham was driving at over ninety miles an hour. We could say that Helmut Kohl got fined almost $150,000.

Which words mean:

a. more than?
b. less than?
c. either more or less than?

Describe the numbers below using the words in the box.

about	almost	around	over

1. 148 kilometres an hour
2. 32 minutes late
3. 323
4. 972
5. between 487 and 513
6. 4961
7. between 99,000 and 102,000
8. between 3,300,000 and 3,640,000
9. 9,970,426
10. 78,030,000
11. 180,000,000

Now listen and check your answers. Practise saying them.

6 | Free practice

Do you know the following numbers? If you don't, guess, using around, over or almost.

1. What's the speed limit on the motorway? Do you know what it is in miles per hour?
2. What's the maximum fine you can get for a parking offence?
3. What's the maximum sentence you can get for robbery?
4. How much money does your president earn per year?
5. What's the average salary in your country?
6. What's the exchange rate of the dollar?
7. What's the population of the second biggest city in your country?
8. What's the population of China?

Using vocabulary

1 Basic crime vocabulary

Complete the short dialogues below with the words in the boxes.

1.

dead	stabbed	murder

A: Did you hear about that (a) .... yesterday?

B: No, what happened?

A: They found this woman (b) .... just near where I live. Apparently, she'd been (c) .... six times.

2.

got away with	raided	robbery

A: Did you hear about that (a) .... yesterday?

B: No, what happened?

A: These guys (b) .... this jeweller's shop in town. They (c) .... around a million pounds' worth of jewellery.

3.

killed	massacre	rampage

A: Did you hear about that (a) .... in the States?

B: No, what happened?

A: Apparently, a kid went on the (b) .... with a gun in a school. He (c) .... eight or nine people.

4.

came up to	ran off	snatched

A: Did you hear about Jim having his bag (a) ....?

B: No, what happened?

A: Apparently, he was just waiting at a bus stop and this guy (b) .... him, grabbed his bag and (c) .... It had his mobile, his wallet, his diary, everything in it.

5.

burgled	kicked in	stolen

A: Did I tell you we had our house (a) ....?

B: No! When did that happen?

A: Last week. I went out shopping on Tuesday and when I got back, I found the front door had been (b) .... and the TV and DVD had been (c) ....

6.

killed	papers	serial killer

A: Did you see they've caught that (a) ....?

B: Serial killer? I haven't heard anything about it.

A: Oh, come on, you must have. It's been in all the (b) .... They call him The Vampire. He's (c) .... about six people in the last year.

Now practise the conversations. Try to continue them for as long as you can.

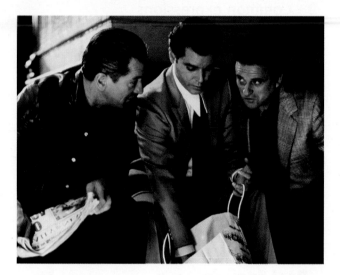

2 Free practice

With a partner, have conversations similar to the ones in Exercise 1. Use these ideas.

1. murder / old man / in his house / beaten to death
2. robbery / security van in Birmingham / five million in cash
3. massacre / young guy / in a shopping mall / shot twenty people
4. bag snatched / standing outside the post office / teenage girl / luckily nothing
5. burgled / two weeks ago / window smashed / computer
6. those robbers / papers / The Great Houdinis / robbed seven banks

Have you heard about any crimes recently? What happened?

Go round the room and talk about the crimes you've heard about.

3 | Before you listen

Match the sentences 1–6 to the pictures A–F.

1. My handbag was snatched.
2. My mobile phone was stolen.
3. I got mugged at knife-point.
4. Someone broke into my car and stole my bag.
5. There's a lot of vandalism in some areas.
6. A lot of kids go shoplifting in the big department stores.

Which of these crimes are common in your country?

4 | Four crimes

🎧 **You are going to hear about four of the crimes in the pictures A–F. As you listen, decide which person is talking about which picture.**

Person 1: ....   Person 3: ....
Person 2: ....   Person 4: ....

Look at the tapescript for Person 3 on page 158. With a partner, correct the language mistakes made by the victim.

5 | Vocabulary

Complete the sentences below with the correct form of the verbs in the box.

cancel	get away with	hold	leave
let	report	smash	snatch

1. They .... a gun to my head. It was terrifying!
2. I came out of the house this morning and saw that my car windscreen had been ....!
3. I was so stupid. I somehow managed to .... my keys at home.
4. They broke into my car and .... my suitcase, which I'd left in the boot.
5. I want to .... that I've had my bag snatched.
6. I'd just left my house when I had my digital camera .... by this man.
7. We'd better .... the police know about that boy we saw shoplifting.
8. All my credit cards were stolen, so I had to have them .... straightaway.

All of the sentences above are slightly different to what happens in the conversations on the recording. Can you correct each one?

🎧 **Listen again and see if you were right.**

135

Using grammar

1 | Third conditionals

In the first of the four conversations on page 135, the man who was mugged was angry that the passer-by didn't stop and help. When he was explaining his decision, the passer-by said: 'I would've helped if I'd been able to.'

This kind of if- sentence is a **third conditional**. It's made up of two parts:

- an if- clause: if I'd been able to
- an imaginary result clause: I would've helped

Here are some more examples:

If we'd left the house earlier, we wouldn't have missed our flight.

It would have been easier if you'd told me about it earlier.

To make the if- clause, we use *if* + subject + **past perfect** (*had* + past participle).
In the imaginary result half of the sentence, we use subject + *would/wouldn't* + *have* + past participle.

Sometimes we put the if- clause part of the sentence first; sometimes we put the result part first. It depends on which half of the sentence we feel is more important or more connected to what was said before.

We use third conditionals to talk about things we would like to change about the past, or ways in which the past might have been different.

2 | Practice

Make third conditional sentences by matching the result clauses 1–8 to the if- clauses a–h.

1. I can't believe my car got stolen! It wouldn't have happened

2. I can't believe my flat got broken into! It wouldn't have happened

3. I can't believe he got five years in prison! It wouldn't have happened

4. I can't believe we missed the flight! It wouldn't have happened

5. I can't believe I didn't get that job I applied for! I'm sure I would've done

6. I can't believe you didn't go and see the Eiffel Tower! I guess you would've done

7. I can't believe I didn't pass! I'm sure I would've done

8. I can't believe we didn't win that game! I'm sure we would've done

a. if I'd parked it in a safer street.

b. if there hadn't been so much traffic on the way there.

c. if he'd pleaded guilty instead of trying to prove he was innocent!

d. if they hadn't substituted me halfway through the first half!

e. if I'd had a burglar alarm!

f. if a different teacher had marked the papers!

g. if you'd had a few more days there, wouldn't you?

h. if I'd dressed a bit more smartly for the interview.

With a partner, discuss what actually happened in each of the situations above. For example, in number 1, my car got stolen because I'd parked it in a dark street with no lighting – the kind of street where lots of cars get stolen!

With a partner, think of other possible if- clauses for 1–8 above. For example:

I can't believe my car got stolen! It wouldn't have happened if I'd closed the back window properly.

> ▶ For more information on third conditionals, see G25.

3 | Free practice

Make four sentences that are true for you following the pattern in Exercise 2 on page 136. You should begin:

I can't believe … .

Explain what you've written to your partner. Then make third conditional sentences using these ideas.

1. (I didn't phone you yesterday because I was really busy.)
   Sorry I didn't phone you yesterday. I . . . . if . . . .

2. (The food was OK, but not great. The problem was, it wasn't salty enough.)
   The food was OK, but it . . . . nicer if . . . . a bit saltier.

3. (I didn't buy that jacket because it was too expensive.)
   A: Did you buy that jacket in the end?
   B: No, I . . . . if . . . .

4. (I asked for her phone number. I didn't know her boyfriend was a boxer.)
   I'm not stupid! I . . . . if . . . .

5. (I bought a second-hand car, but then the police stopped me and said it was stolen.)
   I'm not a criminal! I . . . . if . . . .

4 | Pronunciation: third conditionals

Listen and practise saying these sentences.

1. If I'd known, I wouldn't have asked!
2. If I'd known, I wouldn't have bothered.
3. If I'd known, I wouldn't have worn it.
4. If you'd told me about it, I would've come.
5. If you'd told me about it, I wouldn't have mentioned it.
6. I wouldn't have believed it if I hadn't seen it with my own eyes!
7. I wouldn't have got into university if it hadn't been for her!
8. I would've been dead if it hadn't been for her!
9. I wouldn't have done it if I'd known I didn't have to.
10. Of course I would've done it if I'd had to.

What do you think the speakers above are talking about?

Go back to page 87 and re-read the story of Janet and Nick. Role-play the conversation you think they had in the police station. Start like this:

Nick: This is all your fault! This wouldn't have happened if you hadn't tried to bribe that policeman!

Janet: Well, if you'd …

5 | Finally

Here are four infamous crimes which made international news. What do you know about them? Which is the most serious?

- The Dunblane Massacre
- The Columbine High School shootings
- The Harold Shipman case
- The Bali bombing

Ask your teacher for more information if you need it.

How are you? • I'm sorry to hear that. • How long will it take to heal? • Do you bleed easily? • I've h
a really bad cold. • You're looking much better. • Have you tried Chinese medicine? • I don't believe
things like homeopathy. • How did you do it? • I'd take it easy if I were you. • I could really do with
break. • I'm not sleeping very well. • I slipped and fell. • I must've sprained my ankle. • Are you tak
anything for it? • She's a keep-fit fanatic. • I think I've fractured it. • The operatic
next week. • I'm feeling a bit run-down. • He's critically ill in hospital.

Using vocabulary

1 Collocations

What problems do you think the people in the pictures below have?

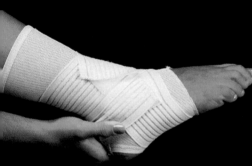

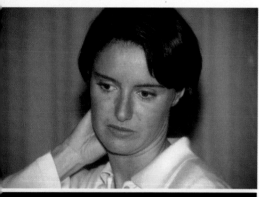

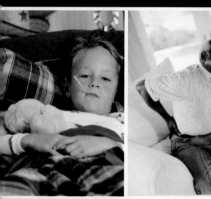

Complete the sentences below with the verbs in the box. You will need to use some verbs more than once.

cut	done	feel	got	sprained

1. I've .... an awful cold.
2. I've .... a terrible headache.
3. Ouch! I've .... my finger.
4. I can't play tennis. I've .... my ankle.
5. I've .... a stiff neck for some reason.
6. I've .... something to my back.
7. I've .... terrible stomach-ache.
8. I .... a bit sick.
9. I've .... a bad toothache.
10. I .... a bit hung-over.
11. I've .... really bad hay fever.
12. I think I've .... the flu.
13. I've .... a bit of a temperature.
14. I've .... something to my knee. It hurts.
15. I've .... my wrist somehow.
16. I've .... myself shaving.

With a partner, decide which piece of advice a–j you would give in response to the statements 1–16. If you think more than one piece of advice is possible, can you agree on which is the best?

a. Maybe you should go and see someone about it.
b. Maybe you should have a glass of water or something.
c. Maybe you should just take it easy, then.
d. Maybe you should take something for it.
e. Maybe you should go and have a lie-down or something.
f. Maybe you should take some aspirin or something.
g. Maybe you should take a day off or something.
h. Maybe you should stick a plaster on it or something.
i. Maybe you should get someone to give you a massage or something.
j. Maybe you should go out and get a bit of fresh air or something.

> **Real English:** Maybe you should ... or something
>
> When we give advice, we often make it sound less strong by beginning with maybe and then finishing the sentence by saying or something.
> *Maybe you should have a glass of milk or something.*
>
> In this situation, or something could mean take some indigestion tablets or take something else which will make you feel better.
>
> What do you think or something could mean in the advice e–j in Exercise 1 above?

2 | What's the matter?

Put these conversations into the correct order.

Conversation 1

a. Oh, no. How long've you had that?

b. For a few days now.

c. No, I know. I've got an awful cold.

d. No, I just need to get a good night's sleep tonight, then I'll be OK.

e. Well, maybe you should take a day off work or something.

f. Are you OK? You don't look very well.

Conversation 2

a. How come? Have you not been well?

b. No, no. I've just had a really stressful day at work. That's all.

c. No, it's all right. I just need some aspirin, then I'll be OK.

d. No, not really. I've got a terrible headache.

e. You look terrible. Are you all right?

f. Well, maybe you should go and have a lie-down or something.

 Listen and check your answers.

Now practise reading the two conversations with a partner.

3 | Further practice

With a partner, write a new conversation using one of the sixteen situations from Exercise 1 on page 138. Start the conversation with one of the following:

What's the matter?
Are you all right?

A: ....
B: ....
A: ....
B: ....
A: ....
B: ....

4 | Health quiz

Read these questions and check that you understand the highlighted words and expressions to do with health. Then answer the questions with your partner.

1. Would you describe yourself as fit?

2. How do you feel about having injections?

3. How many fillings have you got?

4. Are you allergic to anything?

5. How often do you have a check-up at the doctor's? At the dentist's?

6. Do you take vitamin pills?

7. Do you wear contact lenses?

8. Have you ever had any stitches? Why?

9. Have you ever had an operation?

10. Do you belong to a gym?

11. Have you ever had acupuncture or a massage or anything like that?

12. Have you ever fainted? What happened?

13. Have you ever pretended to be ill so that you could take a day off work?

5 | Cures

Do you know any good ways of ...

1. getting rid of hiccups?
2. getting rid of a cold?
3. losing weight?
4. stopping a nosebleed?
5. soothing aching muscles?
6. staying young-looking?

Which of the treatments in the box below would you use if you ...

7. had terrible arthritis?
8. had a bad cold?

- a massage
- a mud bath
- a nice hot bath
- acupuncture
- camomile tea

Discuss these questions with a partner.

9. What other problems are the treatments used for?

10. Which countries are these most popular in?

11. Do you think any of them are particularly effective?

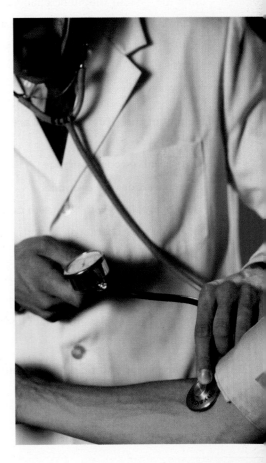

Listening

1 | The NHS

The NHS – the British National Health Service – was one of the first free health services in the world. Compare what you have heard about it with a partner, then read this text.

The National Health Service was started in 1948 to provide free health care for everyone. Before that, all doctors charged fees, so only those who could afford it got medical care. Today, the NHS is still free. Nobody has to pay when they go and see a doctor or when they have an operation or need any other kind of hospital treatment. It's all paid for by taxes. However, there are lots of problems with the present system. People don't like paying high taxes and so you often have to wait a long time before you get to see a doctor and some people have to wait over a year before they can have an operation. Some things are charged for now, like prescriptions, eye tests and dental checkups. Thousands of doctors and nurses leave every year, complaining that they are overworked and underpaid. Some people think the system should be changed. They would like everybody to take out health insurance and would like some parts of the service to be privatised.

Tick any of the situations that are true for your country.

1. free health care for everyone ☐
2. free operations for everyone ☐
3. lots of problems with the health care system ☐
4. long waits for operations ☐
5. prescription drugs no longer free ☐
6. doctors and nurses leaving their jobs ☐
7. poor rates of pay in the health service ☐
8. the government plans to privatise parts of the health care system ☐

Compare what you ticked with your partner.

Do you think the health service in your country sounds better or worse than the NHS? Why?

Have you ever had to go to a doctor in a foreign country? When? What happened?

> **Real English:** the NHS
>
> When we say the NHS, we stress each letter in the abbreviation.
> Do you know what the following abbreviations stand for? Practise saying them.
>
> the UN   the WHO   the BBC   the EU
> the US   the IMF   UFO   CV

2 | While you listen

You are going to listen to two friends. One of them is talking about some recent experiences at the doctor's. Cover the conversation below. As you listen, try to answer these questions. Then compare your notes with a partner.

1. What health problems does Ken mention?
2. How did the doctor deal with these problems?

Listen again and complete the gaps.

At the doctor's

Ken: It was a pint you wanted, (1) . . . . ?

David: Yeah, cheers. Do you want a cigarette?

Ken: Yeah, thanks. Oh, I need this.

David: Have you had a (2) . . . . or something?

Ken: Yeah, I've been really busy trying to catch up with work after last week.

David: Oh, yeah?

Ken: I was ill all last week. It was awful. I had this terrible flu. I couldn't sleep, I (3) . . . . all through the night, and I'd get up in the morning and my whole body would be stiff and aching. It was terrible. I thought I (4) . . . . die. Honestly, it was awful.

David: Yeah?

Ken: So I rang the doctor and he said he didn't have any (5) . . . . till this Tuesday, so I said, 'What good is that? I'll probably be better by then – or dead!' So he said, 'Well, you (6) . . . . see me, then,' and put the phone down. I couldn't believe it. Doctors these days are just so unhelpful.

David: Yeah.

Ken: You know, my mum ... she's seventy and the other day she was coming home from the shops and she slipped and fell over and when she woke up the following day, she had a really sore back. She could (7) . . . . She rang the doctor to ask him to come out, but he wouldn't, so then she had to go all the way to the surgery (8) . . . . Then, when she got there, she had to wait around for about an hour with all these really ill people coughing and sneezing and spreading their germs. When she finally saw the doctor, he (9) . . . . for about ten seconds and he just told her to go home and lie down for a few days. That was it! No pain-killers, no physiotherapy, nothing! And then (10) . . . . , he told her she should maybe lose some weight.

David: No!

Ken: Yeah! And then two days later, she got this nasty chest infection, which she probably picked up in the waiting room, so she went back and this time he just told her to (11) . . . . and drink lots of water. She wanted some kind of medicine, but he said it wouldn't work for some reason. I don't know! It seems as if we pay all these taxes so we can have a free service, but all we really get from them is advice about giving up smoking, getting more exercise, (12) . . . . fatty food and anything else which makes life worth living. Doctors? They treat you as if you're two years old!

David: I know ... do you want another cigarette?

Ken: Well ... I shouldn't really. I'm trying to give up. Oh, all right. Just one last one!

Do you think the doctors who spoke to Ken and his mum were right? Why/why not? Is your own experience of doctors positive or negative?

3 | So what did the doctor say?

Make sentences that give typical pieces of doctor's advice by matching the beginnings 1–10 to the endings a–j.

1. She just told me to drink
2. She told me to keep
3. He told me I'm going to have to have
4. He told me I should try to lose
5. She told me I really should stop
6. He told me to cut down on
7. He told me to make sure I get lots of
8. She gave me some painkillers
9. She gave me some ointment to rub
10. He just told me to go home and take it

a. an operation.
b. some weight.
c. smoking.
d. sleep.
e. for it.
f. lots of fluids.
g. on the rash.
h. the weight off my foot for a few days.
i. dairy products like cheese and butter and milk.
j. easy for a while.

What problems do you think the patients above had?

Now with a partner have similar conversations to the one below:

A: I've got this really bad backache.

B: Oh, no. Have you been to see anyone about it?

A: Yeah, I went to the doctor and he just told me to take it easy for a while and gave me some painkillers for it.

Using grammar

1 | Giving advice

Earlier in this unit you met this structure:
Maybe you should … .
Should is often used to give advice. Can you remember two other ways to give advice? Look back at page 60 to remind yourself.

In pairs, take turns reading out the problems 1–9 below and giving each other advice using the ideas in the box.

- buy a bike
- cut sugar out of your diet
- eat more slowly
- get a notebook and use it!
- get rid of them
- look for another flat
- look in the chemists for something
- tell him you'll report him to the Council
- try acupuncture

1. My landlord has just put my rent up to a hundred pounds a week.
2. I'd love to stop smoking, but I can't!
3. I keep getting terrible spots all over my face!
4. I'm getting fat! I've put on ten kilos since Christmas.
5. My flatmates are useless! They never do anything round the house!
6. I want to get fit. I've tried going to the gym, but I just find it so boring!
7. My landlord's useless! It takes forever to get him to fix anything!
8. I keep forgetting all the new words we've studied in class!
9. I don't know why, but I always burp a lot after dinner! It's so embarrassing!

Do this activity again, but this time think of your own advice. Take two minutes to prepare.

▶ For more information on giving advice, see G26.

Real English: burp

If you burp, you make a noise as you open your mouth to let air out from your stomach, after eating. Some cultures think this is rude, others do not. After making the noise, it is polite in English to say excuse me.

2 | Should, have to

We use should to tell people what we ourselves think is desirable – often to give advice. For example:

You should try to lose a bit of weight.

If we are talking about official advice, rules and regulations, we usually use have to **or** have got to – advice you can't ignore.

You have to apply for your passport months in advance.

You've got to enclose the £20 fee with your application.

Complete these sentences with should **or** have to/have got to.

1. Remember that if you want to see the doctor, you . . . . register with the surgery first.
2. That looks nasty! You . . . . get someone to have a look at that for you.
3. It's a really nice flat, but the landlord has told us we . . . . pay two months' deposit up front for it! There's no way we can afford that!
4. If you're serious about losing a bit of weight, maybe you . . . . cut out all the chips and the beer!
5. If you're going to work in Russia, I think you . . . . have a blood test first, before they'll give you a visa.
6. I . . . . go into hospital next week for an operation on my knee.
7. It's terrible if you get ill there, because you . . . . pay all the medical bills yourself.
8. If you want the doctor to see you today, I'm afraid you'll . . . . take a number and wait till it's called.
9. If you're interested in architecture, you . . . . go and have a look at the old church round the corner. It's amazing!

3 | *Should* for talking about the future

Should is often used to give people advice and to make suggestions, but it can also be used to talk about what you think the future will probably be like.

You should try that new Italian place that has just opened. It sounds great. (suggestion)

It should be finished by the end of the week. (future)

Which sentence in each pair gives advice/makes a suggestion and which talks about what the future will probably be like?

1. a. If you get the job, we should have a big party or something to celebrate.
   b. That party tomorrow should be good.
2. a. This shouldn't hurt. It should only take a second or two.
   b. If it's hurting, you should take it easy for a few minutes.
3. a. They should make lessons more interesting if they want us to come to them every day.
   b. That lecture tomorrow should be interesting. He's supposed to be a great speaker.
4. a. I've got to go to the optician's later, but it shouldn't take that long. I should be finished by nine.
   b. I really should go to the optician's. These new lenses really don't feel right.

4 | Matching

Make sentences by matching the beginnings 1–8 to the endings a–h.

1. There should be lots
2. It should only cost
3. They shouldn't take
4. It should be
5. It should only take me
6. There shouldn't be
7. You should have quite a good
8. It should be well worth

a. good.
b. a minute or so.
c. any problem with that.
d. that long.
e. chance.
f. of people there.
g. seeing.
h. ten pounds or so.

Now complete these conversations using the sentences above.

1. A: Will it be OK if we check out at one o'clock instead of twelve? It's just that our plane doesn't leave till four.
   B: I'll have to confirm it with my boss, but . . . .

2. A: That new French movie's out next week, isn't it?
   B: Yeah. It's had rave reviews, so I guess . . . .

3. A: I'm really looking forward to tomorrow night. It's ages since we've eaten out.
   B: I know. . . . . , shouldn't it?

4. A: I'm not sure I'm going to go tonight. I haven't got that much money left.
   B: Come on. We're going home the day after tomorrow. . . . . to get in and you don't have to spend any more money after that.

5. A: Are you ready yet?
   B: Nearly, I just need to make a really quick phone call. . . . .

6. A: It's Mike's leaving party tonight, isn't it?
   B: Yeah, I'm looking forward to it, actually. . . . .

7. A: Do you think it's worth me taking the exam?
   B: Yeah, why not? You've been working really hard this term, so . . . . of passing.

8. A: The doctor will see you in a few minutes.
   B: Thanks.
   A: He'll just need you to fill in these forms first. There's only a couple to do, so . . . .

5 | Pronunciation: sentence stress

Match the comments 1–6 to the responses a–f.

1. This is going to cost us a fortune.
2. It's going to be in the nineties in Egypt, I'm sure.
3. It's going to be well below zero by the time we land in Finland.
4. I'm terrified of injections! It's really going to hurt.
5. That meeting's going to be awful!
6. It's going to take hours.

a. It shouldn't be <u>that</u> painful.
b. No. It shouldn't be <u>that</u> expensive.
c. No. It shouldn't be <u>that</u> cold.
d. No. It shouldn't be <u>that</u> hot.
e. No. It shouldn't take <u>that</u> long.
f. No. It shouldn't be <u>that</u> bad.

🎧 **Now listen and check your answers. Then practise reading out the conversations with a partner. Pay particular attention to the stress in the responses.**

Review: Units 17-20

1 | Grammar review

Choose the correct form.

1. I've known him / I met him since I was a child.
2. He mustn't / can't be more than fifty. He hasn't got a grey hair on his head.
3. I'm used to / I used to play the recorder when I was a kid, but I was useless, so I gave it up.
4. I never used to / I not used to drink coffee before I went to live in Spain.
5. Sorry I missed the party. I would've come / I had come, but I finished work late.
6. It would've been easier if I would've done / I'd done it myself.
7. The doctor told me that I take / to take it easy for a few days.
8. You look terrible. Maybe you have to / you should go to the doctor's.
9. It's OK. I just need to take an aspirin and then I'm / I'll be all right.
10. I need to make a phone call. It shouldn't / It should take too long.

Compare your answers with a partner and explain your choices.

2 | Word order

Rewrite each sentence, putting the word in brackets in the most natural spot.

1. Do you believe that? (honestly)

   ....

2. Listen, we're never going to agree. (obviously)

   ....

3. Let's agree to disagree. (just)

   ....

4. I need an aspirin or something. (just)

   ....

5. He wants to know where I am. I hate it. (always)

   ....

6. Oh, come on! Because you're English, it doesn't mean you have to be cold and distant. (just)

   ....

7. He can't be more than about twenty-one. He's in his second year at university. (still)

   ....

8. He's a nice guy, but I'd go out with him. (never)

   ....

3 | What's the missing word?

Complete the texts with one word in each space.

1. When I was younger, I (a) .... to go running a lot. I (b) .... most Sundays and I (c) .... sometimes go in the week (d) .... well, but then I injured (e) .... back playing football and I had to (f) .... an operation. After that, I never went again.

2. I went to see that Robert de Niro film (a) .... came out on video recently. It (b) .... really disappointing. He was awful. He used to (c) .... so good. I'd always (d) .... and see his films as soon (e) .... they were on at the cinema, (f) .... now I don't bother.

3. My mum had an accident the (a) .... day. She was coming home from the shops (b) .... it was still a bit icy. She slipped and (c) .... over. She thought she was OK, but when she woke up the (d) .... morning, she (e) .... a really sore back.

4. I want someone (a) .... likes clothes. I work in the fashion (b) .... in Milan, so the way someone dresses is really important to me. I (c) .... never go out with someone (d) .... didn't care about the (e) .... they looked. I (f) .... to like really good-looking men, but I've changed my (g) .... about that, because they (h) .... to be so big-headed!

4 | Look back and check

Look back at Exercise 1 on page 132. Tick all the words and expressions you can remember. Ask your partner about anything you have forgotten.

With a partner, do Exercise 2 on page 134 again. Try to use as much of the language that you remember as possible.

Can you use any of the vocabulary from this page to talk about recent crimes?

5 Verb collocations

Match the verbs 1–10 to the groups of words and phrases they collocate with a–j.

1. ask ▢
2. get back ▢
3. make ▢
4. get ▢
5. go ▢
6. have ▢
7. leave ▢
8. raise ▢
9. take ▢
10. get rid of ▢

a. contacts / a big profit
b. your husband for another man / school
c. money for charity / taxes
d. them to court / a day off
e. her out on a date / someone to help
f. my words mixed up / what I deserve
g. out of habit / on the rampage
h. hiccups / my old car somehow
i. together with her ex / from work late
j. my bag snatched / my car stolen

You have one minute to memorise the collocations a–j. Now cover the exercise above. Your partner will read out the verbs 1–10. How many collocations can you remember?

With a partner, try to think of one more common collocation for each of the verbs 1–10.

6 Adjectives

Complete the sentences below with the adjectives in the box.

commercial	exact	nasty	snobbish	two-faced
dull	harsh	slight	sporty	typical

1. A: I'm sorry I didn't make it to the meeting yesterday.
    B: Don't worry. You didn't miss much. It was very .... and it went on far too long.

2. Don't come too near me. I've got this really .... cold. I don't want you to catch it.

3. A: Didn't you think it was a bit .... getting ten years for that. I mean, she didn't kill anyone.
    B: No, not really. I think she got what she deserved.

4. Isn't Belinda here yet? ....! She's always late.

5. You can tell he's from abroad, because he's got a .... accent. It's not very noticeable, though.

6. I don't really like boy bands and that kind of music. It's too .... They're only interested in making money.

7. I don't really trust him. He can be really .... He'll smile and laugh with people one moment and then he'll complain about them when they're gone.

8. Honestly, his wife's the .... opposite to him. She doesn't say a word and he never shuts up.

9. I have to admit, I'm not a very .... person. The only exercise I do is pick up the TV remote control!

10. I have to say, some English people are incredibly .... They won't say 'Hello' to you if you didn't go to the right public school or if you don't have the right kind of job.

7 Questions and answers

Match the questions 1–10 to the answers a–j.

1. What do you think of her? ▢
2. What was that club you went to on Friday like? ▢
3. What did you do in the class I missed? ▢
4. What was the name of that hotel you stayed in in London? ▢
5. Do you know what you call that thing? It's like a cupboard and you keep papers in it. ▢
6. Were you any good? ▢
7. Why did you give up? ▢
8. What's your sister like? Do you get on? ▢
9. Have you been to the doctor's? ▢
10. What's the population of your city? ▢

a. Yeah, much better than we used to. She's much less moody now and generally more out-going.
b. Yeah, I used to play in the school team. I was the captain, actually.
c. She's nice, but I don't fancy her or anything.
d. Yeah, I know what you mean, but I can't remember the word off the top of my head.
e. Yeah, she gave me some antibiotics, but they don't seem to be doing much good.
f. I don't know exactly, but it's well over five million.
g. I've forgotten for the moment. It was 'The Majesty' or something like that.
h. I can't remember! I've got a handout for you somewhere, though.
i. It was OK, I suppose, but the music was pretty awful.
j. I injured my leg in a car accident and I couldn't really play to the same standard afterwards.

8 | What can you remember?

With a partner, note down as much as you can remember about the texts you read in Units 17 and 19.

What's your type?

Rich and famous or rich and dangerous?

Now compare what you remember with another pair of students. Who remembered more? Which text did you enjoy more? Why?

9 | Common expressions

Complete these sentences with the words in the box.

ask	die	lightly	police	sees
court	not	eventually	say	wrong

1. He got off . . . .
2. Don't . . . . me why!
3. I thought I was going to . . . .
4. He took them to . . . . for unfair dismissal.
5. I don't know what she . . . . in him.
6. I guess he'll grow out of it . . . .
7. I'm the . . . . person to ask, really.

8. He's . . . . exactly the most intelligent man in the world.
9. You should report it to the . . . .
10. How can you . . . . that!

Discuss these questions with a partner.

11. Can you think of any criminals who got off lightly?
12. Have you ever thought you were going to die? When? What happened?
13. Do you know anybody who's not exactly the most intelligent person in the world?
14. Do you know anybody who's ever taken anyone to court? Why? What happened?

10 | Revision quiz

Discuss these questions in groups of three.

1. What's the difference between a half-brother and a stepbrother?
2. Is a niece a boy or a girl?
3. What might a couple do if they're getting serious?
4. Does a slob do lots of exercise?
5. What do you do if you're very fashion-conscious?
6. What could you have pierced?
7. What do you usually see in a parade?
8. Is it polite to swear a lot?
9. When do you need a lingua franca?
10. Are stereotypes true?
11. What do vandals do?
12. What can you do to get rid of hiccups?
13. What do robbers raid?
14. Can you think of three ways you could be murdered?
15. Why would you need stitches?
16. Can you think of three things you can have at the dentist's?
17. If nurses are underpaid, can other jobs be overpaid?
18. What do you usually put on a rash?
19. Can you think of five things you might celebrate?
20. Is 'gorgeous' usually used to describe men or women?

Learner advice: Recording and revising vocabulary

One creative way of trying to remember words is to try and associate them with things. Check with a partner that you understand the language below. Then discuss which country or place you most associate each item with. For example, maybe you could associate *She moved away when I was young* **with Australia because a friend of yours moved there when you were young. Or perhaps you could associate** *give you an injection* **with a clinic near your home. Spend five minutes making your decisions. Then explain your associations to your partner.**

She moved away when I was young. ....

He's so big-headed. He's always showing off. ....

He's quite chatty once you get to know him. ....

I've fancied her for ages. ....

There was a huge economic boom. ....

outrageous costumes ....

It was a bit of a dump. ....

a lingua franca ....

one of the most conservative places I've ever
    stayed in ....

a very remote area ....

an island off the west coast ....

He was found guilty of vandalism. ....

It was a harsh sentence. ....

I don't know the first thing about it. ....

go on the rampage ....

If I'd known, I wouldn't have bothered. ....

I managed to get stuck in the lift. ....

It dries my skin out. ....

He's so out of shape. ....

give you an injection ....

It's a health risk. ....

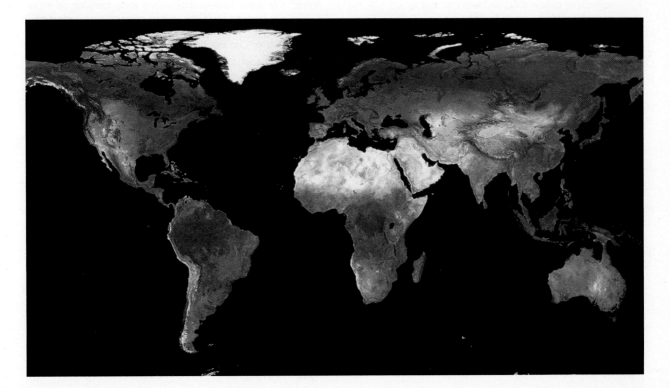

Tapescript

Unit 1

Listening (page 9)

Jack:	Do you mind if I join you?
Lisa:	No, of course not. Go ahead.
Jack:	I'm Jack.
Lisa:	Lisa. Hi.
Jack:	So, were you here last term?
Lisa:	No, it's my first time here. What about you?
Jack:	No, I started in September.
Lisa:	Oh, right. Do you live near here?
Jack:	Yeah, in Highbury.
Lisa:	Oh, yeah. Whereabouts exactly?
Jack:	Saints Road. It's just off Gillespie Road, near the big supermarket.
Lisa:	Yeah, I know it. I live in Old Street.
Jack:	Right. You're not from here originally, though, are you?
Lisa:	No, I was brought up in Scotland, but I've lived down here for about ten years now.
Jack:	Right, right. I was going to say, I thought I could hear your accent. It's not very strong, though.
Lisa:	I know. I've lost most of it.
Jack:	So what do you do?
Lisa:	I'm a teacher. I work at St Philip's, the school down the road.
Jack:	St Philip's! I used to go there!
Lisa:	Really!
Jack:	Yeah. Is it still as bad as I remember it being?
Lisa:	I don't know. I think it's all right.
Jack:	I hated it. I left when I was sixteen.
Lisa:	Oh, right. What do you do now, then?
Jack:	Nothing much. I work in Safeway's stacking shelves. I hate it. That's why I'm here. I want to get out and do something different. Go and work in Italy or something. Maybe teach English even.
Lisa:	Good idea.
Jack:	What about you? Why do you want to learn Italian?
Lisa:	Oh, my boyfriend's Italian.
Jack:	Yeah? What do you need to come to class for? He should teach you.
Lisa:	Yeah, maybe. It's a bit difficult, though, because he speaks English really well and he gets frustrated listening to me when I speak Italian.

A quick quiz (page 11)

accent   coast   design   whereabouts

Unit 2

Follow-up questions (page 15)

1. A: What did you do last night?
    B: I went to the gym.
    A: Oh, I didn't know you did that. How often do you do that, then?

B: Quite a bit. About two or three times a week, I suppose.

2. A: What did you do last night?
    B: Oh, I went to my yoga class.
    A: I didn't know you did that. How long have you been doing that, then?
    B: For quite a while now. It's really good.

3. A: What did you do last night?
    B: I went for a swim.
    A: Oh, really? Where do you do that, then?
    B: At the new Olympic pool down in New Market.

4. A: What did you do last night?
    B: I went to the Arsenal–Liverpool game.
    A: Oh, wow! Was it very expensive?
    B: Yeah, quite. It cost us about twenty-five pounds a ticket.

5. A: So what did you do last night?
    B: I went to a friend's house and we just played PlayStation all night.
    A: Oh, really? I love PlayStation. Are you any good?
    B: Not very, but I enjoy it anyway.

6. A: What did you do last night?
    B: I went out to the cinema to see *The Black Hand*.
    A: Oh, I'd like to see that. Was it any good?
    B: Oh, it was all right.

Unit 3

Summer holidays (page 22)

Rose:	Are you going away this summer?
Steve:	Yes, we're going to Portugal.
Rose:	Oh, really? Whereabouts?
Steve:	We're not sure exactly. We're going camping, so we've just booked the flight. We're going to rent a car when we get there. I suppose we'll probably go north of Lisbon – up the coast.
Rose:	That sounds great. It's supposed to be lovely there. Have you ever been there before?
Steve:	No, but my girlfriend's wanted to go for ages, so we thought we'd give it a try. What about you? Are you doing anything special?
Rose:	We haven't really decided yet. There's some really cheap offers to Ibiza at the moment. Or we might just go to Cornwall again.
Steve:	Oh, yes, Cornwall. It's really nice down there. We went a few years ago and had a great time.
Rose:	We rented a cottage for a week last year. But you never know what the weather's going to be like, do you?
Steve:	No, I suppose not. But Ibiza? Really? Are you serious?
Rose:	Well, maybe. Why? Have you ever been there?
Steve:	No, but I've never really wanted to go, to be honest. It just sounds awful, from what I've heard. It's supposed to be full of British tourists getting sunburnt and drunk.
Rose:	Yes, I know, but at least we'd get some sun, and it's not all like that. A friend of ours went last year and said there were lots of places where you can get away from all the clubbers.
Steve:	Oh, right.

Rose: And there are package holidays there for a hundred and fifty pounds for a week. And it's really cheap when you get there.

Steve: Oh, well, it might be worth a try, then.

Unit 4

Two uses of the present continuous
(page 30)

Lauren: Hi, it's Ben, isn't it? How's it going?

Ben: Oh, hello. Yeah, not too bad, thanks. How're you?

Lauren: Oh, all right, I suppose. So what're you doing here? Are you doing some shopping or something?

Ben: Yeah, I am. What about you?

Lauren : Oh, I'm just having a wander around, you know. There's not much you can do with all this rain, is there?

Ben: Oh, I know. It's awful.

Lauren: Yeah. I'm really fed up with it! I mean, it rained all day yesterday, we couldn't do anything.

Ben: Yeah.

Lauren: I came here to get some sun. You know, lie on the beach and take it easy, not sit around all day inside. I could've done that at home in England. I mean, we went out to the market the day before yesterday, but we just got soaked.

Ben: Yeah, I know what you mean. Anyway, listen, I've got to go. My wife's waiting for me. We're actually going to the market now.

Lauren: I'd give it a miss, if I were you. It's not very good.

Ben: Well, anyway, I'll see you.

Unit 5

What do you do? (page 36)

1. I work as a painter and decorator. I'm self-employed.
2. I'm a student at the moment, but I'd like to work for a big publishing company as a graphic designer when I graduate.
3. I work for a small clothes company as a designer.
4. I'm a housewife now, but I used to work in a bank as a cashier.
5. I work part-time in a local hospital as a nurse.
6. I'm a student, but I work part-time in a restaurant as a waitress.
7. I work part-time in a local school as a teacher.
8. I'm unemployed at the moment, but I used to work for a dotcom company as a computer programmer.

So, what do you do? (page 40)

Ken: So, what do you do, Maria?

Maria: Oh, I'm a drugs worker.

Ken: Right, so what does that involve? Do you work in a rehabilitation centre or what?

Maria: No, no. I work in an area of Bristol where there are a lot of drug addicts. We go out in a van and give out clean needles, food and things like that. We also give them information about how to stay healthy, or give them help if they need to see a doctor.

Ken: So you don't try to make them stop?

Maria: No, not if they don't want to. If we tried to make them stop, they wouldn't want to know us. I mean, if they want to stop, sure, we help them find a place in a rehabilitation centre, but we don't try to persuade them or anything. We try not to make judgements.

Ken: Not at all? So what's the point? Aren't you making things worse? You know, encouraging them to take more drugs?

Maria: No, I don't think so. You can't really persuade them. They have to want to give up. What we do is make sure they stay as healthy as possible so they don't spread diseases like AIDS and they don't leave dirty needles lying around.

Ken: Mm, maybe. You must get a bit depressed, though, seeing all those people wasting their lives.

Maria: Yeah, I do sometimes, but it can also be very rewarding when you help people sort out a problem. And the money's quite good as well.

Ken: So you like it, then?

Maria: Yeah, it's OK. There's lots of good things about it. I mean, I work in the afternoons and evenings, so I don't have to get up early, and the people I work with are really nice, so you know . . .

Ken: Well, that's the main thing, isn't it?

Maria: What do you do, then?

Ken: Oh, I work for Barclays Bank.

Maria: Doing what?

Ken: Buying and selling currency.

Maria: Yeah? I have to say, that sounds a bit boring.

Ken: It can be, and I have to work really long hours, but then again, the money's really good.

Maria: Mm, right.

Ken: And I get to travel quite a lot. We've got an office in New York that I go to every month.

Maria: That must be good.

Ken: Yeah, it is.

Unit 7

While you listen (page 48)

Ed: So, how was York, then?

Gill: Oh, it was good. We had a great weekend. It's a brilliant place to spend a few days. It's a shame about the hotel, though!

Ed: Why? I thought you said you were going to be staying in the best place in town.

Gill: Well, that's what the brochure said, yeah. And when we first got there, everything was great. The staff at check-in were lovely – really efficient. And our rooms were amazing – absolutely spotless.

Ed: So what was wrong with the place, then?

Gill: Well, before we went out for dinner on the Friday night, I wanted to have a shower. The trouble was, I hadn't brought any soap or shampoo or anything like that – and there were no free toiletries at all. Can you believe it? I thought that was standard in every hotel now. Anyway, I rang Reception and they said that the maid would bring me some up. Well, I waited for forty-five minutes and nothing arrived, and then, when I rang to ask what had happened to her, they told me she'd gone home! I couldn't believe it. In the end, I just decided to do without the shower and went out smelling a bit sweaty, which wasn't exactly romantic!

Ed: That all seems a bit odd. So, did you manage to get some toiletries the next day, then?

Gill: Yeah, but I had to go and buy them myself in town. And then, the next morning, after breakfast in bed, which was nice, when I'd finally had my shower, I noticed there was something funny about the towels.

Ed: Don't tell me! They were dirty?

Gill: Exactly! They hadn't been changed since the person before.

Ed: But that's disgusting! So did you complain about it?

Gill: Oh, yes – and I must say, they were very apologetic. I actually ended up feeling sorry for the boy on the desk. I got pretty angry with him!

Ed: So, apart from a couple of hiccups, then, was everything else all right?

Gill: Well, yes and no. We couldn't believe how cheap the bar was – almost half the price things are down in this part of the world – and the barman was fantastic – a really, really nice guy!

Ed: So what are you complaining about?

Gill: Well, we decided to eat in on the Saturday. They had this special Saturday dinner menu, and it looked very reasonable. There wasn't a huge choice or anything, but it all looked quite interesting. Anyway, I had the salmon and Veronica had the steak. Well, you should have seen it when it came. She asked for it well done, but when it arrived, it was absolutely swimming in blood! She couldn't touch it. I thought she was going to be sick. So I called the waiter over and he took it away.

Ed: And brought it back well done?

Gill: Well, you could say that! It wasn't exactly well done. It was more well burnt! It was totally inedible – it was shocking, actually. I've never seen anything like it.

Ed: So did Veronica complain?

Gill: Well, that's the trouble. She did. And do you know what happened? The chef himself came out of the kitchen and told her she was ignorant and said he was wasting his time cooking for someone who didn't appreciate good food. Well, by this time, poor Veronica was in tears. All her make-up was running down her face and everything. It was awful! We just had to get out of there and escape.

Ed: So I take it you won't be going back again, then?

Gill: Too right! It's sad, really, though, because it *was* a lovely place. But there's no way it was worth £80 a night, what with all that hassle!

Problems (page 53)

1.
Waiter: Is everything all right, sir?
You: I'm afraid there's a fly in my soup.
Waiter: Oh, you're right. Is it dead?
You: I don't care if it's dead or alive. Just take it away, please, and bring me some more – but without a fly!
Waiter: I'm very sorry, sir.

2.
Assistant: Thank you. 1p change.
You: I'm sorry, but I think I gave you a £20 note.
Assistant: No, I think it was a ten pound note.
You: I'm sorry, but I think if you check, you'll see it was a twenty.
Assistant: You're absolutely right. Sorry about that. There you are.
You: That's quite all right. Thank you.

3.
Assistant: That's £49.99, sir.
You: Wait a minute. Did you say £49? The label says £29.99.
Assistant: Mm. Let me see. You're absolutely right, but my screen says it's £49.99. There must be a mistake. Just a moment. I'll check . . . Yes, you're right. I'm very sorry.

Unit 8

While you listen (page 58)

Paul: Come in, come in. You can leave your bags in the hall for the moment. Take your coat off. Just hang it up on the back of the door there.

Angela: Paul, why don't you take it? Honestly, he can be so rude sometimes. Hello. Nice to meet you at last. I'm Angela.

Au pair: Hello.

Angela: Did you have a good journey? I was starting to get a bit worried about you.

Au pair: It was OK, but the plane was … what did you say, Paul?

Paul: Yeah, I think she had a bit of a bumpy flight from the sounds of things. It was almost an hour late getting in. A storm or something.

Angela: Oh, poor you. Sit down. You must be exhausted.

Au pair: Sorry?

Angela: You must be very tired.

Au pair: Yes, yes.

Angela: Can I get you something to eat?

Au pair: No, thank you. I had something to eat on the plane. I'm just tired.

Angela: Yes. I'm sure. The children wanted to stay up to meet you, but they've got school tomorrow.

Paul: Do you want me to show you round the house now or shall we do it in the morning?

Au pair: No, I'm very tired, so maybe …

Paul: So, we'll show you where everything is tomorrow?

Au pair: Is it OK if I just go to bed?

Angela: Yes, yes of course. It is very late. I need to get to bed myself. Paul, do you think you could take her bags up?

Paul: Yeah, of course.

Au pair: Thanks. Goodnight.

Angela: Yes. Sleep well. By the way, have you got an alarm clock? The children really do need to have their breakfast by seven thirty.

Au pair: Seven thirty?

Angela: Do you want me to get you up tomorrow? Maybe that'll be easier as it's your first day.

Au pair: I . . . er . . . yes.

Unit 9

Recommending a website (page 64)

Simon: Are you booking your summer holiday already, then?

Pete: Oh, hello, Simon. I didn't see you there. No, no. It's Karen's birthday in a few weeks' time and I was thinking of taking her away somewhere for the weekend. There's not much on offer, though.

Simon: Well, have you got access to the Internet?

Pete: Yeah, well, we're connected at work.

Simon: Right. Well, why don't you try that? You can sometimes get some really good last-minute deals online.

Pete: To be honest, I've never really had much luck buying things on the Internet. The other day, I tried to book some train tickets on Ticketline.com, but it was just so complicated. It took so long! In the end, I just gave up and did it over the phone.

Simon: Yes, I know what you mean. That site's not very user-friendly. Have you tried any of the cheap airline sites, though?

Pete: No, never.

Simon: Well, if I were you, I'd try some of them. I've booked lots of flights online and it's always been really easy. I've never had any problems and it's usually cheaper than going to a travel agent's. You usually get a discount for online booking.

Pete: So, which ones are the best?

Simon: Well, it depends where you want to go. You could try British Airways first. They're sometimes just as cheap as the budget airlines. Their address is BA.com. And the other one I've used quite a lot is easyJet.com, but they don't fly to as many places as BA.

Pete: Right, that sounds much better than standing here in the pouring rain. Thanks.

Simon: Well, if you want any more help, why don't you e-mail me. It's spencersimon@shotmail.com.

Pete: Thanks. Hey, while we're talking about it, actually, do you know any good sites for buying CDs? When Karen and I first met, there was a song called 'You've been gone too long' playing in the bar and I thought it would be really nice to try to get it for her birthday.

Simon: Very romantic!

Pete: Yeah, well, I do my best. The only problem is I'm not sure who it's by and I've never seen it in any record shop.

Simon: I'm not sure. You could try looking at dustygroove.com. My brother's always talking about them. Otherwise, if I were you, I'd go to one of those music chat sites and see if anyone there can help you.

Pete: Right, OK.

E-mails and website addresses (page 65)

7. lemongrass2272@shotmail.com
8. nsgo7891@shotmail.com
9. www.jazzman/CDs.co.uk
10. dellerh@wmin.ac.uk

Unit 10

Rachel's birthday (page 72)

Jamie: Well, Rachel, happy birthday!

Martin: Yeah, happy birthday, Rachel!

Rachel: Oh, flowers! They're lovely! Thanks. I'll just go and put them in some water.

Jamie: So, what would you like to do tonight, then?

Rachel: To be honest, I haven't really decided yet. I've been so busy all day I haven't really thought about it. What do you fancy doing?

Jamie: I'm easy. It's up to you, really. It is your birthday, after all.

Rachel: I know, but I hate making decisions.

Martin: How about going to see that musical which is on at the King's?

Rachel: We could do, I suppose.

Jamie: Oh, no, that's supposed to be awful. A friend of mine went and she left halfway through.

Martin: Oh, right. OK, well, how about Ben's cafe? They do jazz on a Wednesday.

Rachel: Yeah, we could do Ben's if you want.

Jamie: Oh, Ben's! Please, no! The food in that place is so expensive, and you only get tiny little portions. Anyway, I hate jazz. I'd rather go somewhere else, if we can.

Martin: Yeah, well, it's not your birthday! Anyway, I thought you said you weren't bothered what we did.

Rachel: No, it's all right if Jamie would prefer to do something else. Listen, I've had an idea, do you fancy going bowling? There's that bowling place in Moortown.

Jamie: Oh, yeah! I know the one. I've been there before. It's really good.

Martin: Yeah, sounds fine.

Rachel: OK, great. Let's do that, then.

Jamie: What time do you want to go, then? Seven? Seven thirty?

Rachel: Can we make it eight? I want to have a bath, get changed and just chill out for a bit first.

Jamie: Yeah, sure.

Martin: Whatever. I'm easy. Listen, though, I told Stella and Mike we might be doing something later.

Rachel: Oh right, great. Do you want to give them a ring and tell them what we're doing?

Martin: Yeah. Where shall I tell them to meet us?

Rachel: You know where it is, don't you?

Martin: Yeah, I think so. It's just near the station, isn't it? On Otley Road.

Rachel: Yeah, that's it. Well, we'll meet them there – just inside the entrance, in the foyer.

Martin: OK. By the way, do you think we'll have to book the lanes?

Rachel: I don't know. I've never actually been there. Do you know, Jamie?

Jamie: I think we should be OK. It's the middle of the week. I doubt it'll be that busy.

Unit 11

Comparatives and superlatives (page 78)

A: When do you want to eat, then?

B: The sooner, the better. I'm starving. Where were you thinking of going? Did you have anywhere special in mind?

A: Well, I was thinking of this place just round the corner, actually. It's one of the best places to eat in town, but it depends on how much you want to spend. It *is* quite expensive.

B: Well, I'm a bit short of money at the moment, so the cheaper, the better, to be honest.

A: OK, well, in that case, there's a nice little café on the other side of town we could go to, but we will have to get a bus.

B: Is that going to take a long time?

A: No, it shouldn't be too bad. There's a bus that goes straight there now, almost non-stop. It's much better than it used to be. You used to have to go a really roundabout way.

B: OK, so shall we go, then?

A: Yeah. Let me just get my things together and then we'll be off.

Listening (page 80)

Journey 1

A: Jimmie! Jimmie!

B: Oh, there you are. Hi. How are you?

A: Fine, fine. How're you? How was your journey?

B: Terrible! Really, it was just awful!

A: Really? Because you're here on time.

B: Yeah, well, that wasn't the problem. It's actually quite a fast line. No, the thing was, it was just so crowded that I had to stand up all the way here.

A: Oh, no. poor you. That's two hours, isn't it?

B: Two and a half actually, and it felt like much longer because I was stuck next to about seventy football fans all smoking and drinking and shouting at everyone who walked past. It was horrible.

A: Oh, no. That must've been the big game that was on in Coventry today.

B: Yeah, maybe. I didn't really ask them too much about which club they supported!

Journey 2

A: Oh, there you are! I was starting to get worried about you! I thought you might've missed the flight or something. How are you? Come in. Come in.

B: No, no. We caught the flight OK, it was just that it was delayed by about two hours before take-off because of the weather.

A: Oh, dear! Was it a bit of a bumpy flight, then?

B: Yeah, it was awful! I really thought we were going to crash at one point.

A: Oh no. I must say, I hate flying at the best of times, let alone when it gets like that.

B: I know! Anyway, we got here in one piece, but then they managed to lose one of our bags somehow, so we had to wait around for an hour or so while they tried to locate it.

A: And did they find it?

B: Yeah – on board a flight to Peru! They're not going to be able to return it until Tuesday or Wednesday, they said!

A: What a pain! So how did you get from Gatwick to here? Did you get the train?

B: No, we were so tired and fed up once we got in that we decided to take a cab. It was fifty pounds. Does that sound about right?

A: Fifty pounds?! That's twice the price it should've been, I'm afraid. I hope you got their number.

Unit 12

Different food (page 82)

1. It's a kind of vegetable. It looks a bit like a strange green flower or something like that. You take off the outside leaves and boil the inside leaves until they're soft. I usually dip them in a little bit of sauce – just oil and lemon and garlic.

2. It's a kind of fruit. It's very common in south-east Asia – and very popular too. It looks really strange. It's got a really strong smell and quite a strange texture. My mum said it's like eating a pillow or a cushion or something!

3. It's a traditional Turkish meat dish, but you also get it in Greece, in Iran, all over the place, really. You use fresh lamb and grill it and then serve it either on its own or in this kind of flat bread, with a bit of salad.

4. It's a kind of traditional Spanish seafood dish. Well, I suppose really it's a *rice* and seafood dish. You have to use a special kind of rice and you add different kinds of fish and shellfish and things. It's delicious. Most areas in Spain have their own special way of cooking it.

5. It's a kind of a salad. You can have it as a side dish or just on its own – in the summer. It's basically just mushrooms and radish and whatever kind of green leaves you've got available.

6. It's a kind of dessert. It's eaten all over the Middle East. It's a bit like a little cake or something. It's covered in pastry and it's filled with nuts and honey. It's quite fattening, I suppose, but it's really delicious.

7. It's a kind of cake. My mum used to make it all the time when I was growing up. She used to put rum or brandy in it, so it was quite rich, quite heavy. You couldn't really eat more than one slice of it.

8. It's a traditional Middle Eastern starter or side dish. It's made from crushed chickpeas and you mix that with a bit of lemon. You dip pitta bread into it. It's really nice.

9. It's a kind of traditional soup. You usually put a lot of beans in it – and then maybe some carrots or whatever other kind of vegetables you have available. It's very filling. It's great in the winter.

Listening (page 86)

Cathy: Do you want any more of this chicken?

Steve: No, honestly, I'm full. Finish it off.

Cathy: Are you sure? You don't seem to have eaten much. Have you tried the fish?

Steve: Yeah, but to be honest, it was a bit too hot for my liking.

Cathy: Oh, sorry.

Steve: Don't worry about it.

Cathy: Well, what did you think of the vegetable dish? That was lovely.

Steve: Yeah, it was OK. A bit too greasy for my liking, but it was OK.

Cathy: Oh, dear, I'm sorry, we should've gone somewhere else.

Steve: No, no. The rest of it was lovely.

Cathy: But we only had rice apart from that.

Steve: There was the soup as well.

Cathy: It's just a shame you spilt most of it when you got up to go to the toilet.

Steve: Yes, sorry about that. I'm sure the stain will wash out.

Cathy: Hopefully. Don't worry. These things happen. But you should've asked for some more. You must still be hungry.

Steve: Honestly, I'm fine. I couldn't eat another thing. Shall we get the bill?

Cathy: I suppose so.

Steve: Excuse me. Excuse me, could we have the bill?

Waiter: Of course, sir. Was everything all right?

Steve: Yes, it was lovely.

Cathy: How much is it?

Steve: Forty pounds.

Cathy: Forty pounds? That can't be right.

Steve: I know, what does that say? Is that a D or an A?

Cathy: Yeah, I think it's a D. They've charged us for the D menu instead of the A. It's almost five pounds more expensive.

Steve: Excuse me … excuse me …

Waiter: Yes, sir?

Steve: I'm sorry, but I think you've got the bill wrong. You've charged us for D menu but we had menu A.

Waiter: I'm sorry, one moment. I'm sorry, you're absolutely right. That should be thirty-one pounds, not forty.

Steve: That's OK. These things happen. Cathy, shall I pay for this on my card and you can pay me back later?

Waiter: I'm sorry sir, we don't take credit cards. Cheques or cash only.

Steve: You're joking. Have you got any cash?

Cathy: Only about ten pounds.

Steve: Oh, no! Is there a cash machine near here?

Waiter: Yes, there's one just down the road outside the supermarket.

Steve: Right, do you want to wait here and I'll go and get some cash out.

Cathy: Yeah. I guess I'll have to.

Steve: I'm really sorry about this.

Waiter: That's OK. These things happen.

Steve: I'll be back in a moment.

Waiter: Has sir returned?

Cathy: No, not yet. I'm sure he'll be back. I can't imagine where he's gone.

Waiter: He has been gone half an hour.

Practice (page 86)

1. A: Mum, I'm hungry
   B: Well, you should've eaten more at dinner.
2. A: Mum, I need to go to the toilet.
   B: You should've gone before we came out.

3. A: I'm cold, mum.
   B: Well, you should've brought a coat!
4. A: I can't eat this. I'm allergic to eggs.
   B: You should've told me before! I could've cooked something else.
5. A: Actually, it's my birthday today.
   B: Really! You should've said. We could've done something special.
6. A: I just stayed in last night and watched TV.
   B: You should've come to the party. It was great fun.

Unit 13

Recommending (page 92)

1. A: I was thinking of trying some of the local food. Can you recommend anywhere?
   B: Well, you could try Agut. It's a great restaurant near the port. They do great fish.

2. A: I was thinking of buying a few souvenirs. Can you recommend anywhere?
   B: Well, you could try Jalan Surabaya. It's a big long street market in town. You can find some real bargains.

3. A: I was thinking of going to an art gallery. Can you recommend anywhere?
   B: Well, you could try the National Portrait Gallery. It's got some beautiful paintings and photos.

4. A: I was thinking of going out to see a show or something tonight. Can you recommend anywhere?
   B: Well, you could try one of the theatres off Broadway. They have some great plays on there sometimes.

5. A: I was thinking of going to have a look round a museum or somewhere like that. Can you recommend anywhere?
   B: Well, you could try the British Museum. It's got a great collection of ancient artefacts.

6. A: I was thinking of maybe getting a bit of exercise later. Can you recommend anywhere?
   B: Well, you could try Shinjuku park. It's a nice place for a jog.

7. A: I was thinking of doing a bit of sightseeing. Can you recommend anywhere?
   B: Well, you could go up to the big Buddhist temple. It's beautiful. It dates back to the tenth century.

8. A: I was thinking of taking the children somewhere. Can you recommend anywhere?
   B: Well, you could try Parc Asterix, just outside the city. It's a really fun theme park.

What's it like? (page 93)

1. A: Have you been to that club in the centre of town?
   B: No, why? What's it like?
   A: It's a bit of a rip-off, actually. It's ten pounds to get in and then all the drinks are four or five pounds each! I'd give it a miss if I were you.
   B: Oh, right. Thanks for letting me know.

2. A: Have you been to that new Portuguese restaurant in the Old Town yet?
   B: No, why? What's it like?
   A: Oh, it's great. It's the best place to eat in town. They do great seafood. It's well worth a visit.
   B: Oh, right. Thanks for telling me. I'll give it a try when I get the chance.

3. A: Have you been to that amusement arcade on the sea front?
    B: No, why? What's it like?
    A: It's a bit of a tourist trap, to be honest. It's full of holidaymakers wasting all their money. I'd give it a miss if I were you.
    B: Oh, right. Thanks for letting me know.

4. A: Have you been to that fast food place just round the corner from here?
    B: No, why? What's it like?
    A: It's a really horrible place. The food's disgusting and the service is awful. I'd give it a miss if I were you.
    B: Oh, right. Thanks for letting me know.

5. A: Have you been to Summertown yet, where Louis lives?
    B: No, why? What's it like?
    A: To be honest, it's a bit of a rough area. There was a shooting there last week. I'd give it a miss if I were you.
    B: Oh, right. Thanks for letting me know.

6. A: Have you been to that street market that they have every Saturday?
    B: No, why? What's it like?
    A: Oh, it's great. You can pick up some real bargains there. I got this bag there for only eight pounds. It's well worth a visit.
    B: Oh, right. Thanks for telling me. I'll go down there when I get the chance.

7. A: Have you been up to the top of Arthur's Seat yet, that big hill in the middle of town?
    B: No, why? What's it like?
    A: Oh, it's amazing! You get a great view of the city from up there. It's well worth a visit.
    B: Oh, right. Thanks for telling me. I'll go up there when I get the chance.

8. A: Have you been to the Ronald Gallery in Rye Street?
    B: No, why? What's it like?
    A: Oh, it's a nice gallery. There's a great exhibition on there at the moment. It's well worth a visit.
    B: Oh, right. Thanks for telling me. I'll go and have a look at it when I get the chance.

A day out (page 94)

Kylie: Morning, David. Victoria. Do you mind if we join you?
David: Hi, Kylie. No, of course not. Go ahead.
Victoria: Did you sleep well?
Kylie: Yes, very well, thanks. They're lovely rooms, aren't they? Really comfortable.
David: Wonderful. We've got a great view of the river from ours.
Kylie: Have you? We can only see the car park from ours.
Victoria: That's a shame.
David: So, what are you planning to do today?
Kylie: We haven't really thought about it, have we Jason?
Jason: No.
Kylie: We'll probably just take it easy this morning, you know, go and have a wander round the shops.
Jason: Yeah.
Kylie: We might go to the Picasso exhibition at the Louvre this afternoon. It depends what the queues are like. I've heard it gets very busy. A friend of ours went and she said she had to wait for over an hour to get in. Isn't that right, Jason?
Jason: Yeah.
Kylie: So, what are you two doing today? Any plans?

David: Yeah, we're going to go up the Eiffel Tower this morning and then we're going to go for a cruise down the river. We don't really like art galleries and museums and things like that, do we, Victoria?
Victoria: No.
Kylie: Right. Well, it sounds like a nice day, anyway. I hope it doesn't rain for you.
David: Why? What's the forecast?
Kylie: Well, they said it's going to rain this morning, but it might clear up later.
Victoria: Well, it was OK when we got up.
David: Are you going to eat here tonight?
Kylie: I don't know. We might go out, it depends what time we get back this afternoon.
Jason: And how much money you spend shopping.
Kylie: Hm. Why? What are you doing tonight?
David: Well, we've booked a table at a restaurant on the Champs Elysée. It's supposed to be amazing. You're welcome to join us, if you like.
Kylie: That's very kind of you. We probably will, won't we, Jason?
Jason: Hm, it sounds a bit expensive.
Kylie: Don't be silly, we can afford it.
Jason: As I say, it depends how much you spend when we wander round the shops.

Unit 14

Listening (page 100)

Conversation 1
Sergei: Frances. Can I ask you a question?
Frances: Of course.
Sergei: Can you give me the thing for the exam?
Frances: What, the application form?
Sergei: Yeah, yeah. I want to do the exam. Do you think I can take it?
Frances: Yeah, of course you can take it, but I doubt you'll pass.
Sergei: Yeah – great, because I need this to go to university in September. I really want to do it now.
Frances: I know that's what you want, but what I'm saying is you're bound to fail if you take it now.
Sergei: Sorry? So you think I won't pass?
Frances: No, probably not, but you never know. Miracles can happen.
Sergei: What? I don't understand. Do you think I can take it or not?
Frances : Look, take it if you want – but don't blame me when you fail!

Conversation 2
Barry: How did the exam go?
Blanca: It was easy. All the questions I expected came up.
Barry: Great. What about the writing? Was that OK?
Blanca: Yeah, I did the letter.
Barry: What about the second piece?
Blanca: You have to do two pieces of writing?
Barry: Yeah! Maria – I must've told you that about fifty times.
Blanca: I didn't see another question.
Barry: So you only did one?
Blanca: Yeah. Oh, no! Do you think I can still pass?
Barry: Well, it's not impossible, but it depends how well you did on the other questions.

Conversation 3

Joan: What's up? You look a bit down.

Antonio: I got my results this morning for my end-of-year exams.

Joan: Oh, dear. Not good news, then.

Antonio: No. No, I failed.

Joan: Oh, no, I'm sorry. What happened? I thought you revised really hard for them.

Antonio: I did, but the questions weren't what I expected and I tried to answer them, but …

Joan: Can you re-take it?

Antonio: Yeah, but I'll have to take the course again next year.

Joan: What? Wait. You have to repeat the whole year?

Antonio: Yeah. It's normal, no?

Joan: Not back home it's not. When we fail an exam at university, we usually get the chance to re-take it, but you don't have to do the whole course again.

Antonio: Oh, right. Well, here you have to repeat the whole course. And pay for it, of course.

I messed up badly! (page 101)

Story 1
A friend of mine always left his revision for his exams till the last minute. Most of the time it worked fine, but one time, the night before a Chemistry exam, he stayed up all night reading through his notes. He took several caffeine tablets to keep himself awake. Unfortunately, in the middle of the exam, the effects of the tablets wore off and he just fell asleep. Needless to say, he failed.

Story 2
I failed my driving test five times. The last time I took it, I was sure I would pass, but halfway round, I saw a friend of mine that I hadn't seen for ages and she started waving at me. I didn't look at her for long, but it was long enough for me not to see the car in front of me pull out. I crashed straight into the back of it, and needless to say, I failed!

Story 3
A friend of mine once tried to get through a test by copying the answers of the girl next to her. She was sure the teacher didn't see her cheating and, as the girl she was sitting next to was one of the best students in the school, she was fairly confident she would pass. Unfortunately, without thinking, she copied the name of the girl as well as the answers! Needless to say, she failed.

Asking for an opinion (page 102)

1. Do you think she'll come?
2. Do you think I'll need a coat?
3. Do you think you'll see Ken later?
4. Do you think we'll be back by eight?
5. Do you think you'll pass?
6. Do you think you'll do a Master's after you graduate?

Unit 15

Further practice (page 106)

1. A: Did you see that they think the peace talks might break down?
   B: No, that's terrible! If that happens, they'll go to war.

2. A: Did you see that they're going to put up taxes on air travel by 200%?
   B: Yeah, I know, I heard. It's terrible. If they do that, we won't be able to afford a holiday.

3. A: Have you heard about this famine in Africa?
   B: Yeah, it's awful. The government should do something to help. If they don't do something, millions will die.

4. A: Did Tony tell you he's thinking of going on a diet?
   B: No, but I'm glad to hear it. Honestly, if he carries on eating so much, he'll end up having a heart attack.

5. A: Did you see that that woman who helped her sick mother to die went on trial yesterday?
   B: Yeah. Did you know she could be convicted of murder? If she's found guilty, she'll get fifteen years.

6. A: Did I tell you that our company might be taken over?
   B: No. How will that affect you if it happens?

7. A: Did I tell you that I've got an interview for a promotion?
   B: No. That's great. Will you get more money if you get it?

People talking about sport (page 108)

Conversation 1

A: Did you see the Mottram match yesterday?

B: Yeah. I can't believe he lost!

A: I know. Five–one up in the last set and serving for the match – he should've won.

B: I know. He just seemed to go to pieces. I mean, how many double faults did he serve?

A: I don't know, but it must've been ten or more. I don't think he scored a point in his last three service games.

B: I know. It was awful. I felt a bit sorry for him, actually. He's never going to win Wimbledon, is he? He just doesn't have the mental strength.

Conversation 2

A: Did you see the fight on Saturday?

B: Yeah, what a fix! I can't believe Clarey lost.

A: I know. They must've bribed the judges or something. I mean, he knocked the other guy down twice and he must've won most of the other rounds.

B: I know. I just don't know how they can say Winton won on points.

A: No. Except, of course, now they're going to make even more money having a re-match. It's all about money, isn't it? The whole thing's just fixed.

Conversation 3

A: Did I tell you I went to see a snooker match the other day?

B: Snooker! Why?

A: Oh, my host father is really into it and he had a spare ticket for this competition, so he asked if I wanted to go along. I didn't have anything else to do, so I thought I'd go and see what it was about.

B: And what was it like?

A: Awful. It's just so boring! All you do is sit in almost complete silence and watch two guys try to hit these different coloured balls into holes. I just don't get it!

B: Hadn't you seen it on TV before?

A: No, we don't really play it in our country. Anyway, after about an hour, I fell asleep and then they had to wake me up because I was snoring!

B: You're joking. That must've been a bit embarrassing.

A: Yeah, it was a bit.

Conversation 4

A: Did I tell you I went dog racing the other day?

B: No. What was it like?

A: It was great! I really enjoyed it. I even won some money!

B: You had a bet?

A: Yeah. Just a pound. Nothing serious. It makes the races a bit more interesting, you know.

B: So, how much did you win?

A: Fifty pence.

B: Wow! So you hit the big time, then! Well, don't spend it all at once!

Conversation 5

A: Did you see the England–Japan game?

B: Yeah. It was awful. England were useless!

A: Yeah? I missed it. I had to go out. What was the score in the end?

B: Japan won five–nil.

A: You're joking! What went wrong?

B: Everything. We couldn't pass, we gave the ball away too much. We just kept kicking it up the pitch all the time, and then when we did have a chance, we couldn't shoot and when we had to defend, we couldn't tackle. Honestly, it was awful. The Japanese played well, though. They deserved to win!

I don't know (page 108)

1. A: I don't know why anyone would want to read 'Hello' magazine.
   B: I don't know. I quite like to see how the rich and famous live.

2. A: I don't know how anyone could eat dog.
   B: I don't know. Why is it any different to eating pork or beef?

3. A: I don't know who would want to go to Iceland for their holidays!
   B: I don't know. It's supposed to be really beautiful.

4. A: I don't know if I'll ever finish this book!
   B: I know. It's so long and boring!

5. A: I don't know what men see in Jennifer Lopez!
   B: I don't know. I think she's quite sexy.

6. A: I don't know where all my socks disappear to! They're all odd pairs.
   B: I know. I thinks it's the washing machine. It must eat them.

Unit 16

Listening (page 114)

Bob: So, who are you going to vote for, if you don't mind me asking?

Miriam: I'm not. I don't see the point! They're all as bad as each other. They're all basically liars, aren't they? They're all only interested in making money for themselves. They're all corrupt. Politicians! I just don't trust any of them.

Bob: Do you really believe that?

Miriam: Of course I do! Look at this government. At the last election, they said they would change everything, but nothing has changed at all since they came to power. The economy's still in a mess, people are still losing their jobs and prices are still going up. In fact, I think the only thing they have done to change anything since they've been in power is to cut taxes for the rich and cut unemployment benefits for the poor. It's a disgrace! They're only interested in their friends in big business.

Bob: I know, but did you vote last time?

Miriam: No, I told you. I don't believe in them.

Bob: Yeah, but don't you see? It's because people like you don't vote that these people get in. By not voting you're really voting for them.

Miriam: No, look, Bob. You're not listening to me! What I'm saying is there's no alternative. Look at all the main parties – they basically all say the same things, and have the same policies. That's my point.

Bob: But they're not all the same, are they? You could vote for the People's Workers Party.

Miriam: What? The People's Workers Party!? You are joking, aren't you!? All they want to do is put up taxes and re-nationalise everything. They're mad.

Bob: They're not. That's what this country needs. If the state was running things like the railways and telephones and things like that, we wouldn't have such high levels of unemployment. We should be putting up taxes on big business and rich people, not cutting them.

Miriam: Maybe.

Bob: Definitely. If we did that, we could invest the money in schools and hospitals and things like that.

Miriam: Maybe, but the government would probably just waste it. They usually do. The other thing is, if they taxed business more, then they'd just go somewhere else, or find some way of avoiding paying it.

Bob: You could stop them somehow.

Miriam: Yeah, maybe, but let's face it, Bob. Nobody's going to vote for them, are they, so it's all a bit hypothetical!!

Unit 17

Adjectives (page 120)

1. A: What's your dad like?
   B: He's all right, but he can be quite strict. He always wants to know where I am and he makes me come home before nine o'clock – even on a Saturday.

2. A: What's your brother like? Do you get on?
   B: Not really. He's so fussy about everything! For example, he won't eat any vegetables except peas. If you suggest going somewhere, he never wants to. He's just so difficult to please. I'm the exact opposite. I'm really easy-going.

3. A: What's your gran like? Do you get on?
   B: Yeah, I suppose so. She's OK. She's very independent. She's eighty-five and she still lives on her own, but she's very religious and I'm not. She's always saying I should go to church or I'll end up in hell, but then at the same time, she can be really generous. She bought me a piano for my birthday once.

4. A: What're your parents like?
   B: They're great. I'm quite lucky because they're quite liberal. They let me do more or less whatever I want.

5. A: What's her boyfriend like?
   B: He's awful! I don't know what she sees in him. He's really big-headed, he's always showing off and saying how good he is at everything, and he's so mean! Do you know what he bought her for her birthday? A bar of chocolate!

6. A: What's her new boyfriend like?
   B: He's gorgeous, really good-looking. He looks like a film star, but he's quite quiet. He doesn't really say anything.

7. A: What's his girlfriend like?
   B: Really nice. She's very chatty and out-going. She's very easy to get on with. She's also really sporty. She plays football and hockey. She's really fit. Honestly, I don't know what she sees in that fat slob. She should be with me!

Used to and would (page 124)

A lot of people don't believe it when they see pictures of me when I was younger, because I used to look really, really different. I used to have quite long hair, and I used to dress quite differently too. I'd wear a lot of really loud clothes and a lot of bright colours. I used to play bass in a band and we used to be kind of famous. We made a few records and we'd go on tour quite a lot. I got to see the world a bit. I used to be a bit wilder than I am. I've really calmed down quite a lot, but when I was eighteen or nineteen, I'd be out every night, clubbing, dancing, drinking, you know. It's funny, because even though I used to be much slimmer than I am now, I think I'm quite a lot fitter now. I used to smoke around twenty a day, but I stopped a few years ago, and took up jogging instead! I think getting married has helped me calm down a lot, too. I used to be a bit of a ladies' man before I met my wife, and I'd always have two or three girlfriends I'd see at any one time, but those days are long gone. I'm a one-woman man now! I'm much happier now, too. When I was that age, I used to feel a lot angrier and more confused about life. I'm so glad I'm not a teenager any more!

Unit 18

Radio interview (page 130)

Presenter: And now we turn to the story of Gareth Davies, which has caused so much discussion recently. As you probably know, Mr Davies lost his job, despite being an award-winning teacher of English, because he failed an exam in Welsh. He lost a court case recently, where he had argued he shouldn't be forced to have a qualification which wasn't relevant to his job. To discuss this and other issues about language we have Gareth himself and Christine Edwards, Professor of Modern Languages at the University of Eastminster. First of all, Gareth, I think quite a few people would say, you live in Wales, you should speak the local language, which is Welsh.

Gareth: Well, I'm not actually sure you can say that Welsh is the local language. I'd say that the majority of people in Conway speak English as their first mother tongue. The second thing is, I am Welsh! OK, my parents moved to London, when I was four because of work, but I was born here and both my parents come from different parts of Wales. It's just that neither of them spoke Welsh. If people want to speak it, fine, but it's no use to me in my normal life, apart from this stupid bit of paper. You can't make people learn languages.

Presenter: Isn't that a point, Christine? People simply express themselves in the way they want and that happens to be English.

Christine: No, I'm sorry, but if you look at all the languages round the world, one is dying out every two weeks and that's because of English. I think people think they have to speak English or they will not be able to get a good job, or succeed in the world. Also, because America is so rich, people see lots of Hollywood movies, and listen to lots of American music, and so for younger people English becomes cool and they start to want to speak it. So then you get languages like French being diluted with English. No, when the language dies you also lose the culture and traditions of that country. Languages need to be protected, and that's all that's happened here in Gareth's case.

Gareth: So what you're saying is that I'm actually somehow damaging Welsh culture by not learning the Welsh language! This is crazy! If kids want to be cool, what's wrong with that? What gives you the right to tell people how to live and how to speak? And anyway, the way you think doesn't change when you're speaking in another language. When I am speaking Welsh – badly, I admit – I still want to say the same kind of things I say in English. I'm still me. I'm not suddenly someone else.

Disagreeing (page 130)

A: You can't get a good job if you don't speak English.
B: Come on! That's a bit of an exaggeration!
A: No, it's not. All the best jobs these days ask you to be fluent in English.
B: So what you're saying is I could be a brilliant medical student, say, and I couldn't get a job as a doctor because I can't speak English.
A: Yeah, more or less.
B: Do you honestly believe that?
A: Yeah. If you don't speak English, you're nothing.
B: How can you say that?
A: Because it's true.
B: That's crazy.
A: Listen we're obviously never going to agree, so let's just talk about something else, shall we?
B: OK, but you do realise you're wrong!
A: OK, whatever. I don't want to argue. Let's just agree to disagree.

Stereotypes and reality (page 131)

1. A: He's a typical Scot – really mean!
   B: Oh, come on! Every Scot I've ever met was really generous.

2. A: He's a typical Italian – really loud!
   B: Oh, come on! I've got a really good friend who's from Rome and he's quite quiet.

3. A: She's a typical Japanese – really quiet and shy!
   B: Oh, come on! That's such a stereotype! Lots of Japanese people are really out-going.

4. A: She's a typical small town girl – really conservative.
   B: Oh, come on! Just because you don't come from the city doesn't mean you can't be open-minded.

5. A: She's a typical Parisian – arrogant and snobbish!
   B: Oh, come on! I've got a friend from Paris and she's really nice.

6. A: The Spanish are much more friendly than most people.
   B: Some of them, maybe! I've met some Spaniards who were really cold and distant.

7. A: People from Osaka are usually really funny.
   B: Oh, come on! They can't *all* be funny! There must be some who are as dull as the rest of us!

8. A: People from the north are much more open and honest than southerners.
   B: Oh, come on! Just because you're a southerner doesn't mean you have to be two-faced.

Unit 19

Numbers (page 133)

1. almost one hundred and fifty kilometres an hour
2. about half an hour late
3. almost three hundred and twenty-five
4. almost a thousand
5. around five hundred
6. almost five thousand
7. about one hundred thousand
8. about three and a half million
9. almost ten million
10. over seventy-eight million
11. almost two hundred million

Four crimes (page 135)

Person 1
Passer-by: Are you OK? That looked pretty nasty!
Victim: Just about, I suppose! Thanks a lot for helping me!
Passer-by: Listen, what do you think I could've done? I would've helped if I'd been able to, but there were five of them … and they had a knife!
Victim: Don't tell *me* about it! I know! They were holding it against my throat.
Passer-by: Well, at least you're OK. That's the main thing, isn't it?
Victim: I suppose so.
Passer-by: Did they get away with much?
Victim: Yeah, everything! They took my watch, my wallet with all my credit cards and cash cards in, about three hundred pounds' worth of cash. The lot!
Passer-by: So you'd better make sure you cancel the cards pretty soon, then.
Victim: Yeah. I'd better do that now. Do you know if there's a phone near here I can use?
Passer-by: Yeah, there's a public phone box just round the corner.
Victim: Right. I suppose I'd better report it all to the police as well. Would you mind if I gave your name as a witness?
Passer-by: A witness? Ah, well … um … the thing is, you see, I don't want to get involved, really, so … um … well, you know how it is.
Victim: Oh, thanks a lot! I hope I can do the same for you one day!

Person 2
Friend 1: Hi, Rachel, how're you?
Friend 2: Don't ask! I've had a terrible morning!
Friend 1: Oh, no? What happened?
Friend 2: It's my car! I came out of the house this morning and the back window had been smashed.
Friend 1: Oh, no. That's awful. What were they after? The car stereo?
Friend 2: Yeah, I guess that might've been it, because they did take that. It would've been OK if that'd been all they got, but they got away with my handbag too. I'd somehow stupidly managed to leave it on the back seat.
Friend 1: Oh, no! Was there much in it?
Friend 2: No, not really, but there was a spare set of keys in there, and my home address.
Friend 1: God! That wasn't a very sensible place to leave them!
Friend 2: I know! I know! I was so worried that they'd come round and burgle my flat that I called in a locksmith and got my locks changed this morning. It cost me a fortune.
Friend 1: I bet it did! Oh, well, you won't be making that mistake again, will you!

Person 3
Police officer: Hello. Bexhill Police. How can I help you?
Tourist: Hello. This is Reo Miyamoto speaking. I want to report that I was stolen my mobile phone.
Police officer: I'm sorry. You want to report something? Is that right?
Tourist: Yes. I was stolen my mobile phone.
Police officer: I'm not sure I understand you, sir. Did somebody take your mobile phone?
Tourist: Yes, yes. I was walking by sea when two boys ran and one of boys take it.
Police officer: Oh, right. I see. You had your mobile phone snatched. It's not the first time that's happened!
Tourist: No, no. The first time.
Police officer: No, I mean. There's been quite a few other people that've had the same problem recently, sir. Anyway, what was your name again, please, sir?

Tourist:	Reo Miyamoto. M-I-Y-A-M-O-T-O.
Police officer:	And whereabouts are you staying, Mr Miyamoto? In a hotel?
Tourist:	No, No. I just do a one-day travel here … from Brighton.
Police officer:	Oh, you're only here on a day-trip. Right, well, if you let me know where you are now, I'll send an officer out to talk to you straightaway.

Person 4

Child:	Mummy, why did that man do that?
Parent:	Why did which man do what, darling?
Child:	That man there. The tall man.
Parent:	Why did he do what, dear?
Child:	Put the thing in his pocket.
Parent:	He put something in his pocket, did he? Are you sure? It might just have been his mobile phone or his wallet or something, mightn't it?
Child:	No. I saw him. He put some things inside his coat pocket. Look, he did it again.
Parent:	Oh, yes … I saw it that time.
Child:	I told you!
Parent:	Well, we'd better let the security guards know, hadn't we? That was well-spotted, Daniel. Well done.
Child:	But why did he do it, Mummy?
Parent:	I don't know. Maybe he doesn't want to pay for it. Ah, there's one now. Let's go and talk to him.

Unit 20

What's the matter? (page 139)

Conversation 1

A: Are you OK? You don't look very well.
B: No, I know. I've got an awful cold.
A: Oh no. How long've you had that?
B: For a few days now.
A: Well, maybe you should take a day off work or something.
B: No, I just need to get a good night's sleep tonight, then I'll be OK.

Conversation 2

A: You look terrible. Are you all right?
B: No, not really. I've got a terrible headache.
A: How come? Have you not been well?
B: No, no. I've just had a really stressful day at work. That's all.
A: Well, maybe you should go and have a lie down or something.
B: No, it's all right. I just need some aspirin, then I'll be OK.

At the doctor's (page 141)

Ken:	It was a pint you wanted, wasn't it?
David:	Yeah, cheers. Do you want a cigarette?
Ken:	Yeah, thanks. Oh, I need this.
David:	Have you had a bad week or something?
Ken:	Yeah, I've been really busy just trying to catch up with work after last week.
David:	Oh, yeah?
Ken:	I was ill all last week. It was awful. I had this terrible flu. I couldn't sleep, I was sweating all through the night, and I'd get up in the morning and my whole body would be stiff and aching. It was terrible. I thought I was going to die. Honestly, it was awful.
David:	Yeah?
Ken:	So I rang the doctor and he just said he didn't have any appointments till this Tuesday, so I said, 'What good is that? I'll probably be better by then – or dead!' So he said, 'Well, you don't need to see me, then,' and put the phone down. I couldn't believe it. Doctors these days are just so unhelpful.
David:	Yeah.
Ken:	You know, my mum … she's seventy and the other day she was coming home from the shops and she slipped and fell over and when she woke up the following day, she had a really sore back. She could hardly move. She rang the doctor to ask him to come out, but he wouldn't, so then she had to go all the way to the surgery by herself. Then, when she got there, she had to wait around for about an hour with all these really ill people coughing and sneezing and spreading their germs. When she finally saw the doctor, he looked her over for about ten seconds and he just told her to go home and lie down for a few days. That was it! No pain-killers, no physiotherapy, nothing! And then on top of all that, he told her she should maybe lose some weight.
David:	No!
Ken:	Yeah! And then two days later, she got this nasty chest infection, which she probably picked up in the waiting room, so she went back and this time he just told her to take it easy and drink lots of water. She wanted some kind of medicine, but he said it wouldn't work for some reason. I don't know! It seems as if we pay all these taxes so we can have a free service, but all we really get from them is all this advice about giving up smoking, getting more exercise, cutting down on fatty food and anything else which makes life worth living. Doctors? They treat you as if you're two years old!
David:	I know … do you want another cigarette?
Ken:	Well … I shouldn't really. I'm trying to give up. Oh, all right. Just one last one!

The authors speak

As teachers of general English, we hear lots of comments that students make about grammar. 'Grammar is very important,' some students say. Others explain that they hate grammar because 'it's very difficult'. A different concern was expressed by another student: 'I know lots of words, but I'm not very accurate.' The most immediate result of all these fears is that countless students over the years have told us, 'My grammar's not good enough yet. I need more grammar,' and have then asked us if we can recommend a good grammar book.

Because of all these concerns about grammar, we believe it is an important area to think about. Let's look at the five issues raised above and try to answer each in turn.

1. 'Grammar is very important.'

If someone said to you, 'I Spain. Teacher Madrid,' you would have a good idea that they mean: 'I am from Spain and I work as a teacher in Madrid.' However, if they said, 'I in a where I am the of. I also to on a lot and I've several,' you almost certainly would not understand that what they were trying to say is, 'I work in a big secondary school, where I'm head of the science department. I also go to conferences on teaching quite a lot and I've given several talks.' What this example shows us is that you can communicate something with a little vocabulary, but with only grammar you can say nothing meaningful.

This does not mean that grammar is unimportant. It's good to notice grammar and to know when something is right or wrong, but as we shall see in the rest of this introduction, doing grammar exercises may not be the best way to use your study time.

2. 'I hate grammar. It's very difficult.'

We both speak other foreign languages as well as English. We speak them quite well, but not very fluently and we both get really tired of people telling us that English is much more difficult, and that their own languages are really easy. The truth is, *all* languages are difficult when they are different from your own, and most students take time to become grammatically accurate in a foreign language. Even very fluent speakers often make small grammatical mistakes. And yet languages which are widely spoken must have fairly simple grammatical rules. Otherwise, how could fluent speakers speak them so quickly? Here are some facts about English grammar to show that it is simpler than you may think.

a. In English, for example, most sentences follow a pattern of having a subject and a verb, followed by an object and/or complement, which tells you the where, when, why, who, what or how of the verb.
I work
I work near here. (where)
I work for a big company. (who for)
I work weekends. (when)
I'm working to pay my way through university. (why)
I'm working very hard at the moment. (how/when)
I like my job. (what)

Sometimes, the subject of a sentence can be quite complicated, but the sentence still follows the same pattern.
A friend of mine, who I went to university with,
subject
works   for a television company.
verb   complement

b. English verbs are also quite simple because they only have three forms.
work   working   worked

There are some irregular verbs, but no more than many other languages.

c. English only has two main tenses – the present simple and the past simple.
I play football every Friday.
I played football last Friday.

d. English can look back on an event using perfect forms. To make this form, we use *have/has/had* + a *past participle*.
I've played for years now.
He'd played for a local team for five years, before Arsenal spotted him.

e. English can also add the idea of 'extended time' by using continuous forms.
I'm living at home with my parents at the moment.
We were living with Rachel's mum before we got married.
I've been waiting for months for my operation.

f. The future in English has no special form. It can be expressed in several different ways, each with a slightly different meaning.
I'll see you tomorrow.
The train leaves at nine tomorrow morning.
She's coming next Thursday.
I think it's going to be OK.

g. An interesting thing about English verbs is that sometimes logical things just don't sound correct. So, for example, these are both correct.
A: Do you want to go and see that new Spielberg film?
A: Do you fancy going to see that new Spielberg film?

However, the second of the following two examples is wrong.

B: Yeah, I've been wanting to see that film for the last few weeks.

B: Yeah, I've been fancying going to see that film for the last few weeks.

Why is this wrong? We don't know. We just don't say it! Often, the best way to become more accurate grammatically is to notice and remember good typical examples of the tenses in use. We try to give you lots of these in this book, and there are more in this grammar section.

3. 'I know lots of words, but I'm not very accurate.'

Accuracy takes a long time, so don't be too hard on yourself. Children take ten or eleven years to become accurate even in their mother tongue! However, one way you can help yourself is to learn words as part of a natural expression or in collocations. Collocation is the way that words go together with some words, but not with others: *big rain* is wrong, but *heavy rain* is correct. All languages have collocations like this. The collocations we make in English may be different from the ones you make in your language. If you just learn the word *rain* without the words that go with it, you are more likely to make mistakes. Also, some words may be more common in a particular tense or with particular structures, so you should try to notice, write down and remember words in their context. For example, you could write:

pick up = collect

or you could write the whole sentence:

I've got to go and pick up some friends from the airport.

You could then translate this whole sentence and notice that *pick up* can go with the structure *have got to* and is often followed by the word *friend* and the preposition *from + place*. Then, next time you see the words *pick up*, you could try to notice whether the sentence follows this pattern or not. The second way helps you to use the words you know more accurately. In this book, most of the vocabulary is presented within a whole sentence or a dialogue so you can see how it's typically used. The grammar exercises also try to use typical vocabulary which may be new to you. The texts are written to include useful new language for your level, in fairly typical phrases.

4. 'My grammar isn't very good. I need more grammar.'

Your grammar is probably not that bad, actually. You've probably already met many of the structures in this book. However, you may still make mistakes because you do not know the natural words and expressions that help you say what you want to say. That's why we have tried to provide examples of the kinds of natural conversations people have. The other thing that you probably need more of is the grammar of spoken English. We do not normally speak the way grammar books tell you. Here, for example, is a typical 'grammar book' exercise:

A: Have you been to France?

B: No, I haven't.

A: Would you like a coffee?

B: No, thank you.

Both are grammatically correct, but in conversation we often add comments to continue the conversation. The examples below are much more natural, but involve less controlled practice of the grammar!

A: Have you been to France?

B: No, but I'd love to go. It's supposed to be beautiful.

A: Would you like a coffee?

B: No, thanks. I've just had one.

Many of our grammar exercises include follow-up comments and offer you 'more grammar'. This is typical of natural conversation. Noticing patterns like this and the kind of *subject + verb + complement* patterns we saw above is probably better than doing more exercises on tenses.

5. 'Can you recommend a good grammar book?'

The answer is almost certainly no! We would always recommend a good vocabulary book and dictionary before a grammar book. We think that at your level, *English Vocabulary Organiser* by Chris Gough and *Keywords for Fluency* by George Woolard are good books to learn from at home. If you still decide you want to buy a grammar self-study book, look through some of its examples or ask your teacher to look at it. Ask yourself: Is the grammar presented in dialogues? Are they realistic? Would anyone ever say these things? When? Who to?

If you cannot really imagine a situation in which you'd use the examples given or if they seem very unusual, then we probably wouldn't recommend that particular book, especially if you want to improve your spoken accuracy. If you want to improve your written accuracy, then ask yourself if this book presents new language in the context of the kind of writing you want to do (letters, e-mails, etc.) If it doesn't, when would you write the examples it provides and why?

So, in summary:

- Record typical examples of grammar in context.

- Notice, record and translate whole expressions and collocations, not single words.

- Notice and learn the follow-up comments and questions that often go with structures.

- Learn how to use words you know first, learn new words in context second, do grammar exercises last.

- Remember, accuracy takes a long time to achieve. Listen, speak, read and write English, but most of all – *enjoy it*!

Grammar commentary

Unit by unit grammar notes

G1 | Past simple and past continuous (page 12)

The most important thing to know about the past continuous is that it is not used on its own very often. It is usually used with the past simple. We use it when we want to say that something which started in the past was in progress when another action – usually a much shorter action – happened. Look at these examples:

A: What happened to your hand? It looks nasty!
B: Yeah, I know. I was chopping carrots the other day and the knife slipped and nearly took my finger off!

A: So, how did you two meet?
B: Well, it was while I was working in San Francisco.

Some books will tell you that past simple action 'interrupts' the past continuous action, but this is not always true. In the first example, the cutting of the finger 'interrupted' the chopping, which presumably stopped after that. In the second, however, the living in San Francisco presumably carried on after the two people met.

Two important words often used with the past simple and past continuous are *while* and *when*. *While* is often followed by a clause which uses the past continuous. *When* is often followed by a clause which uses the past simple. These examples should make this clearer:
It started snowing while you were sleeping.
The attacks happened while I was living in Chicago.
I was talking to Frank when Jane phoned.
I was jogging round the park when suddenly this mad dog appeared from nowhere and started attacking me!

With lots of stories, it's usually only the first two or three verbs which are in the past continuous, as these set the scene – they give some background and context. All the action is usually in the past simple:
I was coming up the escalator at the station and this guy was going down the other one on the left when suddenly he tripped and fell and went crashing downwards. It was awful! Then suddenly, this women near me started shouting, 'I'm a doctor. Get out of my way!'

The most common verbs in English are irregular – their past simple form is not made by adding *-ed*. You've probably studied lots of these words already – *got, took, went, had, made,* and so on. The most important thing to do is to try and learn typical collocations for each verb to help you use them in as many natural ways as possible. It's a good idea to keep a list of these verbs with common collocations. For example:
I got home quite late last night.
We got into a big argument over dinner.
I think she got lost while she was wandering round town.

G2 | Present perfect continuous and past simple (page 18)

We usually use the present perfect continuous to talk about an action or activity which someone started doing in the past and which they still do now. It is very common in questions beginning with *How long*.
A: So, how long've you been living here, then?
B: Oh, it must be nearly twenty years now.

A: How long've you been working there?
B: It's about six years now, nearly.

It is also often used to talk about an activity over a period of time up to now which has a present result. Look at these examples:
I've been studying Japanese for six years now, and I still don't understand all the different kinds of writing!
They've been going out together for years, and he still hasn't told her that he loves her!

We often use a time expression with the present perfect continuous to show either when the activity started or how long it has been happening. We use *since* to do the first and *for* to do the second:

I've been living there	since I was a kid.
	since my dad died.
	since 1993 or 1994.
	since last year.
I've been playing netball	for ages.
	for years.
	for three or four years now.
	for a month.

There are lots of other time expressions we commonly use with the present perfect continuous, all of which show that the actions described have happened a lot in the recent past.
I've been working really long hours these last few months.
I've been getting quite depressed about it recently.
She's been writing to him a lot over the last couple of weeks.

The past simple is often used to talk about an activity which happened a lot in the past, often over a period of time, but which is finished now and which has no connection to the present. It is also used to talk about states which were true for a long time in the past, but which no longer are.
I went ice-skating a lot when I lived in Balham.
I visited her three or four times a week when she was in the Old People's Home.
I lived in Malaysia for six years in the nineties.
I had really long hair all through my teenage years.

Using the past simple to talk about these things makes them sound like facts about the past.

G3 Present perfect simple (page 24)

The present perfect talks about something that happened in the past, but which has a connection to the present.
Mary won't be in today. She's gone to Warsaw for a few days.

I've had a word with him about it and I think he understands the situation better now.

We often use this form to talk about how many times something has happened in a period from the past up to now. Again, there is often a present connection.
I've seen that film about three hundred times! I really can't face watching it again. Isn't there anything else on?

A: Have you ever been to Vietnam?
B: Yeah, about twenty times. I've got family living there. Why? Are you thinking of going there?

The present perfect simple is also sometimes used to talk about how long something has happened from the past to now, although it is more common to use the present perfect continuous to do this. There are only a small number of verbs which we use in the present perfect simple like this.
I've always loved spicy food.

I've never liked Alex Ferguson.

I've known him since I was a kid.

I haven't always had long hair. It's quite a recent thing for me.

Did you notice that these are all 'state' verbs, not 'action' verbs? That's why we prefer the simple form.

One other important thing to remember about the present perfect simple is that when we answer 'Have you ever …?' questions, we don't normally use the present perfect in the answer very much. We give details in the past simple. The question asks us about our whole life experience, from when we were born to now, but when we answer, we are usually talking about one particular time in the past.

A: Have you ever been to Latin America?
B: Yeah, I have, actually. I spent three weeks in Nicaragua a few years ago. Why?

A: Have you ever been to a live game?
B: Yeah, quite a few times. I started going maybe six or seven years ago. The last thing I went to was the semi-final the other week.

G4 Present continuous (page 30)

We often use the present continuous to talk about things that started in the past, but which have not yet finished. The present continuous suggests something temporary, not something permanent. These could be things actually happening at the moment we speak.
A: Is it still raining outside?
B: Yeah, it's pouring!

A: Can you help me with this?
B: One minute. I'm brushing my teeth!

Or they could be something not actually happening at the time you speak, but happening in the time around now.
I'm reading this amazing book at the moment.

She's doing a computing course in Bournemouth this month.

We also use the present continuous to talk about something in the future, usually in the near future. These are usually things we have arranged to do with our friends or family, or maybe things we have already paid for or booked. Look at these examples:
A: So, what're you doing this weekend? Any plans?
B: Yeah. I'm going out for dinner with my wife tonight and then tomorrow morning we're taking the train up to Trieste and spending the weekend up there with some friends.

A: What time are you getting in?
B: I'm catching the seven fifteen, so I should be with you by nine-ish.

There are not many verbs used to talk about future arrangements, so it is a good idea to look out for typical collocations of the most common ones.

I'm going	out for dinner with some friends / to the cinema with my sister.
I'm having	some friends round for dinner this evening / lunch with a client.
I'm meeting	my boss next week to talk about it / an old friend of mine this evening.

G5 Get used to/be used to (page 38)

The most difficult thing about these forms is the fact that there are quite a few different phrases in which we use them. It is important to try to learn to use these phrases as whole chunks of language. Look at these examples and try to notice the other words and phrases we use with *get used to/be used to*:
A: How do you find the food here? It must be quite different from what you're used to back home.
B: Yeah, it is, but it's OK. I'm used to everything now.

A: How do you find working from home? Is it OK?
B: Yeah, it's great, but it took me quite a long time to get used to it.

A: I can't believe how expensive everything is here!
B: Don't worry. You'll get used to it.

We often use *'Don't worry. (I'm sure) you'll get used to it'* to try to make people feel better when they are finding something difficult or strange. We often say *'It's OK. I'm used to it'* when someone asks us if we find something strange or difficult.
Don't confuse *get used to/be used to* with *used to + verb*. Even though these forms look similar, they are completely different in meaning. If you used to do something, you did it a lot in the past, but do not do it any more. For example:
I used to smoke, but I stopped after my doctor told me I should.

We used to be really close, but we've lost touch over the years.

You will learn more about *used to + verb* in Unit 17.

G6 | Opinions with *must* (page 41)

Probably the most common use of *must* is to make guesses about what we think things are like, based on what we know, what we have heard or what we have seen. Look at these examples, and notice how we answer guesses like this:

A: It must be very stressful, working seven days a week.
B: Yeah, it can be. It really gets to me sometimes!

A: It must get quite hot in Korea in the summer.
B: Yeah, it does. It reaches eighty or ninety sometimes.

We often begin sentences with phrases like *I think, I suppose* or *I guess* when we use *must* for guessing.
I guess he must be about forty, forty-five, something like that.

I suppose it must be very difficult to become a heart surgeon.

I think he must be German or Austrian, judging from his accent.

G7 | Must/mustn't (page 46)

Using *must/mustn't* for talking about obligation is a lot less common than using *must* for making guesses. In this context, *must* means something like '*I think it's very important.*' Because it conveys a strong idea of personal opinion, we generally only use it to talk about things we feel we need to do ourselves. There's quite a limited number of verbs we use *must* with in this context.
I must remember to phone him this week.
I must make sure he's heard about the meeting.
I must just finish this letter I'm writing.
I mustn't forget to visit her when she goes into hospital.

Remember that we use *must* to talk about obligation in the present. To talk about obligation in the past or the future, we usually use *had to* or *will have to*.
I was running late for my flight, so I had to get a taxi to the airport.

If you want to get into the team, you'll have to start playing better than that!

We sometimes use *you must* to strongly recommend something like a film or a book.
It's an amazing restaurant. You really must go down there, if you get the time.

It's a great book. You must read it.

However, usually, if we want to recommend something, we use *should* as it sounds less aggressive.
It's a great place. You should go there if you get the time.

The whole CD is brilliant. You should give it a listen.

If we are talking about rules – school rules, office rules, company rules, etc., we usually use *have to* or *'ll have to*.
To collect your certificate, you have to go up to Room 301 and talk to David.

If you want to see the doctor, you'll have to register first and then take a number and wait.

If you *don't have to* do something, it means you can if you want to, but there's no obligation.
Isn't it lovely, not having to get up early for a change!

Here's your homework, but it's optional. You don't have to do it if you don't want to. It's up to you.

If we want to sound slightly apologetic and less direct when telling people about rules, we often use *supposed to/not supposed to*.
A: Sorry, madam, but I'm afraid you're not supposed to smoke in here.
B: Oh, I'm so sorry. I didn't realise.

A: Sorry, but if you're coming from a non-EU country, you're supposed to join that queue over there.
B: Oh, really? Thank you for telling me.

We usually use 'If I were you, I'd … ' when we want to give friends or people we know some advice.
If I were you, I'd phone first and check they're open today.
I'd leave it until later if I were you.

We use *allowed to/not allowed to* to talk about things that official rules let us do – or don't let us do.
A: Do you know how many cigarettes you're allowed to bring into the country?
B: Yeah, I think they let you bring two hundred in, tax-free.

It's so stupid where I work. They've got this new rule saying women aren't allowed to wear trousers. It's so sexist!

G8 | Had to/didn't have to (page 50)

We use *had to* to talk about things in the past which we didn't want to do, but which we had no choice about due to rules, laws, problems or a sense of duty.
They told me I had to go back again a week later.

He told me I had to take the form to a post office and sort it all out there.

There was a huge queue, so we had to wait forty-five minutes before we could get in.

There was snow on the line, so we had to take a different train.

Sorry I didn't come to your dinner party. I had to help a friend of mine move that day.

Sorry I missed your call. I had to take some books back to the library.

We use *didn't have to* to talk about things we thought we would be forced to do in the past, but which we were lucky enough not to be made to do.
It was great. We didn't have to pay to get in. They just let us walk straight in.

It was great at my school. We didn't have to wear a school uniform after we were fourteen.

German was an optional subject at my school. You didn't have to do it if you didn't want to.

G9 | Present continuous: habits (page 57)

If we want to complain about someone's typical behaviour, the annoying things they do a lot, we often use the present continuous with *always* to emphasise the idea that this happens a lot.

A: He locked himself out of his car yesterday.
B: Oh, he's always doing things like that! He's very forgetful.

A: I can't stand the way she's always sending text messages in class!
B: I know! It drives me mad as well!

We also sometimes use the present continuous with *always* to emphasise someone's positive habits.

A: She's a lovely person, isn't she?
B: Oh yes. She's always smiling, always happy.

She's incredibly generous – always giving the kids little presents and things like that.

G10 | Make, let (page 58)

Bosses, teachers and parents often make employees, students and children do things they don't want to do.

My boss is making me work weekends at the moment.

I hate the way she's always making us repeat everything ten times in class.

My dad makes me clean his car every Sunday – and he doesn't even pay me for it!

If the bosses, teachers or parents aren't quite so strict or are quite liberal, then they may let employees, students and kids do things that some other people in their position wouldn't allow. This is a guaranteed way of making people happy!

My boss is great. She lets me take time off whenever I need it.

Our teacher's great. He lets us call him by his first name and he calls us by ours.

My mum's very liberal. She lets me stay out late at weekends and things like that.

G11 | Present perfect and past simple (page 66)

Most of what you need to know about these two forms has already been mentioned in the notes for Unit 3. One useful thing to know is the way to answer questions in these tenses. There are lots of very common, fixed responses to questions about time. Look at these examples:

A: How long have you known him?
B: It must be about thirty years now.
B: It must be almost fifteen years now.

A: How long have you lived here, then?
B: Ever since I was a kid.
B: Ever since I can remember.

A: How long've you wanted one?
B: For ages.
B: For at least a year now.
B: Only for a couple of months.

A: When did you start doing that, then?
B: It must've been in 1982 or 1983, I suppose.
B: It must've been maybe twenty years ago.

A: When did you first meet her?
B: Maybe six or seven years ago.
B: A couple of months ago at a party.
B: It was only last week, at work.

It is also quite common to introduce a subject using the present perfect simple – which connects it to now – and then go into details, using the past simple.

I've always been keen on collecting erasers. It all started when I was at primary school and my grandmother gave me one for a birthday present one year.

G12 | Giving advice (page 68)

When we want to suggest one possible solution to a problem, we often use *'Have you tried –ing?'* to make our first suggestion. If this idea isn't useful, we often then suggest a second one using *'Why don't you try -ing?'* Look at these examples:

A: I can't work out how to open this file.
B: Have you tried clicking that bit there?
A: Yeah, I know, but nothing happened.
B: Oh, right. Well, in that case, why don't you try asking someone at the Help Desk.

A: My cat's overweight. I can't believe it!
B: Oh, no! Have you tried putting it on a special diet or something?
A: Yeah, it's on one already, but it doesn't seem to make much difference.
B: Oh, right. Well, in that case, why don't you try making it go out a bit more often?
A: Yeah, maybe I should. I don't know. It seems a bit cruel to me.

G13 | The *-ing* form and the infinitive (page 74)

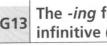

There is no reason why some verbs are followed by a verb in the *-ing* form while other verbs are followed by verbs in the infinitive. It is just the way things are! You have probably already picked up quite a lot of examples of both types of words without knowing it, just through meeting lots of English. The best way to deal with this area of English is to try to note down and remember natural examples of words which go together. Here are some examples of the kinds of things you should already know. It is a good idea to keep a list of these and add new examples each time you find them.

Do you fancy going out somewhere tonight?

Have you tried talking to him about it?

I really like reading.

I can't stand having to get up early.

I don't remember seeing him there.

I'd really like to visit Ghana next year, if I can.

I'd love to see you again sometime.

We could go out if you really want to, but I'd prefer to stay in.

I must remember to pay my gas bill this week.

Often the other parts of the sentence are as important as the choice of the –ing form, the infinitive with to or the infinitive without to. For instance, I must remember is always followed by the infinitive with to, but I don't remember and I can't really remember are followed by the -ing form.

G14 Let's ... (page 75)

We use Let's to make suggestions. It is also often used as a response to a question about plans.

A: Do you want to eat out tonight or shall we cook something?
B: Let's cook. I can't afford to eat out again!

A: Shall we take a break now, then?
B: Yeah, let's. I really need a coffee.

A: We could ask Susie to look after the keys.
B: Yeah, maybe, or we could ask Kenzo if he'd mind staying in the flat for a day or two.
A: Yeah, that's a good idea. Let's do that, then.

G15 Comparatives and superlatives (page 78)

When we are making decisions, we often use comparatives to explain the reasons for our decision. Where there are two choices, we generally use adjective + -er or more + adjective. For example:

A: Shall we take the bus?
B: No, let's walk. It'll be cheaper.

A: Shall we tell her about it?
B: No, let's keep it as a surprise. That'll make things a bit more interesting later!

When there are several choices, we generally use the + adjective + -est or the most + adjective. For example:

A: Do you know any good hotels in town?
B: Well, the nearest one to here is the Grand, but if you want something cheaper (than the Grand), you're best going down towards the station.

A: Do you know any good hotels in town?
B: Well, the most central one is the Parador. It's right in the main square, but if you'd like something a bit smaller and more friendly (than the Parador), then the Rincon is really nice.

The rules for when to add -er/-est and when to add more/most are quite complicated. Words of three syllables take more/most, and most shorter adjectives of one or two syllables take -er/-est, but this is not always true. Participle adjectives (ones which end in -ing and -ed), for example, always take more/most – even if they have a short sound (e.g. bored, crowded), and so do adjectives ending in -ful and -less (e.g. helpful). Don't worry too much if you make mistakes with comparatives and superlatives – native speakers break the rules quite a lot anyway, and it's not unusual to hear less educated people say things like: 'It's more better than it used to be' or 'It's more colder here than it is there'!

G16 Comparative phrases (page 79)

The structure The + comparative, the + comparative, is common in spoken English and very useful. It means we can make long sentences much shorter. For instance, if you want to say that you've been studying a lot recently and that even though you've been studying hard, you find you keep forgetting things, and that this problem is just getting worse, you can just say:
The more I study, the less I remember.

Here are some other examples of how quite complicated ideas can be expressed very precisely using this structure.

The more I see of her, the more I like her.

The longer I stay here, the more used to the food and the weather I get.

As far as music's concerned, I personally think the louder, the better.

The harder I work, the more I want to go out and spend money!

The more I think about it, the worse it seems to get!

G17 Should've/shouldn't have (page 86)

This is the grammar of regret and missed opportunities. There are expressions often used with should've/shouldn't have which clearly show its function of looking back on the past from the perspective of now.

A: Looking back on it, I can see now I shouldn't have done it.
B: Oh, well. You live and learn, don't you?

A: With hindsight, I realise that maybe I should've tried to help her with things a bit more.
B: Yeah, but it's always easy to be wise after the event, isn't it?

We also often use should've/shouldn't have with I wish + past perfect and with third conditionals (see the grammar notes for Unit 19). This allows us to talk about imaginary results in the past as if the mistakes we made had never happened.

A: You should've come. It was great.
B: Yeah, I wish I had. It sounded great.
A: I'm sure you would've enjoyed it.

A: I should never have tried to bribe the policeman.
B: I know! He wouldn't have arrested us if you hadn't!
A: Don't remind me! I wish it had never happened!
B: Me too, but it's a bit late for all that now.

If we want to emphasise mistakes we made in the past, we can use should never have instead of shouldn't have.

I should never have given him my number! He won't stop calling me now!

I should never have listened to you! I should just've done things my own way!

G18 Going to, will, might (page 96)

1. Going to

Lots of learners are also confused about the difference between using the present continuous to talk about future arrangements and using *going to + verb* to talk about decisions about the future. In most cases, there's hardly any difference. For example, both of the following sound fine.

A: What're you doing tonight? Any plans?
B: Yeah, I'm going out for dinner with some friends/I'm going to go out for dinner with some friends.

Most native speakers would probably choose the first option here – the present continuous – to talk about things that have already been arranged with other people, but it is not wrong if you use *going to + verb*.

When we are reporting decisions that we have made on our own and that we haven't really discussed or planned with any other people, we tend to use *going to + verb*.

This year, I'm going to try and stop eating so much chocolate.

I've made up my mind already. I'm going to take the first job I'm offered.

2. Will

Lots of English learners overuse *will*. You may have been told that *will* is the future tense in English. This is not strictly true. It is actually just one of several different ways of talking about the future. It is often used in promises or threats.

I'll bring the money tomorrow, OK.

I won't forget, I promise.

If he does that one more time, I'll scream!

If it happens again, we'll have to sack you, I'm afraid.

We often use *I will* – or its more normal spoken form, *I'll* – when we have just suddenly decided to do something, at the moment of speaking.

A: That's the phone!
B: OK, OK. I'll get it.

A: I really need that book I lent you. Do you think you could bring it tomorrow?
B: Listen, what I'll do is I'll pop it round to you later on today, OK.

3. Might

We often use *I might* as a short answer in response to a question about our future plans. It means *'Maybe I will. I don't know yet.'*

A: Are you going to go to that dinner tomorrow night?
B: I don't know. I might. I'm not sure yet.

A: What're you doing over the holidays? Are you going to go anywhere nice?
B: I don't know. I might. It depends if I can find a cheap flight or not.

G19 The future: seven important verbs (page 102)

Because these verbs for talking about the future are all used in the present continuous, the idea is that the actions they describe have already started and are still continuing as we speak. If you're dreading something, that feeling of dread probably began when you first realised you would have to do this horrible thing in the future, and it probably won't stop until it is out of the way!

The nouns these verbs collocate with are quite limited. For example, the kinds of things you might be dreading include a test or an exam and a visit to the doctor's or the dentist's. It's a good idea to keep a list of any new collocations you meet for each verb.

G20 First conditionals (page 106)

First conditionals talk about things in the future that we think are likely to happen. The *if*- part of the sentence talks about the possible action in the future and is usually in the present simple; the other part of the sentence talks about the result you expect. Either part of the sentence can come first. It all depends on which piece of the sentence connects most to what has been said before or on what you want to emphasise. When the *if*-part comes first, we usually add a comma after it when we are writing.

A: I'm going to try and do a German course this year.
B: Oh, really. If you do, let me know, and I'll join you.

A: I'm going to try and do a German course this year.
B: Oh, really? That's a shame! I won't see as much of you if you do!

The result part of first conditionals often uses *will/won't*, but can also use *going to* and *should* as well.

If they let their dog into our garden one more time, I'm going to go round there and have a word with them about it!

If there's no problem with the traffic, we should arrive before night falls.

You should also notice the way we don't repeat conditions that have already been mentioned if they are obvious to the person we are speaking to.

A: Did I tell you our company might be taken over?
B: No. How will that affect you if it happens?

A: The government should do something to help the miners.
B: I know. If they don't, things are going to get really nasty!

G21 Second conditionals (page 114)

We use second conditionals to imagine ways in which the present or the future could be different. Second conditionals talk about the hypothetical results of imaginary actions. They have two parts – the *if*- part, which expresses the imaginary action, and the result part, which expresses the hypothetical result. You can put the *if*- part of the sentence first or the result part of the sentence first in exactly the same way as you can with first conditionals.

The *if-* part uses the past simple or the past continuous. The other part often uses *would + verb*, but can also use *might + verb* or *could + verb*. Look at these examples:

A: Life might be a whole lot easier if we didn't live here any more.
B: Yeah, I know.

A: If I wasn't working so much at the moment, I'd be able to spend more time at home with you and the kids.
B: I know. That'd be really nice.

If I had a degree, I could maybe try and find a better job.

Just as with first conditionals, we don't usually repeat conditions that have already been mentioned if they are obvious to the person we are speaking to.

A: I wish they'd ban smoking in this office. It's driving me crazy.
B: If they did, it'd start a riot!

A: If they spent a bit more money decorating the place, it'd be much nicer working there.
B: Yeah, maybe, but the work itself would still be deadly dull!

G22 Opinions with *can't* (page 123)

We saw in Unit 5 that we often use *must* to make guesses about what we think things are like, based on what we know, what we have heard or what we have seen. The negative or opposite of *must* in this kind of context is *can't*. Look at these examples:

A: I think he must be in his early fifties.
B: No, he doesn't look it. He can't be older than forty-five.

A: It can't be much fun having to share a room.
B: No, it's not. It's horrible.

A: I don't know how she manages with eight kids. It must be really difficult.
B: I know. It can't be easy, can it?

G23 Used to, would (page 124)

You have already seen that we can use the past simple to talk about things we did a lot in the past, but don't do any more. There is not really much difference between these two sentences:

When I was a kid, I went swimming every Wednesday after school.

When I was a kid, I used to go swimming every Wednesday after school.

The only real difference is that the first sentence just gives the facts; the second sentence sounds as if you are enjoying talking about these memories. Both are correct, but native speakers are more likely to use *used to + verb* if they want to emphasise the fact that they are talking about habits or states. It just sounds nicer – as simple as that! There is also the fact that if you use the past simple here, you usually have to add a time phrase – *when I was younger, when I was growing up* – but if you use *used to*, you don't. It is automatically understood that you're talking about the past. Look at these examples:

I always used to want to stay up late on Fridays, but my mum never used to let me.

When I was a kid, I always wanted to stay up late on Fridays, but my mum never let me.

I never used to worry about what I ate, but since I turned thirty, I've started thinking about it a bit more.

When I was younger, I never worried about what I ate, but since I turned thirty, I've started thinking about it a bit more.

Remember that *used to + verb* has nothing to do with *get used to/be used to*, as you studied in Unit 5.

When we use *would* to talk about the past, it is only to talk about past actions, not past states. That is why we can say '*I used to have really long hair*', but not *I'd have really long hair*. Usually, we use *would/'d* to add details about a habitual action in the past after we've introduced it using *used to*.

I used to love going to the beach. I'd go down there every Saturday morning with my mum and dad and we'd go swimming in the summer or we'd just walk around and look at all the shells and things. It was great.

It is not wrong to use *used to* in all of the examples above. It just sounds more natural to use *would*!

G24 Relative clauses (page 128)

In these sentences, we do not need to use a relative pronoun, though it is not wrong if we choose to.

She's the girl (that) I was telling you about.

I didn't get that job (that) I applied for.

It's one of those things (that) you can cut glass with.

In the examples above, a personal pronoun – *we, you, I, she, he*, etc. – follows the main noun in the sentence, so we can leave out the relative pronoun – *who, which, that*. This is because the complement of the main clause – *the girl, that job, one of those things* – is not the subject of the relative clause.

However, in these sentences the object/complement of the main clause – *that shop, one of those alarms, this strange area* – is the subject of the relative clause, so we need to use a relative pronoun to link it to the verb that follows it.

He works in that shop that sells those amazing sandwiches.

She's got one of those alarms that nearly deafen you when they go off!

He lives in this strange area that has a kebab shop on almost every corner!

That is the most common relative pronoun in spoken English.

It is not wrong to use *which* instead of *that* in the sentences above, but in spoken English, we do not use *which* as often, unless we want to refer back to what we have just said. Look at these examples:

I failed the exam, which means I'm going to have to re-take it in the autumn.

I bumped into an old friend of mine in the Italian shop the other day, which was nice.

If the subject of the relative clause is a person, we link it to the verb using *who*.

Why were you rude to that old woman who asked you for directions?

I got talking to this man who lived in my old street.

I met somebody who knows your brother.

G25 | Third conditionals (page 136)

We can change the order of the two parts of third conditional sentences in exactly the same way as we can with first and second conditionals. The *if-* part of the sentence uses the past perfect simple or the past perfect continuous, while the other part of the sentence uses *could/would/might + have + past participle*. We often use *never* in this part of the sentence instead of *not*. Look at these examples:

A: If you hadn't been driving so fast, the accident might never have happened.

B: Oh, so it was all my fault, then! Maybe if you hadn't been talking so much, I would've been able to concentrate on the road more!

If it hadn't been for my old English teacher, Miss Briggs, I'd never have gone into teaching.

Third conditionals are often used with *should've/shouldn't have* and *I wish + past perfect*.

A: I wish you'd told me about it earlier.

B: I know. I'm sorry. I can see now that I should've done.

A: I might've been able to change my plans a bit if I'd known in advance.

A: I wish I'd never started.

B: I know. You shouldn't have done, really.

A: I could've saved a fortune if I hadn't! Oh, well, that's life, isn't it!

G26 | Giving advice (page 142)

Should is a very common way of giving advice – both to other people and to ourselves. *Shouldn't* is used to talk about things that we think are bad ideas.

I know I shouldn't eat cream cakes, but one won't kill me, will it?

My dad keeps telling me I should be grateful, and I guess he's probably right.

If you're into Jamaican music, you should check out The Dub Club. You'd love it.

A word of advice: you shouldn't really use your left hand for passing things in Indonesia. It's considered a bit rude.

We can also use *should* to talk about the future in a limited number of contexts. It always means 'This is what I think things will be like'. It's only used with positive things. For example, the opposite of: It shouldn't take too long. is It's bound to take ages.

Look at these other opposites:
It should be good.
I can't imagine it'll be much good.

There should be lots of people there.
I don't think there'll be many people there.

It should only cost you about fifty pounds.
It'll probably cost you a fortune.

Expression organiser

This section helps you to record and translate some of the most important expressions from each unit. It is always best to record words in phrases, rather than individual words. Sometimes you can translate very easily. Sometimes you will need to think of a similar expression in your own language. In each section, there is space for you to add any connected expressions or collocations you want to remember.

Unit 1

What do you do? ....

How long've you been here? ....

How long've you been learning English? ....

Have you got any brothers or sisters? ....

How long are you staying here? ....

if you don't mind me asking ....

Don't worry too much about it. ....

I had to do a bit of shopping. ....

Could you give me a hand with my homework? ....

Where's the stress? ....

How do you pronounce it? ....

How many syllables are there? ....

It happened while I was sleeping. ....

I was driving home when I heard. ....

Sorry, but I was in the middle of cooking. ....

....

....

....

....

....

Unit 2

I just stayed in and took it easy. ....

I just stayed in and tidied up my flat. ....

I went out for dinner. ....

I went out clubbing. ....

I went to the cinema last night. ....

I went to a friend's house for the evening. ....

How often do you do that, then? ....

Where do you do that, then? ....

Are you any good? ....

For quite a while now. Maybe four or five years. ....

Quite a bit. Maybe once or twice a week. ....

I got given it for my birthday. ....

I support (Barcelona). ....

I like to keep fit. ....

I've been really busy working. ....

....

....

....

....

....

Unit 3

We had a week in Greece. ....

We went on a skiing holiday. ....

We rented a cottage. ....

We went camping. ....

We ate out every night. ....

It was really good value for money. ....

The scenery was amazing. ....

It's a great place to live. ....

It's a great place for a picnic. ....

It's supposed to be lovely. ....

No, but I've always wanted to. ....

No, but I've never really wanted to. ....

No, but a friend of mine has. ....

I've always liked her. ....

I've never tried it. ....

....

....

....

....

....

Unit 4

How's it going? ....

I'm exhausted, to be honest. ....

Actually, I'm a bit fed up. ....

I'm in a really good mood. ....

I got really behind at work. ....

He got really depressed after that. ....

I find it really frustrating. ....

I was really annoyed about it. ....

It's making me really stressed-out. ....

It was really upsetting news. ....

It's a very exciting development. ....

I don't really feel like it. ....

I'm meeting him tomorrow. ....

It's pouring with rain outside. ....

What are you doing here? ....

....

....

....

....

....

Unit 5

I'm a housewife. ....

I work part-time as a nurse. ....

I used to work in a cafe as a waitress. ....

I get to travel a lot. ....

I get to meet lots of interesting people. ....

I have to wear a suit. ....

I don't have to wear a uniform. ....

What's the money like? ....

What are the hours like? ....

I work from home. ....

I work shifts. ....

I could never get used to that. ....

You'll get used to it eventually. ....

How're you finding it so far? ....

That must be really rewarding. ....

....

....

....

....

....

Unit 6

Have you tried that big shopping mall? ....

I got it cheap in a second-hand shop. ....

That place is a rip-off. ....

I've just got to sort my things out. ....

I've got to do a few things in town. ....

Is there a post office near here? ....

There's one just down the road. ....

I need to do some photo-copying. ....

They've got such a wide choice. ....

I was left the money when my dad died. ....

I must remember to do that later. ....

I mustn't forget to call her. ....

I wouldn't if I were you. ....

You're not supposed to smoke in here. ....

I'm glad I don't have to work there. ....

....

....

....

....

....

Unit 7

They were very apologetic. ....

The prices were very reasonable. ....

That's disgusting! ....

I'm sorry, but this is rather cold. ....

I'm sorry, but this isn't very strong. ....

I'm sorry, but my room is absolutely filthy. ....

Do you think you could ...? ....

I'm terribly sorry about that. ....

I didn't want to, but I had to. ....

It was compulsory at my school. ....

He had to do one year's military service. ....

It really drives me mad! ....

I can't understand people who do that! ....

I can't stand that kind of thing! ....

I wonder if you can help me. ....

....

....

....

....

....

Unit 8

I live on the ground floor. ....

She lives in a big block of flats. ....

They've got a huge detached house. ....

It's out in the suburbs. ....

It's only a tiny little studio flat. ....

I still live at home. ....

How old were you when you left home? ....

It's very convenient for the shops. ....

It's quite a rough area. ....

There's hardly any crime. ....

It's quite a posh area. ....

He's always doing that! I hate it! ....

She never helps me with the shopping. ....

How do you get on with them? ....

Not very well, actually. ....

....

....

....

....

....

Unit 9

I'm connected to the Internet at home. ....

I deleted the file by accident. ....

My computer has just crashed! ....

I just need to check my e-mail. ....

I got a virus. ....

the other day ....

in a few weeks' time ....

I've never had any problems with it. ....

I've almost finished. ....

We've been friends since we were at school. ....

I've always liked that kind of thing. ....

How long have you had it? ....

How long did you do that for? ....

It keeps doing that! ....

If I were you, I'd … ....

....

....

....

....

....

Unit 10

Where do you want to meet? ....

Sorry I'm late. The traffic was awful. ....

Have you been waiting long? ....

Whereabouts? ....

I'll pick you up from the airport. ....

I'll meet you at the hotel in the foyer. ....

Do you fancy going out somewhere tomorrow? ....

Would you like to go out for dinner with me? ....

I'd rather do something else. ....

to be honest ....

Do you want to leave now or shall we wait a bit? ....

I'm easy. It's up to you. ....

Can we make it a bit later? ....

Can we make it next week instead? ....

I'm not bothered. ....

....

....

....

....

....

Unit 11

I can't drive. ....

What kind of car have you got? ....

It's a ten-minute walk. ....

It's a twelve-hour flight. ....

He didn't indicate! ....

She went through a red light! ....

It's better than it was before. ....

It wasn't as good as the last time I went. ....

The bigger, the better. ....

Better late than never. ....

It's one of the cheapest places in town. ....

It's one of the biggest in the world. ....

We got delayed for six hours! ....

We got lost outside London. ....

It was so crowded, I couldn't find a seat. ....

....

....

....

....

....

Unit 12

It's a kind of fish dish. ....

It's a kind of pudding. ....

It's quite fattening. ....

It's very filling. ....

It's a bit too rich for me. ....

I find that kind of food a bit bland. ....

She looks anorexic. ....

Millions of people are starving to death. ....

I got food poisoning. ....

You eat too much junk food. ....

It's really good for your health. ....

It should be banned! ....

She's a vegetarian. ....

I'm allergic to it. ....

I should've done it earlier. ....

....

....

....

....

....

Unit 13

I was thinking of buying some souvenirs........................

I was thinking of doing some sightseeing.......................

Can you recommend anywhere? ....

You could try the big mosque in the old town.................

You could try the street market in the centre..................

I must remember to book a table. ....

The restaurant was fully booked. ....

They've sold out of tickets. ....

It's a bit of a tourist trap. ....

I'd give it a miss if I were you. ....

You get a great view of the city from up there.................

It's well worth a visit. ....

What was the weather like while you were there? ....

Terrible! It rained the whole time. ....

Maybe. It depends how I feel. ....

....

....

....

....

....

Unit 14

I'll never forget my old English teacher.......................

I was caught cheating in a test. ....

She used to skip class a lot. ....

He threatened me with a knife! ....

They made us stand outside. ....

I complained to the manager about it. ....

He always used to give us detentions ....

She was always very encouraging. ....

I did a lot of revision. ....

I failed my entrance exam. ....

I had to re-take two exams. ....

I had to have a blood test. ....

I've just passed my driving test! ....

I doubt it'll happen. ....

You're bound to be OK. ....

....

....

....

....

....

Unit 15

I play a lot of tennis in the summer. ....

I go jogging every other day. ....

I play baseball quite a lot. ....

There's a sports centre near where I work.....................

There's a court in the park near my house......................

There's a pool quite near here. ....

I can't stand team sports. ....

I avoid red meat and fatty foods. ....

I eat a lot of fruit and vegetables. ....

It was a really exciting game. ....

I'll give you a hand if you want. ....

I'll go if I really have to, but I'd rather not......................

We don't have to, if you don't want to. ....

I know! I can't believe it! ....

I don't know how you can eat that! ....

....

....

....

....

....

Unit 16

He's really good at dealing with his employees. ....

I have to work very long hours. ....

She has to deal with a lot of bureaucracy.......................

They've cornered the market. ....

She supports the whole family. ....

It's against company policy. ....

They employ over a thousand people. ....

It's a waste of money. ....

I'm a bit short of money at the moment......................

I owe a lot of money to the bank. ....

They've invested a lot in property. ....

The English language market is booming......................

Little companies get squeezed out of the market..............

I'd love to if I had the money. ....

If it was up to me, I'd say yes. ....

....

....

....

....

....

Unit 17

That's my stepbrother and his wife. ....

I've got two half sisters. ....

He's very liberal. ....

She's gorgeous! ....

She's eighty-five, but still very independent. ....

I've known her since I was a child. ....

I asked him out on a date. ....

Did you go on your own? ....

He's not really my type. ....

I want someone who's about the same age as me. ....

I'd never go out with someone like that. ....

He can't be older than thirty. ....

I used to when I was younger. ....

Why did you stop? ....

What were you doing there? ....

....

....

....

....

....

Unit 18

There's a big parade through the centre of town. ....

There's a huge film festival every autumn. ....

There's a big religious festival next month. ....

I only do it out of habit. ....

It commemorates all those who died in the war. ....

We're going out to celebrate. ....

I find it a bit embarrassing. ....

I didn't get that job I applied for. ....

There's that guy I was telling you about. ....

What's the house you're buying like? ....

What're the people you work with like? ....

You swear too much. ....

He's got quite a strong French accent. ....

That's a bit of an exaggeration. ....

It's just a stereotype. ....

....

....

....

....

....

Unit 19

He was found guilty of tax evasion. ....

He was found guilty of lying in court. ....

There's a lot of vandalism round there. ....

He should've got life for that. ....

He got what he deserved. ....

around a couple of thousand ....

almost half a million ....

The fans went on the rampage after the game. ....

He was stabbed to death. ....

They've finally caught that serial killer. ....

I had my bag snatched. ....

They got away with over a million dollars. ....

Have you reported it to the police? ....

Make sure you cancel your credit cards. ....

If you'd told me about it, I would've come! ....

....

....

....

....

....

Unit 20

Are you OK? You don't look very well. ....

I think I've got the flu. ....

I've sprained my ankle somehow. ....

I've done something strange to my back ....

I've got a bit of a temperature. ....

Maybe you should take the day off. ....

I've got to go and have a check-up. ....

I had to have two fillings. ....

I think she wears contact lenses. ....

I've got to keep the weight off my foot. ....

She told me to drink lots of fluids. ....

They want to privatise it. ....

The dinner tonight should be good. ....

It shouldn't take that long. ....

There shouldn't be any problem with that. ....

....

....

....

....

....

4

Unit 9 Computers, Using grammar

1 | Three classic mistakes (continued from page 66)

The second classic mistake was not to back up my work on a regular basis. I remember one day I lost a whole morning's work with one press of a button! The first and most obvious thing you can do is save your work every couple of minutes. The second is to copy all your document files on a daily basis onto an external drive, which you then keep in a safe place. If you do not have an external drive, you can copy files onto an on-line hard drive. If your house or office burns down, all you do is re-access your files via the Internet.

Thirdly, I used to open all e-mail attachments without thinking – until one day I got a virus which wiped my hard drive clean. A really bad virus can destroy years of work. If you don't want a virus, don't open any attachment without first checking who has sent it to you. It's easy to give this sort of advice – especially if – like me – you've made all these mistakes yourself!

So, just to summarise – the three classic mistakes are firstly to load lots of programs you're not going to use on to your hard drive; secondly not to back up your work on a regular basis; and thirdly to open e-mail attachments without first checking who they're from!

Unit 19 Law and order, Reading (page 132)

Rich and Famous or Rich and Dangerous?

They say that in the end we're all the same. You can have money and fame, but in the end you still have to do the same kind of things as everyone else – sleep, eat, fall in and out of love, and, apparently, commit crimes! Yes, when you look at the world of celebrities, it's amazing how many have had trouble with the law. Here's just a few of the ones we could remember, but the Internet has lots more!

Pavarotti

Apparently, Pavarotti has about £300 million. Probably one of the reasons he has so much is that he didn't pay any tax to the Italian government for quite a long time. He said he didn't realise he had to!! He was arrested and taken to court for tax evasion before he finally agreed to pay around $4.5 million.

Jeffrey Archer

Jeffrey Archer is a millionaire author. He was a very successful politician and one of Margaret Thatcher's favourite people. At the same time as being highly successful, he was being unfaithful to his wife. When this story appeared in a newspaper, he denied it and took the paper to court - and won! He was awarded £500,000 in damages. But the truth came out eventually and he ended up in prison for four years for lying in court. Obviously, Archer's story-telling had got a bit out of control!

Paul McCartney

Even the Queen likes Sir Paul McCartney now, but thirty years ago he was arrested in Japan for possession of marijuana. He spent nine days in jail, and could've got seven years and a two-thousand-dollar fine if it had gone to court, but in the end, the police released him and he was sent back to Britain. McCartney said he had no idea why they decided to release him. Do you?

Helmut Kohl

The fact that a politician was found guilty of accepting illegal donations to his party is perhaps not that surprising. What is amazing is that, in this case, the politician paid a one-hundred-and-forty-thousand-dollar fine. He also apologised, which is something most of these other celebrities didn't do!

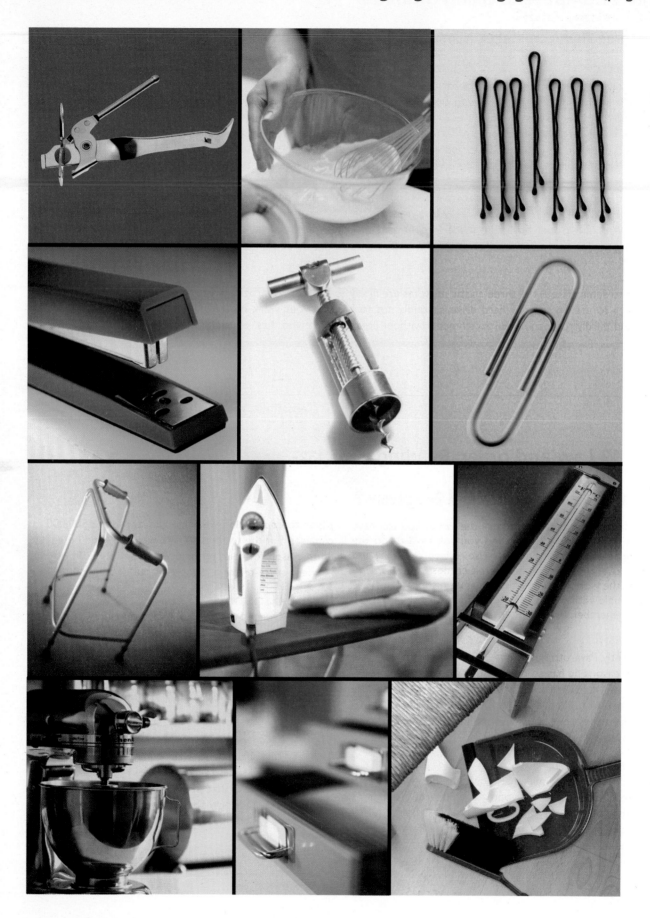